PERGAMON INTERNATIONAL LIBRARY
of Science, Technology, Engineering and Social Studies

*The 1000-volume original paperback library in aid of education,
industrial training and the enjoyment of leisure*

Publisher: Robert Maxwell, M.C.

Science and Gender

THE PERGAMON TEXTBOOK
INSPECTION COPY SERVICE

An inspection copy of any book published in the Pergamon International Library
will gladly be sent to academic staff without obligation for their consideration for
course adoption or recommendation. Copies may be retained for a period of 60 days
from receipt and returned if not suitable. When a particular title is adopted or
recommended for adoption for class use and the recommendation results in a sale
of 12 or more copies the inspection copy may be retained with our compliments.
The Publishers will be pleased to receive suggestions for revised editions and new
titles to be published in this important international Library.

THE ATHENE SERIES
An International Collection of Feminist Books
General Editors: Gloria Bowles and Renate Duelli-Klein
Consulting Editor: Dale Spender

The ATHENE SERIES assumes that all those who are concerned with formulating explanations of the way the world works need to know and appreciate the significance of basic feminist principles.

The growth of feminist research has challenged almost all aspects of social organization in our culture. The ATHENE SERIES focuses on the construction of knowledge and the exclusion of women from the process—both as theorists and subjects of study—and offers innovative studies that challenge established theories and research.

ON ATHENE – When Metis, goddess of wisdom who presided over all knowledge was pregnant with ATHENE, she was swallowed up by Zeus who then gave birth to ATHENE from his head. The original ATHENE is thus the parthenogenetic daughter of a strong mother and as the feminist myth goes, at the "third birth" of ATHENE she stops being Zeus' obedient mouthpiece and returns to her real source: the science and wisdom of womankind.

Volumes in the Series

MEN'S STUDIES MODIFIED
The Impact of Feminism on the Academic Disciplines
edited by Dale Spender

MACHINA EX DEA
Feminist Perspectives on Technology
edited by Joan Rothschild

WOMAN'S NATURE
Rationalizations of Inequality
edited by Marian Lowe and Ruth Hubbard

SCIENCE AND GENDER
A Critique of Biology and Its Theories on Women
Ruth Bleier

NOTICE TO READERS

May we suggest that your library places a standing/continuation order to receive all future volumes in the Athene Series immediately on publication? Your order can be cancelled at any time.

Also of interest

WOMEN'S STUDIES INTERNATIONAL FORUM*
A Multidisciplinary Journal for the Rapid Publication of Research Communications & Review Articles in Women's Studies
Editor: Dale Spender

Free sample copy available on request

Science and Gender

A Critique of Biology and Its Theories on Women

Ruth Bleier
University of Wisconsin

Pergamon Press

New York • Oxford • Toronto • Sydney • Paris • Frankfurt

Pergamon Press Offices:

U.S.A.	Pergamon Press Inc., Maxwell House, Fairview Park, Elmsford, New York 10523, U.S.A.
U.K.	Pergamon Press Ltd., Headington Hill Hall, Oxford OX3 0BW, England
CANADA	Pergamon Press Canada Ltd., Suite 104, 150 Consumers Road, Willowdale, Ontario M2J 1P9, Canada
AUSTRALIA	Pergamon Press (Aust.) Pty. Ltd., P.O. Box 544, Potts Point, NSW 2011, Australia
FRANCE	Pergamon Press SARL, 24 rue des Ecoles, 75240 Paris, Cedex 05, France
FEDERAL REPUBLIC OF GERMANY	Pergamon Press GmbH, Hammerweg 6, D-6242 Kronberg-Taunus, Federal Republic of Germany

Copyright © 1984 Pergamon Press Inc.

Library of Congress Cataloging in Publication Data

Bleier, Ruth, 1923–

   Science and gender.

   (Athene)
   Bibliography: p.
   Includes index.
   1. Women – Physiology – Philosophy.   2. Human biology –
Philosophy.   3. Sex discrimination against women.
4. Feminism.   5. Sexism. I. Title.
QP34.5.B55 1984   305.4′2   83-22054
ISBN 0-08-030972-0
ISBN 0-08-030971-2 (pbk.)

To
Sadie and Abe
and
Kathy and Mark

Reprinted 1984, 1985.

Printed in Great Britain by A. Wheaton & Co. Ltd., Exeter

Contents

Preface

This book is concerned with the role of science in the creation of an elaborate mythology of women's biological inferiority as an explanation for their subordinate position in the cultures of Western civilizations. The theme of women's biological inferiority has been both implicit and explicit in biological science since the time of Aristotle. It is, I would contend, an essential theme for the ideology and cultural practices of societies that require women's subordinance both in the home, as homemakers and mothers, and in the marketplace, as underpaid workers in the nurturing, helping, and domestic professions. It has been the particular task assumed by some scientists to devise ways to measure, demonstrate, and explain how the sexes are different and to establish biological bases for the striking differences in their social, economic and political positions.

In the United States and Europe, science has historically performed similar functions with respect to race and religion—looking for, defining, and measuring differences that could serve to explain the position of people of any race, color, ethnicity, or religion not of the dominant or ruling class. In theory, except for the special attention it has paid to race in regard to questions of IQ and brain size, science has appeared evenhanded in its theorizing about the nature and abilities of women, finding us all, irrespective of our differences, equally inferior. In practice, however, applied science in the forms of medicine, medical care and services, and the professional institutionalized *doing* of science has discriminated against women of color with a force of monumental proportions. To be female *and* black or poor in this society is to be surrounded by barriers that are formidable in every aspect of life and struggle.

As social movements threaten the social order, it is a recurrent phenomenon that corresponding scientific theories emerge that implicitly defend the *status quo*. In the face of the contemporary vigorous resurgence of the women's movement and feminist scholarship, biological determinist theories have become a conspicuous part of our scientific and popular cultures. In the following chapters, I explore the scientific and ideological bases of important contemporary theories that "explain" gender differences and postulate their biological and evolutionary origins.

I have chosen for discussion those areas in the natural sciences that have been among the most influential in molding popular views of gender differences in achievement and their presumed biological origins: sociobiology, sex differences in brain structure and cognitive function, human cultural evolution and anthropology, and sexuality. Common to these areas have been the ethnocentric and androcentric biases of their premises and interpretations, of their universalistic assumptions, and of their world view, as well as their acceptance of ideas of innate *natures* and the separability of biology from culture.

The introductory first chapter touches upon the main themes in the book and also indicates the relationships between science, scientists, and the scientific method in general and their specific historical and cultural contexts. In particular, it suggests that biological determinist ideas emerge as dominant explanations for economic, social, and political inequality during periods of unrest and struggles for autonomy. In the 1970s and 1980s, theories that attempt to explain human behaviors and potentialities by reducing analysis to the level of the gene have emerged once again as dominant cultural influences.

Chapter 2 presents a detailed critique of the premises, methodologies, and theories of Wilsonian sociobiology. While the field of sociobiology has provided valuable insights into the social behaviors of animals, E. O. Wilson introduced Sociobiology in 1975 as the ultimate discipline of human behavior. It considers all human behaviors, characteristics, and social relationships to be biologically, genetically, and evolutionarily determined. Prominent is the special attention Sociobiology pays to the issues and goals raised by the contemporary women's movement. I show that Sociobiology is deeply flawed *as* science, and also that the genes-environment dichotomy underlying biological determinist theories is scientifically meaningless and, hence, useful only for political and ideological purposes.

Chapter 3 describes the evolutionary, embryological, and postnatal development of the human brain. This development has resulted in a brain with an enormous capacity to learn, invent, remember, symbolize, make choices; to have self-awareness, beliefs, convictions, intent and motivation; and to create and transmit cultures. During fetal and postnatal growth, the brain *requires* input from the external world for normal structural and functional development. It is, consequently, not possible to separate biological from cultural factors in any adequate explanation of the development of human behaviors and characteristics nor to defend the notion of an immutable core of *instinct* or *nature* beneath and outside of culture and learning. Paradoxically, it is not our brains or our biology but rather the cultures that our brains have produced that constrain the nearly limitless potentialities for behavioral flexibility provided us by our brains.

Chapter 4 shows that studies linking hormones with aggressivity, achievement, and intelligence or linking brain lateralization with sex differences in verbal, mathematical, and visuospatial abilities have been methodologically and conceptually unsound and inconclusive. From experiments on rodents, an important concept developed that androgens, the sex hormones associated with males, have an organizing effect on the developing brain during the fetal and newborn period and, consequently, on particular sex-differentiated adult behaviors and characteristics, such as mating and fighting. This work has provided a conceptual model for wide-ranging theorizing about the hormonal and neural basis for human sex differences in such characteristics as aggressivity, dominance, intelligence, sexuality, and gender identity.

Chapter 5 discusses theories of human cultural evolution, in particular, Man-the-Hunter. Since its enunciation in the 1960s, the Man-the-Hunter theory of human evolution has been the predominant evolutionary explanation of how we have come to be the way we are and behave as we do. This chapter describes available evidence from archeology, primatology, and anthropology that suggests that the social hunting of large animals is a relatively recent development and could not explain either human origins or the uniquely human aspects of our cultures. I present alternative, more inclusive interpretations of the evidence and suggest that no Single Cause theory can fully explain human cultural evolution.

Chapter 6 examines the work of feminist anthropologists that challenges traditional anthropological concepts and universalist assumptions, such as the subordinate position of women, that underlie biological explanations of women's subordinate position in Western industrial societies. It also describes some historical circumstances that may have characterized the emergence of patriarchal cultures.

Chapter 7 explores sexuality, ideology, and patriarchy. Science and medicine have been important forces in the social construction of sexuality and, through their discourses on sexuality, in the social control of women. This chapter defends the thesis that sexuality and the heterosexual structuring of consciousness and institutions underlie all forms of the violent control of women and their physical, economic, political, legal, emotional, and ideological oppression in patriarchal cultures.

The final chapter examines concepts of objectivity, truth, and the dualistic structuring of reality as patriarchal modes of thought that are intrinsic to science and have also defined science as a male enterprise. It counterposes a feminist science that begins by discarding dualistic assumptions as well as concepts of control and dominance and of linear causality. A feminist science proceeds instead with an understanding of the constant change, complexity, contextuality, and interaction that characterize natural and social phenomena and our lives.

Acknowledgments

In 1971 Joan Roberts, who initiated the first cross-disciplinary departmental course in women's studies at the University of Wisconsin-Madison, first confronted me with the necessity to turn my critical feminist attention to research being done in the area of the brain, hormones, and behavior. Pauline Bart and Jeanne Marecek further propelled me down this path by incorporating me into their national symposia.

This book owes an enormous debt to Judy Leavitt, who has read every chapter, including some in their chaotic first draft form, and consistently asked incisive questions and gave warm support; to Susan Friedman, who first helped to clarify my approach to the book, supplied enthusiasm, and later offered important commentary and criticism; and to Zillah Eisenstein, who has read many chapters and made a number of critical suggestions. Anne Fausto-Sterling, simultaneously involved with her own manuscript on the subject of the biological sciences, has also read most of the chapters and been an important source of ideas and support.

I am deeply grateful to others, Elaine Marks and Rena Gelman, who also had to struggle through the first drafts of my first chapters at a time when the shape of the book was not at all clear, and who, nonetheless, offered encouragement and gentle criticism. Particular chapters in this book benefitted enormously from the advice and suggestions of Diane Kravetz, Susan Millar, Janet Spector, and Wally Welker. I am most grateful to other friends and colleagues who have read chapters and made important suggestions: Bill Byne, Claudia Card, Cindy Cowden, Claire Fulenwider, Kris Guyot, Ruth Hubbard, Biddy Martin, Marion Namenwirth, Maggie Osler, Sue Rosser, and Gina Sapiro.

I wish to thank Larry Jacobsen for the graciousness and efficiency with which he and his staff made materials available to me from the library of the Wisconsin Regional Primate Research Center and other libraries. I thank Renate Duelli Klein and Gloria Bowles, the co-editors of the Athene Series, for their helpful suggestions for some chapters. I am deeply grateful to them and to Phyllis Hall of Pergamon Press for their timely and unconditional enthusiasm that made my book a part of the Athene Series.

I am most appreciative of the skilled photographic work of Shirley Hunsaker and the manuscript typing of Nancy Solterman and Nancy Henderson, and the conscientious compiling of the author index by Wendy Uhlmann.

I am grateful for the semester leave of absence to begin work on this book in the Spring of 1980, made possible by a Faculty Development Award from the

University of Wisconsin Board of Regents, through the efforts of Associate Vice Chancellor MaryAnn Yodelis Smith.

Finally, I should like to express my appreciation for my colleagues in the Department of Neurophysiology, which, beginning with a tradition established by its first chair, Clinton Woolsey and carried on by Joseph Hind, has valued and judged merit in a gender-free way and has protected the autonomy of its members. The department has provided me with a safe place to do my science as well as to criticize and change the institutions that oppress women.

Chapter 1
Introduction

Through dialectical interaction science and culture develop as an organic whole, fragmenting and reintegrating out of both social and intellectual tensions and tendencies.
Carolyn Merchant, 1980, p. xviii

For the past few decades, historians and philosophers of science have effectively described science and its history as an integral part of a social context, growing out of and responding to the needs, values, ideas, technology, and hopes of particular forces within any culture. At the same time, all important scientific ideas have an intellectual history of their own—a long line of ideas developing within their social contexts and leading, over previous decades or centuries, to the present. Today we view certain ideas as great and progressive, and we view them thus because they were influential in molding a cultural reality—our world view—that values such ideas as great and progressive and that remains largely ignorant or unappreciative or uncomprehending of other great ideas that fell by the wayside.

In Merchant's (1980) view, there exists in any historical period an array of available intellectual ideas. Of these, some spread, and some appear to die out. While there are important factors intrinsic to the sciences, to scientists, and to scientific ideas themselves that affect the acceptance and influence of any particular idea or theory at any moment in history, as Kuhn (1970) argues, it is also true that "the direction and cumulation of social changes begin to differentiate among the spectrum of possibilities so that some ideas assume a more central role in the array, while others move to the periphery" (Merchant, 1980, p. xviii). For example, the metaphor of the earth as nurturing mother, which was central to Renaissance imagery, became replaced as the Scientific Revolution mechanized and rationalized the world view. The view of nature as disorder provided a rationale for the need to control and master it. As both Haraway (1979) and Merchant (1980) have developed, under the effects of the ideology and technology of developing capitalism, beginning in the mid-fifteenth century, a new representation emerged of the body, society, nature, and the cosmos as machines that are manipulable and require control and domination. Ideas of order and predictability, of natural laws acting on inert atoms and bodies, superceded ancient philosophies of vitalism and animism, skepticism, change, and uncertainty.

Over the past few years, it has been the particular contribution of feminist scholarship to show that this influence of cultural context on the ideas, questions, methods and interpretations of science, and of scholarship in general, is not only

1

the influence of a particular, constantly changing set of temporally and geo-graphically bounded social concerns in any given time and place. It is, rather, of overriding importance that in the patriarchal civilizations that have been our cultural context for the past several thousand years, a particular, consistent, and profound bias shapes scientific theories in general, theories about women in particular, and scientific explanations of the perceived social and cultural differences between women and men. While the dominant and changing scientific trends in thinking can be painted in broad sweeps coinciding with particular changing historical eras—the Reformation, the Renaissance, the Scientific Revolution, the Industrial Revolution—one unchanging feature of our Western history as we know it is that all the dominant cultures have been patriarchal, whether enlightened, reformed, feudal, capitalist or socialist. Science, like all culture, reflects that consistent historical bias.

The 1970s and 1980s have witnessed powerful movements by women in general and by women and men of color to break out of positions of subordinance to and dependence upon a ruling class of white males. The forces of patriarchal authority have responded, and science has been no less sensitive than other aspects of our culture. From the array of ideas and theories that attempt to explain human behaviors and potentialities, those that reduce analysis to the level of biology, in fact, to the gene, have emerged once again as dominant cultural influences.

SCIENCE AND SOCIAL VALUES

It seems anachronistic in the extreme that the nature-nurture, heredity-environment controversy need be addressed today as a serious intellectual issue. The theme, raised recurrently over the past century, remains frighteningly the same despite enormous advances in general scientific sophistication: Women's efforts to do other than what they are destined to do—by biology and evolution, by nature and temperament—threaten the health and survival of the human race. A theme stated explicitly by nineteenth-century physicians, it is today hinted at darkly by modern biological determinists who predict incalculable harm from "tampering" with nature. The last half of the nineteenth century saw a peaking of Social Darwinist thinking that viewed the body politic—the political and social order—along with each person's place within it, as having evolved according to Darwinian laws of natural selection. Within this milieu, the view of woman's innate tem-perament—maternal, pure, pious, compassionate—underlay the debate by phy-sicians, natural and social scientists, and educators about the size and functioning of the female brain and the desirability of women pursuing formal education, since exercising the female brain would drain limited energy from her true roles of reproduction and motherhood. The nature-nurture controversy flared again in the psychological and biological sciences, particularly in the United States, in the period between the two world wars, but had once again become a dead issue by the early 1940s, as scientists acknowledged the "continual interaction and interrelatedness of nature and nurture" (Cravens, 1978, p. 270).

From our vantage point, scientific theories of previous generations often appear ludicrous. Clearly much of what we know at a given time is limited by both technological and conceptual abilities that are subsequently overcome, but the more ludicrous theories are flawed because of their underlying social ideas. Sound and valuable observations of the structure of the cell were made a hundred years ago with optical microscopes that provided magnifications up to only 500 to 1000 times and have simply been superseded by the observations made possible by magnifications of 200,000 with the electron microscope. The magnifying power of the microscope however, was not the limiting factor in the observations of leading scientists of the seventeenth and eighteenth centuries, such as the accomplished microscopist van Leeuwenhoek, who asserted that he had *seen* "exceedingly minute forms of men with arms, heads and legs complete inside sperm" under the microscope (Hillman, 1977, p. 221). Rather, it was the 20-centuries-long *concept* and tradition, stemming from Aristotle, that women, as totally passive beings, contribute nothing but an incubator-womb to the developing fetus that springs full-blown, so to speak, from the head of the sperm. One's conceptual framework, a certain state of mind, permits one to see and accommodate certain things but not others.

One problem for scientists is the common affliction of becoming emotionally committed to their hypotheses and theories. Thomas Chamberlin, a geologist, was president of the University of Wisconsin in 1890 when he described that phenomenon:

> The moment one has offered an original explanation for a phenomenon which seems satisfactory, that moment affection for his intellectual child springs into existence; and as the explanation grows into a definite theory, his parental affections cluster about his intellectual offspring, and it grows more and more dear to him, so that, while he holds it seemingly tentative, it is still lovingly tentative, and not impartially tentative. So soon as this parental affection takes possession of the mind, there is a rapid passage to the adoption of the theory. There is an unconscious selection and magnifying of the phenomena that fall into harmony with the theory and support it, and an unconscious neglect of those that fail of coincidence. The mind lingers with pleasure upon the facts that fall happily into the embrace of the theory, and feels a natural coldness toward those that seem refractory. Instinctively there is a special searching-out of phenomena that support it, for the mind is led by its desires. There springs up, also, an unconscious pressing of the theory to make it fit the facts, and a pressing of the facts to make them fit the theory. When these biasing tendencies set in, the mind rapidly degenerates into the partiality of paternalism. (1965, p. 755)

The second important problem is that scientists, like everyone else, are born and raised in a particular culture of beliefs, biases, values, and opinions, and, to one degree or another, they will be affected in their work by what they hope, believe, want, or need to be true. When the area of research involves matters that touch very sensitively, indeed often explosively, on scientists' own daily lives, it is even more difficult to maintain, or unrealistic to expect, a neutral, value-free, objective science. But this objective, value-free stance is precisely what our culture claims to be *the* characteristic both of the male mind and science. As the historian of science, Margaret Osler, expresses the problem, "Scientific activity always takes place within a framework of assumptions about the nature of the world and the kind of knowledge it is possible for us to acquire about that world. . . . [T]he conceptual framework which [the scientific community] chooses to adopt reflect[s] the values of the scientists" at any given period (1980a, pp. 277, 279). Consequently, all sciences bear a heavy load of social values, "since they are linked to the people who create them and to the social concerns of those people" (1980b, p. 123). "The history of science teaches us that the choice of assumptions and of methods as well as the choice of questions to be investigated are choices based on values" (1980a, p. 281).

But, it can be argued, even if scientists have personal biases, surely it is a purpose of *the* scientific method to protect research and its conclusions from the investigator's biases, values, and beliefs. Unfortunately, there is no single correct scientific methodology; these biases, values, and beliefs—a scientist's world view as well as mundane daily life circumstances—can and do affect scientific methodology itself. Even though scientific methodology is meant to constantly examine and challenge established scientific beliefs, including the investigator's own, it can be manipulated to support and strengthen those beliefs. The actual questions that a scientist finds interesting to ask and chooses to investigate may be biased; the questions may presume certain truths and premises that are not supportable but incorporate the informal opinions, values, or judgments of the scientist. Thus, the question both precludes asking valid and fundamental questions and also determines the nature and limits of the answers, which were predetermined; in fact, production of those answers was the reason for asking the questions in the first place.

For example, the question, "Why are all males aggressive?" produces very different answers from one asking, "Are males of all species aggressive, and under what circumstances and how is 'aggressivity' displayed?" Scientists' biases, values, and beliefs also affect the nature of the assumptions, usually unspoken and unacknowledged, that are being made. The methodology itself may be flawed if it assumes order, logic, and hierarchy. Furthermore, the scientist's values, beliefs, and cultural experiences will affect the language used to pose the questions and to describe observations; the observations that are made and those that are not made; the controls that should be but are not used; the interpretations that *are* made and the contradictory data and alternative interpretations that are *not* mentioned. Because of these world views, biases, and beliefs that are so integral a part of our consciousness that they may remain forever unexamined and unspecified, many of the premises of research that bear on questions of human behaviors and characteristics are flawed by ethnocentric and androcentric or anthropocentric assumptions. In our culture such assumptions include the ideas that all normal males are aggressive, that women are inferior, and that dominance and control are natural categories.

Until quite recently, assumptions such as these were unchallenged, and they molded and distorted the observations, interpretations, and conclusions of research in the fields of primatology and anthropology and became unexamined premises for research in the biological sciences, as will be shown in the following chapters.

Even though there has always been a strong current of biological determinist thinking in the sciences of human behavior, it surges at times of political and social upheaval. In the mid-nineteenth century, the antislavery, women's rights, and suffrage movements were accompanied by a flourishing of the recurrently discredited science of craniology; human brains were weighed, measured, and remeasured in an effort to find some index of quantitative inferiority of the brains of women and exslaves and other blacks (Fee, 1979; Shields, 1975). Anatomists in one decade found females to be deficient in the lobe of the brain believed to be the "seat" of intelligence. The next decade had to reverse the measurements when it was decided that another lobe accounted for "man's" highest achievements. After a half-century of pronouncements about female and "Negro" brains and futile efforts to demonstrate consistent quantitative differences, the science of craniology faded away. But there were many other physicians and scientists throughout the last half of the nineteenth century and up to the present who remained dedicated to the task of explaining why women and blacks are naturally fitted, biologically destined, for the social roles they indeed fill and, consequently, for social inferiority and economic dependence. It is in woman's nature to do the caring, tedious jobs.

In recent decades several important areas of biology have produced explanations and theories of sex differences in behaviors and characteristics: the field of sociobiology, the sciences of human cultural evolution, and research on the effects of sex hormones on the developing brain and on subsequent adult behavior. While these areas will be discussed in detail in later chapters, I should like to use here the example of sociobiology in demonstrating the relationship between a particular contemporary field of science and its social context.

Even though the field of sociobiology has provided important insights into the social behaviors of animals, E. O. Wilson introduced Sociobiology in 1975 (the capitalized form will be used here to specify Wilsonian sociobiology) as the ultimate discipline of human behavior, the "new synthesis" that will "reformulate the foundations of the social sciences" (Wilson, 1975, p. 4). Sociobiology considers all human behaviors, characteristics, social relationships and forms of social organization to be biologically, genetically, and evolutionarily determined.

Human characteristics and relationships are explicitly programmed in our genes, having evolved over millions of years because they were adaptive for survival. The very fact of their existence proves they have to exist, otherwise they would not have evolved. Not only do Sociobiologists claim to establish the innateness of racism and wars, but also sex differences in social roles and position. Prominent in their writings is the specific attention they pay to the issues, concerns, viewpoints and goals of the contemporary women's movement. In fact, such issues become central to Sociobiological theory-making. "Sociobiology relies heavily upon the biology of male-female differences. . . . Ironically, mother nature appears to be a sexist" (Barash, 1977, p. 283). Sociobiology announces certain characteristics of the female and male "nature" to be universal and then explains why they are universal: why women are genetically predisposed to be "attached" to home and nursery and men to business and professions; why men are hasty, fickle, and promiscuous and women are faithful and selective; why men are aggressive and dominant and women nurturant and coy. And as a final message to women everywhere, Sociobiologists explain the "naturalness" of rape. Barash implicitly dismisses the entire women's movement with manly contempt and sarcasm:

> It strains belief that around the globe and throughout history women have been the victims of a coordinated and sustained plot by churlish males who have conspired to manipulate the social structure to exploit women by forcing them into unwanted roles. (1979, p. 72)

The significance of Sociobiological theories lies not only in the seriousness of the political implications but in the fact that Sociobiology uses shoddy and deceptive methodology. A central problem is an ethnocentrism that generates unexamined assumptions, biased questions, the selective use of animal models, anthropomorphism of concepts and language (*machismo* in insects, *prostitution* in apes and birds, *homosexuality* in worms), and distortions and misrepresentations in the use of data. Their basic premises are flawed: the universal behaviors, characteristics, and sex differences of humans that they presume to explain as biological and innate are *not* universal either within or between cultures; the behaviors of animals *cannot* be taken to indicate innate behaviors of humans, "uncontaminated" by culture, since animals learn and have cultures; nor are the animal behaviors they describe universal. But, most importantly, it is *not* possible to tease apart genetic and other biological factors from environmental and learning factors in human development. This is, in fact, a meaningless way to view the problem, since, from conception the relationships between the actions of genes and the environment of fetus are inextricable. The very structure and functioning of the brain, the organ of mind and mediator of behavior, are influenced by environmental input both before and after birth. Thus, whatever the genetic and hormonal influences are on the development of our fetal and newborn brains, they are inextricable from the influences of the environmental milieu, from sensory input and learning. In addition, in its structure and function, the human brain is qualitatively and quantitatively different from the brains of other animals. Its capacity for learning, consciousness, memory and intent, motivation, intelligence, innovativeness, and flexibility frees us from predetermined and stereotypic behavior patterns, and it also has created cultures of staggering complexity and sophistication that affect our behaviors from the time of birth. No science or discipline can peel off layers of culture and learning and find an untouched core of biological *nature*. Rather than biology acting to constrain and limit our potentialities, it is, in fact, the supreme irony that our magnificent brains, with their nearly limitless structural and functional potentiality for learning, flexibility, and choice-making, have produced *cultures* that constrain and limit those potentialities.

Distinctions of human characteristics and temperaments into *innate* male and female natures have been social, *cultural* constructs and are not *natural*. They are part of an ideology that attempts to make what are in fact social and political distinctions appear to be natural and biological and, therefore, to justify differences in social roles and also relationships of dominance and subordination. Furthermore, that which can be "shown" to be natural easily becomes the norm that justifies rules and mores from which deviance warrants disapproval or punishment.

GLOBAL POLITICS AND BIOLOGICAL DETERMINISM

The underlying scientific issue in evaluating any theory of biological determinism is the feasibility of isolating biological from learned influences in the determination of physical characteristics, behaviors, social relationships, and social organization. The effort to separate genetic and environmental influences continues to plague thinking in many fields. Yet it represents a false dichotomy that does not reflect biological processes, but like other dualisms I shall discuss later, may serve reactionary social and political purposes in certain social-scientific contexts, like the Sociobiological discourse on human nature and female and male natures.

The evident lack of scientific usefulness of the gene-culture dichotomy is belied by the penetration of these ideas into all of the social sciences and by the massive media exposure that Sociobiology has received as a scientific "break-through" in major newspapers, television, radio, and popular weekly and monthly magazines. A front-page article in the *New York Times* announced the "revolutionary" implications of Wilson's first book before it appeared (Alper, Beckwith, and Miller, 1978). Sociobiologists Irven DeVore and Robert Trivers have made a film (*Sociobiology: Doing What Comes Naturally*) and a science curriculum (*Exploring Human Nature*), which have been incorporated into high school science courses throughout the country. Articles have appeared in *Home and Garden*, *People*, *Time*, *Psychology Today*, the *New York Times Sunday Magazine*, the *Boston Globe*, and the *National Observer* (Lowe, 1978, p. 124). *Newsweek*

(May 18, 1981) carried profiles of a woman and a man on its cover and the bold-face caption, "The Sexes: How They Differ and Why." Its message about biologically determined sex differences in ability and achievement reached a quarter of a million *Newsweek* subscribers. Through its reproduction in the *Reader's Digest* (September, 1981), 31 million more readers in 16 languages were reached.

If this amount of attention, which also includes the continuing production by Sociobiologists of new books that say nothing new and are aimed at the lay public, is being paid to a question with neither intrinsic scientific or intellectual merit nor hope of definitive proof, we can suspect that it is a question of great political, social, or economic merit and most likely all three. It seems, then, important to explore the circumstances that can help to explain why a significant part of the biological and social scientific enterprise is devoted to the teasing out and measurement of gender or sex differences, in efforts to find genetic, hormonal, or other biological bases of behaviors and characteristics that are claimed to be differentiated by sex. Who cares and why? How do reputable scientists come to advance or support theories of human behaviors and social organization on the basis of scientific assumptions and methods so flimsy that they would be unacceptable to themselves and to the scientific community if the studies were in their own fields of expertise, such as entomology (Wilson's field)? The answers are many and complex and require analysis at levels from the most personal to the more universal. As I have already suggested, we need to look to a patriarchal social, political, and economic system that gains much in power, privileges, and profits for itself and for individual men from the subordinate position of women and now finds itself faced with the first serious historic threat to its dominance. The women's movement and feminist scholarship can create revolutionary changes in our political/social/economic system and in the entire body of human knowledge and epistemology—*and there is no end in sight*. Even for those participating, the potential is awesome; to those on the outside who see or believe themselves to be, sooner or later, the losers, that potential, as well as today's realities, may be intolerable to contemplate.

Wilson and other Sociobiologists deny that Sociobiological theories have "a reactionary political message" or can be "construed as a support of the status quo" (Wilson, 1978, pp. 292-3) or that they can be held responsible for the abuse and misinterpretation of their conclusions. There are, however, innumerable examples of the explicitly sociological and political content of Sociobiologists' writings as it is incorporated in their underlying assumptions, their perceptions and descriptions of human behaviors and social relationships, and the conclusions they draw within their logical system. It is, after all, making a particular political analysis to say that male aggressivity and dominance over women, territoriality and xenophobia (that is, national chauvinism and racism), conformity and in-doctrinability, are innate human traits, specifically because such assertions withdraw these issues from the political arena. The claim makes these issues biological rather than sociological, even though claims for the innateness of these and other human characteristics are not supported by evidence, but are inferences drawn from fallacious analogies, speculations, subjective belief, and illogical thought processes. Thus, they are not scientific assertions. Such explanations are very soothing to some liberal humanists, which many scientists and academicians believe themselves to be, who decry injustice and inequalities but are relieved of the necessity of action, since wars, oppression, and discrimination are natural and inevitable. Biological determinist theories are, in addition, uncritically embraced as self-confirming by all who prefer and defend the *status quo* and welcome its legitimization by science.

Biological determinists may appear to be apolitical because they carefully avoid discussion or recognition of any political, cultural, or social factors that could account for the presumably innate characteristics that interest them, just as they avoid acknowledgment of the existence of any class or group that oppresses others or controls and manipulates the media (which account for a major share of the "trait" for *indoctrinability*), or benefits from oppressing, exploiting, or controlling. Ignoring political and social factors in analyzing the origins of political and social relationships is, in fact, taking a very specific political position under the guise of science: it is not only useless but biologically hazardous to do social "tampering" and to have political programs that fly in the face of our genetically programmed natures. And indeed Sociobiologists are sometimes explicit in that conclusion:

> It's time we started viewing ourselves as having biological, genetic and natural components to our behavior, and that we start setting up a physical and social world to match those tendencies. (Trivers, from film, *Sociobiology: Doing What Comes Naturally*)

When "those tendencies" are defined to be male aggressivity, female passivity, dominance hierarchies, sex roles, territoriality, racism, xenophobia, competitiveness, and conformity and are the descriptive litany of behaviors and relationships that exist in the particular social orders of which we are a part, it takes no imagination to see how Sociobiological views can form, unchanged, the ideological base for any conservative or reactionary political programs.

And indeed they do. The extreme right in France and the openly fascist National Front in Britain have embraced Wilson's Sociobiological views as the scientific basis for their racist, sexist, and antisemitic programs.

> Against this destructive theory [Marxism], we racialists declare that man and society are the creation of his biological nature. We insist not only that genetic inheritance determines inequality—not social environment—but that social organisation and behaviour themselves are essentially the product of our biological evolution. . . . The theory that behaviour and social organisation are determined to a crucial extent

by genetic inheritance is now central to that most progressive branch of the biological sciences called "sociobiology." (Verrall, 1979, p. 10)

While Sociobiologists themselves acknowledge the racist and chauvinist implications that could be drawn from their interrelated theories of altruism, kin selection and inclusive fitness,[1] the spokesmen for the National Front translate these theories explicitly into their outspokenly racial program:

> Of a far greater significance is the basic instinct common to all species to identify only with one's like group; to in-breed and to shun out-breeding. In human society this instinct is *racial* and it—above all else—operates to ensure genetic survival. (Verrall, 1979, p. 11)

This statement did not require any tortured extrapolation from the claim of the Sociobiologist, W. D. Hamilton:

> I hope to produce evidence that some things which are often treated as purely cultural in man—say racial discrimination—have deep roots in our animal past and thus are quite likely to rest on direct genetic foundations. (1975, p. 134)

National Front theorists have revived nineteenth-century brain-science in support of racism:

> We all know that differences between races in the capacity for rational thought are explained by inherited differences in the physical structure of the brain. (Verrall, 1979, p. 10)

They also spell out the implications of Sociobiological research on sex differences, stating that the obvious existence of male dominance and aggression and of female passivity and domesticity in the animal world

> . . . quickly demonstrate that "feminist" talk of sexual roles being conditioned by society itself is the most puerile Marxist rubbish. Sexual and other behaviour differs between man and woman simply because of differences in male and female hormone secretions. . . . This is why men and women think and behave differently. (Ibid., p. 10)

While scientists, in this case, are one step removed from the reactionary political applications of their biological determinist theories, supplying only the ideological underpinnings, this was not always the case. As early as 1895 German

---

[1] The presumably genetically based tendency to help relatives who carry some of your own genes, since that enhances your own reproductive fitness; that is, it enhances the survival in others of genes identical to some of your own.

scientists and physicians were formulating theories of "racial hygiene" (also known as *eugenics*) and suggesting medical practices that could weed out the poor, feebleminded, criminal, and other biological "misfits" who threatened Nordic superiority (Proctor, 1982). Their Society for Racial Hygiene became one of the more important biomedical societies in Germany. Along with racist social anthropologists, it welcomed the rise of Hitler, who could implement its policies wholesale. By 1938, the medical wing of the Nazi party, the National Socialist Doctor's Association, had a membership of over 30,000 doctors, about 60 percent of all practicing physicians. Laws for the sterilization or "mercy killings" of institutionalized "misfits" were passed and carried out, claiming hundreds of thousands of victims. The Nuremberg and Buchenwald trials finally revealed the role of physicians and scientists in the experimentations, carried out in Nazi concentration camps to the endpoint of death, on Jews, women, homosexuals, Poles, and others considered to be biological inferiors.

Biological determinist thinking is also an important part of the philosophy underlying the political program of the New Right in the United States today, expressed in its efforts to reinforce the patriarchal family and reinstate it as women's exclusive sphere by withdrawing programs for social welfare, removing women from the labor force, and bringing their sexuality and reproductivity more fully under state and male control (Eisenstein, 1982). Woman is to be legally defined and socially confined as mother, reproducer, and nurturer; dependent and subordinate.

While it may be argued that scientists cannot be held responsible for all of the uses to which their published scientific work is put or for distortions it may suffer, they *are* responsible for the quality of the work they publish, for the honesty and validity of the questions they ask, the reliability of the data and the assumptions they use, the methodology and logic by which they pass from premises to conclusions, and the breadth or openmindedness of their interpretations and conclusions. Thus, by choosing public and political arenas to aggressively propagate their ideas and by violating basic tenets of scientific methodology and integrity, Sociobiologists have made unfounded theories accessible for use and abuse by reactionary political ideologists. The European and American political Right has not had to distort either the words or the implications of Sociobiological writings in order to make them relevant as scientific justification for New Right political ideology.

BIOLOGICAL DETERMINISM IN FEMINIST THOUGHT

Finally, it must also be acknowledged that biological determinist or Sociobiological assumptions either implicitly or explicitly underlie, in varying degrees, a broad spectrum of feminist thought and writings that includes both lesbian separatists and liberal reformers in the United States, psychoanalytic and Marxist essentialists in France, and some American academicians who are engaged in the critical reinterpretation of traditional scholarship in their fields of sociology, biology, and psychology. Their writings represent a range of views. These include the position that gender differences are deep and irreconcilable, and that women's characteristics and temperaments are superior and should be celebrated. Another, probably more pervasive and heterogeneous position holds that even though there are biologically based gender differences, they do not imply superiority or inferiority nor do they justify inequities in social, economic, and political policy and practice. Rather they call for public education and reform of sexist policies, laws, and practices.

My argument is not against having a range of programs and approaches generated by a variety of viewpoints; the effectiveness of any movement for social and political change can only be enhanced by its capacity to encompass such a range (i.e., by its capacity to include people holding a variety of ideas and preferences for political and social styles, tactics, and strategies). However the ultimate effectiveness of movements and programs can only be weakened if they rely upon theories of biological determinism. This is both because such theories are seriously flawed and basically scientifically meaningless and because essentialist thinking (i.e., belief in the existence of an ultimate essence within each of us that does not change) has always functioned as a central feature of ideologies of oppression. The "voice of the natural," to use Barthes' phrase, has always been a voice for the *status quo* (Sturrock, 1979, p. 60). That is, essentialism is flawed because it presents a limited and limiting perspective on nature and human potentialities and because it is a poor strategy, a view expressed as well by the Combahee River Collective: "As Black women we find any type of biological determinism a particularly dangerous and reactionary basis upon which to build a politic" (Hull *et al.*, 1982, p. 17). It is always used by ruling orders as a justification for their seizure or possession of power and control. Questions of biological difference are raised for political reasons and frequently are given legitimacy by being posed as scientific issues. We may indeed value the characteristics that in our Western societies are associated with femaleness—and, indeed, *need* to celebrate them, since they seem to be the only force standing in the way of our society's plunge into self-destruction—but we need not justify them as natural, biological, or innate. That we start learning our characteristics and temperaments from the time of birth already burdens them with the possibility of more permanence than is good for our biological potentialities for development, growth, and change. The chance for liberating ideas lies not with trying to turn traditional or misogynist or racist ideologies 180 degrees around and in our favor, but in turning them under completely, destroying their roots. We cannot replace one false illusion with another when our central task is demystification and when our power to transform lies in clear-eyed knowledge and an appreciation of complexity, integration, and change.

Since in this book I go beyond a critique of biological determinist theories to offer alternative interpretations and contradictory evidence, I actually engage in the very activity I warn readers to question, if not distrust. Put differently, I present "facts" to refute "facts," which I claim have been made (up) in the interests of the dominant group—white men. I offer feminist interpretations to replace patriarchal interpretations, which I say reflect the ideology, desires, and necessities of a particular interest group. I am indeed caught in my own trap!

But perhaps I am not. As I will try to maintain throughout my work, I see any theory—feminist or patriarchal—as flexible and open to change. In fact, as a scientist and a political being, my "mind lingers with pleasure" when I encounter theories that allow for constant change, interaction, contradiction, ambivalence. They have always appealed to me enormously. I have interpreted my own experimental research results accordingly and have been much more interested in the work of those scientists whose work is motivated by a desire to demonstrate the flexibility rather than the biological limits and rigidity of the brain and its resulting behavioral possibilities.

Holding a view or a philosophy of flux in science is in harmony with a philosophical position that endorses political movements and attitudes that aim at social change by means of opposition to prevailing opinion and the status quo. But I maintain that the revolutionary force and the open spirit of inquiry that underlies any striving for change is no more "partisan" or "biased" than so-called objective philosophical and intellectual positions. But as it actively aims for change, it opposes the Powers That Be. Feminism is a prime example: it posits that women are oppressed and it openly works for social change. It is developing a profound philosophical world view that will point to change in all systems based upon racial, class, and sexual oppression.

I would argue that the nature of my world view, as it influences my approach in this book, is its own justification. That is, while biological determinists—in the face of overwhelming contradictions—assert the genetic, hormonal, and evolutionary determinism of human nature and our behaviors, it is my aim to describe all those myriad contradictions that make such theories totally inadequate as explanations of behaviors and forms of social relationships. Even if some of the "facts" I cite in support of my arguments are disputable, I will have made the case—and I hope convincingly so—that there is no simple "truth" as Sociobiologists and other supporters of the status quo would have us believe. In the absence of clear paths to truth and social justice, the one hope for bringing about change for the better lies in the capacities of the human brain to make it possible to break out of the cultural constraints that some human beings have constructed to the detriment of others.

REFERENCES

Alper, J., Beckwith, J., and Miller, L. Sociobiology as a political issue. In A. Caplan (Ed.), *The sociobiology debate*. New York: Harper & Row, 1978.

Barash, D. *Sociobiology and behavior*. New York: Elsevier, 1977.

Barash, D. *The whisperings within*. New York: Harper & Row, 1979.

Chamberlin, T. The method of multiple working hypotheses. *Science*, 1965, *148*, 754-759. (Old series, 1890, *15*, 92).

Combahee River Collective. A black feminist statement. In G. T. Hull, P. B. Scott, and B. Smith (Eds.), *But some of us are brave*. Old Westbury: The Feminist Press, 1977.

Cravens, H. *The triumph of evolution*. Philadelphia: University of Pennsylvania Press, 1978.

Eisenstein, Z. The sexual politics of the new right: Understanding the crisis of liberalism for the 1980s. *Signs*, 1982, *7*, 567-588.

Fee, E. Nineteenth century craniology: the study of the female skull. *Bulletin of the History of Medicine*, 1979, *53*, 415-433.

Hamilton, W. Innate social aptitudes of man: an approach from evolutionary genetics. In R. Fox (Ed.), *Biosocial Anthropology*. New York: Wiley, 1975.

Haraway, D. The biological enterprise: sex, mind, and profit from human engineering to sociobiology. *Radical History Review*, 1979, *20*, 206-237.

Hillman, J. *The myth of analysis*. Evanston: Northwestern University Press, 1972.

Kuhn, T. *The structure of scientific revolutions*. 2nd ed. Chicago: University of Chicago Press, 1970.

Lowe, M. Sociobiology and sex differences. *Signs*, 1978, *4*, 118-125.

Merchant, C. *The death of nature, women, ecology and the scientific revolution*. New York: Harper & Row, 1980.

Osler, M. Apocryphal knowledge: the misuse of science. In M. Hanen, M. Osler, and R. Weyant (Eds.), *Science, pseudoscience and society*. Waterloo: Wilfrid Laurier University Press, 1980. (a)

Osler, M. Sex, science, and values: a critique of sociobiological accounts of sex differences. *Proceedings third annual meeting Canadian research institute for the advancement of women*, 1980, 119-124. (b)

Proctor, R. Nazi science and medicine. *Science for the People*, 1982, *14*, 15-20.

Shields, S. Functionalism, Darwinism, and the psychology of women. A study in social myth. *American Psychologist*, 1975, *30*, 739-754.

Sturrock, J. Roland Barthes. In J. Sturrock (Ed.), *Structuralism and since*. Oxford: Oxford University Press, 1979.

Verrall, R. Sociobiology: the instincts in our genes. *Spearhead*, 1979, *127*, 10-11.

Wilson, E. O. *Sociobiology: the new synthesis*. Cambridge: Harvard University Press, 1975.

Wilson, E. O. *On human nature*. Cambridge: Harvard University Press, 1978.

Chapter 2
Sociobiology, Biological Determinism, and Human Behavior

Science, it would seem, is not sexless; she is a man, a father, and infected, too.
                                                          Virginia Woolf, 1938, p. 139

Because Wilsonian sociobiology is a particularly dramatic contemporary version of biological determinist theories of human behavior, because it is powerful and persuasive, because it is a particularly good example of bad science, because it provides "scientific" support for a dominant political ideology that directly opposes every goal and issue raised by the women's movement, and because it has been aggressively marketed and perceptibly incorporated into our culture, it seems a fitting area with which to begin the examination of science and scientific theories of biological determinism.

While the general field of sociobiology has a long and solid tradition of studying the social behavior of animals, in 1975 E. O. Wilson, whose area of expertise is insect behaviors, sought to establish sociobiology "as the systematic study of the biological basis of all social behavior." He stated his conviction that "It may not be too much to say that sociology and the other social sciences, as well as the humanities, are the last branches of biology waiting to be included in the Modern Synthesis" (Wilson, 1975b, p. 4). Thus, Wilson and those in his school of human sociobiology believe that all human behaviors, social relationships, and organization are genetically evolved adaptations, as I will describe below. Before proceeding, however, to a critique of the work of Wilsonian sociobiologists, it is important to distinguish it from the general field of sociobiology. There are many other scientists who study the social behaviors and characteristics of animals and are therefore sociobiologists but do not make reckless extrapolations to human social relationships and behaviors. Their observations and interpretations form an important part of the evidence I use to support my arguments concerning the inadequacies and distortions inherent in the "science" that Wilson and his followers popularize.

By reducing human behavior and complex social phenomena to genes and to inherited and programmed mechanisms of neuronal functioning, the message of the new Wilsonian Sociobiology becomes rapidly clear: we had best resign ourselves to the fact that the more unsavory aspects of human behavior, like wars, racism, and class struggle, are inevitable results of evolutionary adaptations based in our genes. And of key importance is the fact that the particular roles

performed by women and men in society are also biologically, genetically determined; in fact, civilization as we know it, or perhaps any at all, could not
have evolved in any other way. Thus the Sociobiologist and popular writer David
Barash says, "There is good reason to believe that we are (genetically) primed
to be much less sexually egalitarian than we appear to be" (Barash, 1979, p.
47)

But it is not only that the direct political and social statements and theories
of Sociobiologists are dangerous to the interests and well being of women and
minorities. If Sociobiology were a valid science, by even traditional standards,
we should have to find ways to cope with the consequences of incontrovertible
"truths." But this Sociobiology is deeply flawed conceptually, methodologically,
and logically *as a science*. It is only *because* it concerns itself with the most
complex aspects of human behaviors and social relationships, about which we
suffer enormous depths of both ignorance and emotion, that Sociobiology achieves
acceptance as a science. The same kinds of logical and methodological flaws in
the sciences, say, of ant or camel behavior would be immediately obvious and
unacceptable.

In this chapter I first review some basic postulates and assumptions of Sociobiological theory and outline the methodologies used for theory building. I then
offer a detailed critique of Sociobiologists' theories and methods and indicate
some alternative observations and interpretations that contradict their assumptions
and conclusions. Finally, since the fundamental scientific issue is the validity
of a theory based on the genetic determination of human behavior, I explore the
relationship between genes and the fetal environment and between biology and
learning.

SOME PREMISES AND APPROACHES OF SOCIOBIOLOGY

Natural Selection of Behaviors Through Gene Transmission

The basic premise of Sociobiology is that human behaviors and certain aspects
of social organization have evolved, like our bodies, through adaptations based
on Darwinian natural selection. It is important to understand Darwin's theory
of evolution of the *physical forms* of animals by adaptation in order to understand
its application by Sociobiologists to *behavior*. In its modern version, the theory
assumes that by some genetic recombination or mutation, a particular anatomical
characteristic appears anew in a species, let us say gray body color in a family
of orange moths. If the gray color in the moths' particular ecological setting
permits more gray than orange moths to survive predation and other causes of
an early demise and therefore to reach sexual maturity so that more gray moths
are reproduced than their relatives of the original orange color, then an increasing

proportion of moths will be gray in successive generations. Over time, the genes for gray will be present in increasing numbers of moths and become a predominant feature of moths in *that* ecological setting. The new genetic feature for gray is then considered, in the language of Darwinian evolution, to be adaptive through natural selection, since it contributes to the maximum fitness of the moths, with *maximum fitness* being defined as the ability to leave many healthy descendants that are themselves able to reproduce and thus spread the genes for gray body color.

Sociobiologists suggest and assume that *behaviors* also evolve in similar ways so that "adaptive" and "successful" behaviors become based in our genes, and that certain genetic configurations became selected because they result in behaviors that are adaptive for survival. Our "innate" predispositions to display these behaviors constitute our human *nature*. It is important to note at this point that to be valid the theory requires that human behaviors be represented by a particular genetic configuration, because evolution through natural selection requires genetic variations (that is, mutant forms) from which to select. But Sociobiologists themselves, as well as geneticists, agree that it is not possible to link any specific human behavior with any specific gene or genetic configuration. The only evidence for such a link is that which is provided by Sociobiologists' circular logic. This logic makes a *premise* of the genetic basis of behaviors, then cites a certain animal or human behavior, constructs a speculative story to explain how the behavior (*if* it were genetically based) could have served or could serve to maximize the reproductive success of the individual, and this *conjecture* then becomes evidence for the *premise* that the behavior was genetically determined.

> This is the central principle of sociobiology: insofar as a behavior reflects at least some component of gene action, individuals will tend to behave so as to maximize their fitness. . . . The result is a very strange sort of purposefulness, in which a goal—maximization of fitness—appears to be sought, but without any of the participants necessarily having awareness of what they are doing, or why. (Barash, 1979, pp. 29 and 25)

Notice the *insofar* clause is key and serves to confuse the issue. All behavior of course reflects at least *some* component of gene action. Individuals of any species of animal behave within the limits of the broad range of biological capabilities defined by their genes. Humans walk rather than fly. Birds peck at their food. When we are frightened, our hearts beat faster. But what is really at issue in Sociobiological theory is not the physical capacity for behavior that biology provides but rather the genetic encoding of the entire range of complex human behaviors and characteristics that are expressed in a nearly infinite variety of ways by different individuals and cultures and often not expressed at all, such as altruism, loyalty, dominance, competitiveness, aggressivity. In addition, Sociobiology claims genetic encoding for such arbitrarily chosen and questionably sexually differentiated "traits" as coyness, fickleness, promiscuity, rapaciousness, or maternalism.

Sociobiologists make a passing attempt to acknowledge that learning, culture, or environment plays a role in human behavior, but it is clear that their hearts (and minds) are not engaged by this idea. David Barash clearly states his position on the contribution of learning to behavior:

> Core elements are the essential person, an entity bequeathed by evolution to each of us; they are the *us* upon which experience acts. The great strength of sociobiology is that its conception of the "core" is grounded in evolution. . . (1979, p. 10)

> Biology and culture undoubtedly work together, but it is tempting to speculate that our biology is somehow more real, lying unnoticed within each of us, quietly but forcefully manipulating much of our behavior. Culture, which is overwhelmingly important in shaping the myriad details of our lives, is more likely seen as a thin veneer, compared to the underlying ground substance of our biology. (1979, p. 14)

Richard Dawkins, the Sociobiologist who coined the catchy anthropomorphic phrase, *selfish genes*, explains that genes and their expression are unaffected by environment:

> Now they swarm in huge colonies, safe inside gigantic lumbering robots, sealed off from the outside world, communicating with it by tortuous indirect routes, manipulating it by remote control. They are in you and in me; they created us, body and mind; and their preservation is the ultimate rationale for our existence. They have come a long way, those replicators. Now they go by the name of genes, and we are their survival machines. (1976, p. 21)

Mary Midgley, the British philosopher, suggests that "Dawkin's crude, cheap, blurred genetics is not just an expository device. It is the kingpin of his crude, cheap, blurred psychology" (1980a, p. 120). She further notes how the message of such "science" was transmitted to the general public by the cover of *Time* magazine's sociobiology number, which showed two puppets making love "while invisible genes twitch the strings above them . . ." (1980b, p. 26).

Sex Differences in Reproductive Strategies

Since a key concept for Sociobiological theory is that behaviors are programmed to maximize the ability of the body's genes to reproduce themselves, an important area for Sociobiological speculation is that of reproduction itself. The second key postulate, then, is that the two sexes have a different strategy for maximizing their fitness through the reproduction of the largest possible number of offspring, and it is to this difference that Sociobiologists are able to attribute what they consider to be differences in female and male *natures*, behaviors, and social roles. Sociobiologists believe that women and men have different strategies and behaviors for assuring the reproduction and survival of their genes because they have an "unequal" biological investment in each offspring. Their reasoning is that since human males produce millions of sperm a day and can theoretically "sire offspring with different women at hourly or at most daily intervals" (Van Den Berghe and Barash, 1977, p. 814), their investment in the future in terms of the maximum reproduction of their genes in offspring lies in inseminating as many women as possible. Also, their relative investment in any one offspring is small. The human female, however, has a much greater investment in each of her offspring because her egg is 85,000 times larger than a sperm (hence more "expensive" to produce), because she ordinarily produces but one egg at a time and only about 400 in her lifetime, and because she usually produces no more than one offspring a year. Furthermore, since she is the one who gestates the fetus in her body, her expenditure of energy for those months and for the subsequent year or two of lactation and infant care is considerably greater than the father's. Therefore, while the *genetic* contribution from each parent is equivalent (23 chromosomes), the mother contributes a larger proportion of her total reproductive potential and a larger investment of time and energy. These facts, according to Sociobiologists, result in different reproductive strategies in the two sexes: women are selective and choosy—they go for quality: men go for quantity. Thus, E. O. Wilson writes:

> It pays males to be aggressive, hasty, fickle, and undiscriminating. In theory it is more profitable for females to be coy, to hold back until they can identify males with the best genes. . . . Human beings obey this biological principle faithfully. (1978, p. 125)

And Barash explains further:

> The evolutionary mechanism should be clear. Genes that allow females to accept the sorts of mates who make lesser contributions to their reproductive success will leave fewer copies of themselves than will genes that influence the females to be more selective. . . . For males, a very different strategy applies. The maximum advantage goes to individuals with fewer inhibitions. A genetically influenced tendency to "play fast and loose"—"love 'em and leave 'em"—may well reflect more biological reality than most of us care to admit. (1979, p. 48)

The Leap to Sex Differences in Human Social Roles and Characteristics

Thus, we can see that Sociobiologists leap from some obvious facts such as the relative sizes and available numbers of eggs and sperm to sweeping and unwarranted generalizations about and explanations for presumed female and male *innate* characteristics: women are coy, choosy, and fussy; males are fickle and promiscuous. These characteristics then are used to ascribe a biological basis to such social phenomena and arrangements as marital fidelity for women and adultery, polygyny (harems), and rape by men. Sociobiologists explain that a woman stands to lose much less by her husband's sexual infidelity and by his fathering of children outside the marriage than a husband stands to lose by his wife's infidelity, since he would, in the latter case, be helping to rear children who do not bear his genes. It is for this reason, they claim, that there is a sexual double standard: a differential valuation of virginity and a differential condemnation of marital infidelity (Van Den Berghe and Barash, 1977).

Sociobiologists derive two other important postulates from the observation that the eggs and sperms that women and men contribute to the process of conception are different. The first is predictable: since a woman has a greater investment in terms of egg size and the time and energy spent in gestation, she also invests the major portion of total parental care in her offspring. She does this in order to protect her biological investment and her genes, since each of her offspring represents a greater proportion of her total reproductive capacity than it does for the father. An added factor is that women know with certainty that their genes have been passed on in their children; men have to take it on faith.

> Throughout their evolutionary history, males have generally been ill advised to devote themselves too strongly to the care of children, since the undertaking might turn out to be a wasted effort. (Barash, 1979, pp. 108-9)

There is a second important Sociobiological postulate derived from the fact that the total number of eggs available for fertilization is far fewer than the number of sperm available to fertilize them: competition among males for females is inevitable, since females, with their limited reproductive potential, are a scarce resource. Because of this competition on the time scale of evolution, the most reproductively successful males came to be those who were larger and more aggressive. It is this inherited male aggressivity that provides the biological basis for male dominance over females, male dominance hierarchies, competitiveness, territoriality, and war.

This, then, is how Sociobiology sees itself as replacing psychology and sociology. It is a social theory in the guise of biology; Sociobiologists provide the biological basis for all social phenomena and, in particular, for the social roles and the cultural representations of women and men. Thus Dawkins blandly declares:

> The female sex is exploited, and the fundamental evolutionary basis for the exploitation is the fact that eggs are larger than sperms. (1976, p. 158)

And Wilson explains:

> In hunter-gatherer societies, men hunt and women stay home. This strong bias persists in most agricultural and industrial societies and, on that ground alone, appears to have a genetic origin. (1975a, p. 47)

This quotation is particularly perplexing in view of Wilson's obvious and known familiarity with the renowned work of his Harvard colleagues, Richard Lee and Irven DeVore and their coworkers, on hunter-gatherer societies extensively documenting the exact opposite of this claim; that, in fact, women gatherers are away from "home" as much as the men. His knowledge of what women do in agricultural and industrial societies appears similarly based in mythic imagery rather than in modern anthropological scholarship let alone in the real world of agricultural and industrial economies where 50 to 100 percent of women may work outside the home. The most generous interpretation may be that extrapolations to human societies from insects is a hazardous (though not unrewarding) intellectual undertaking even for eminent entomologists. And, finally, to complete the unanimity of the Sociobiological voice, Barash speaks:

> . . . women have almost universally found themselves relegated to the nursery while men derive their greatest satisfaction from their jobs . . . such differences in male-female attachment to family versus vocation could derive in part from hormonal differences between sexes. . . . (1977, p. 301)

I should like to call attention to the last quotation as an example of Sociobiologists' tendency to play loose with both language and logic. Barash speaks of women being *relegated* (assigned, banished) to the nursery, while men *derive satisfaction* from their jobs, hardly equivalent states, conditions, or situations; he then proceeds to base them *both* in biology as though they *were* equivalent. It is like claiming that repeatedly jailed offenders have an innate attachment to their cells.

SOCIOBIOLOGICAL METHODOLOGY IN THEORY BUILDING

Having stated the basic postulates of their theory, Sociobiologists then go on to catalogue the behaviors they consider to be universal and characteristic of humans and thus to be either explainable by or supportive of their theory. These behaviors and characteristics are never defined so that we all can know that we are talking about the same thing, nor are they selected according to any agreed upon criteria from psychology, anthropology, or sociology. The behaviors and characteristics they choose to discuss and explain as universals of human societies are what upper/middle class white male North American and English scientists consider to be characteristic: male aggressivity, territoriality, and tribalism; indoctrinability and conformity; male competitiveness and entrepreneurship; altruism and selfishness. The existence of these supposedly genetically determined human characteristics ("traits") then obviously and logically explains such social phenomena as national chauvinism, xenophobia and war; slavery and capitalism; ethnocentrism and racism; dominance hierarchies and sexism.

SG–B

In order to establish that these presumed universal human characteristics and social phenomena have evolved genetically, the next step in Sociobiological theory building is to demonstrate their existence throughout the animal world. The methodology consists essentially of flipping through the encyclopedic catalogue of animal behaviors and selecting particular behaviors of fishes, birds, insects or mammals that can be readily made to exemplify the various categories of human "traits" and social arrangements that Sociobiologists claim to be universal and genetically based. It is this step that introduces a number of methodological flaws into a theory already suffering from the conceptual ailments I have described.

But before discussing these flaws, I should like to place this critical next step within the context of the basic postulates and methodology of Sociobiology that I have described thus far. First, a picture is presented of human social organization and relationships. These are said to have universal elements that are based upon the existence of universal human behavioral traits that have evolved through natural selection because they were optimally adaptive; that is, the best alternative for survival from among several genetic variations. This assumes a specific genetic coding for specific behavioral "traits" and characteristics. It is not possible to adduce scientific proof for the presence or absence of specific behavioral traits in evolving hominids since traits leave no fossil record. Therefore, there is no way to identify the possible genetic variations from which current behavioral solutions have been selected. This forces Sociobiologists to demonstrate biological and evolutionary continuity by establishing similarities with other living nonhuman species that are viewed as representing an evolutionary continuum culminating in the human species. This is done by then describing carefully selected behaviors of particular species that represent and demonstrate some presumed human universal, such as female "coyness." But since we also do not know what the environmental, ecological, or reproductive problems were that such behaviors or characteristics were solving over the past several hundred million years, Sociobiologists attempt to reconstruct evolutionary history by inventing plausible stories that attempt to show how a particular behavior or social interaction in humans or other species *could* have or *would* have been adaptive and therefore favored by natural selection and genetically carried through subsequent generations. Basically, the aim is to establish the biological "innateness" and inevitability of present-day human behaviors and forms of social organization.

FLAWS IN SOCIOBIOLOGICAL THEORY AND METHODOLOGY

In the methodology and arguments used by Sociobiologists and other biological determinists, one can detect a number of recurring and interrelated flaws. The problems begin with the categories and definitions of behaviors that they consider characteristic of all people. When they proceed to draw analogies to animal behaviors, the problems are compounded by their selective use of particular animal models and by the language and concepts they apply to their descriptions of animal behaviors. We will find that these problems are intimately interrelated, but I shall try to analyze each, giving examples from important Sociobiological concepts, and then discuss two other kinds of methodological problems: the scientific tests one uses to validate hypotheses, and the classical and recurring issue of gene-environment, biology-culture interactions.

Ethnocentricity of Behavioral Description

The first problem lies in the Sociobiological descriptions of presumably universal human behaviors and social relationships, which are curiously similar to social organizations in the white Western industrial capitalist world. In this sense, Sociobiology is in fact an anachronism. It incorporates into its methodology the naive ethnocentric, androcentric, and anthropocentric fallacies discarded at least a decade or two ago by most competent and aware anthropologists and primatologists. Throughout Sociobiological writings there is a pervasive sense of the investigator's perception of his own self as a universal reference point, as equivalent to humanity, viewing all others—the other sex, other classes, races, cultures and civilizations, species, and epochs—in the light and language of his own experiences, values, and beliefs. He and his fraternity become the norm against which all *others* are measured and interpreted. (I use the male pronoun since Sociobiologists with few exceptions are male.) Thus, Sociobiologists make unwarranted generalizations about characteristic human behaviors, such as that "men would rather believe than know" (Wilson, 1975b, p. 561) or that women are coy and marry for upward social mobility. This means that much of the argument of Sociobiologists is devised to explain what *they* define as universal behavioral traits, the existence of which is, however, highly problematic to many students of human behavior. As the anthropologist Nancy Howell has said, " . . . they seem to be innocently ignorant of much of the complexity of human social life and cultures that sociobiology sets out to explain" (1979, p. 1295), though one wonders, when they see rape in the reproductive mechanism of flowers and war as a collective expression of individual male's innate aggressivity, just how "innocently ignorant" they can be. At the same time they seem also to be unconscious of any of the methodological problems that pervade attempts to describe human behavior, problems with which social scientists continue to struggle. As Richard Lewontin has pointed out, "anthropologists have long been acutely conscious of the difficulites of describing human behavior in such a way as not to dictate the analysis by the categories of description" (1976, p. 24). Sociobiologists simply declare what they consider to be categories of behavioral description, for example, entrepreneurship, territoriality, aggression, dominance, without relationship to any cultural or historical context, and then proceed to arbitrarily assign examples of human and animal behavior to that category to demonstrate its universality in the animal world.

The concept of dominance hierarchies is an example of both ethnocentrism of descriptions of human "traits" and the trap of dictating analysis by the use of arbitrary categorization of behavior. Barash asserts that we are "a species organized along distinct lines of dominance" (1979, p. 186). But as Ruth Hubbard points out:

> We in the industrialized countries have grown up in hierarchically structured societies, so that, to us, dominance hierarchies appear natural and inevitable. But it is a mistake to apply the same categories to societies that function quite differently and to pretend that differences between our society and theirs can be expressed merely as matters of degree. . . . To take widely and complexly different social manifestations and scale them along one dimension does violence to the sources and significances of human social behavior. Western technological societies have developed in their ways for their own historical reasons. Other societies have *their* histories that have led to *their* social forms. (1978, p. 134)

As I discuss in detail in Chapter 6, many anthropological studies suggest that dominance hierarchies have not uniformly characterized the organization of human societies either in the past or today. In order to prove both the universality and the evolutionary inevitability of male dominance and dominance hierarchies, Sociobiologists and other biological determinists cite the example of the prototypical primate troop with its chest-pounding leader that has become familiar to us all. I shall discuss the fallacies of this approach in a section to follow on anthropomorphism.

Another example of the ethnocentric and androcentric application of concepts of human behavior to animals can be found in Sociobiological explanations of polygyny (marriage of one man to many wives) and hypergamy (marriage for upward mobility). I have already alluded to the Sociobiological postulate that men, being producers of millions of sperm a day, maximize their fitness by impregnating as many women as possible and, therefore, have traditionally established systems of polygyny, and that women have evolved to be more selective. Van Den Berghe and Barash (1977) describe the fact that in some bird species the females "prefer" polygynous males (here used to mean males that mate with many females) over bachelors. Wondering why, biologists have concluded that it is because the polygynous males command better territory than bachelors, more land providing more food and more protection for the young. This leads Van Den Berghe and Barash (1977) then to another Sociobiological universal of female behavior, hypergamy, marrying males of higher socioeconomic status for upward social mobility:

> Extrapolating to humans, we suggest that men are selected for engaging in male-male competition over resources appropriate to reproductive success, and that women

are selected for preferring men who are successful in that endeavor. Any genetically influenced tendencies in these directions will necessarily be favored by natural selection.

It is true, of course, that social advantages of wealth, power, or rank need not, indeed often do not, coincide with physical superiority. Women in all societies have found a way of resolving this dilemma by marrying wealthy and powerful men while taking young and attractive ones as lovers: the object of the game is to have the husband assume parental obligations for the lover's children. Understandably, men in most societies do not take kindly to such female strategies on the part of their wives, though they are not averse to philandering with other men's wives. The solution to this moral dilemma is the double standard, independently invented in countless societies. In any case, ethnographic evidence points to different reproductive strategies on the part of men and women, and to a remarkable consistency in the institutionalized means of accommodating these biological predispositions. (pp. 814, 815)

In this way the authors postulate a genetic tendency and a "biological pre-disposition" for women to marry men of wealth, power, and rank. Yet it is perfectly obvious that this "predisposition" can govern the behavior of only a small percentage of the world's women, since only a tiny minority of men in all countries of the world have any wealth, power, or rank. Thus, the vast majority of women everywhere, who are in lower socioeconomic classes and marry within their class, are excluded from biological universality. Their "universal" hypergamy is what happens only in romantic fiction. Sociobiologists attempt to establish human *species universals* of behavior by using an extraordinarily ethnocentric and class-biased model based on the behavior of a relatively small group of people in their own countries and others where the sexual and marital exploits of the rich and powerful are familiar topics in the international press. Furthermore, they also imply that there exists a related biological predisposition that expresses itself in the sexual double standard "independently invented in countless societies" because of men's unwillingness to assume obligation for the offspring (genes) of their wives' lovers. There is no suggestion that the double standard could have social origins independent of genes, that it may be but one more reflection of the economic and political domination of men over women in "countless" patriarchal societies.

Since even biological determinists recognize that many so-called human characteristics or behaviors are *not* universal, they postulate "predispositions," that is, traits that are genetically determined but not always expressed. It is very difficult, however, to take seriously the existence of a "predisposition" if it is not manifested in the majority of human beings. Just as Sociobiologists claim territoriality to be an evolutionary predisposition even though it is not manifested in a large number, perhaps the majority, of species, one could use their reasoning to argue that the *sharing* of territory is based on a biological predisposition, since the majority of species do just that.

It is a remarkable feature of Sociobiologists' descriptions of human "traits" that there appears to be no recognition of the possibility that there may be something arbitrary, selective, or subjective in their characterizations of females and males; that if some other group, for example, women or black males or American Indian males, were to list what they consider to be characteristics of women and men, the lists would be quite different. There is no acknowledgment, for example, that there are many women who are *not* coy and would use other adjectives to describe women. Also my guess is that it would come as a surprise to Sociobiologists to know that many American women because of *their* experiences, would include in their list of male characteristics helplessness, impracticality, and dependence. One is then left to wonder why this kind of list is any less "scientific" than the list of "human" characteristics Sociobiologists have chosen to describe.

Lack of Definition of Behavioral Units

A further difficulty that one encounters in Sociobiological accounts of human behavioral categories is the absence of any precise description or definition of the behaviors Sociobiologists are seeking to explain. It is a requirement for any science to define the units or the phenomena that are the subjects of its investigations so as to ensure that different scientists, writers, and their readers are using the same terms to mean the same thing. Certainly a theory of social behavior needs to describe the behaviors it explains. But Sociobiologists do not describe or define what they mean, for example, by entrepreneurship or aggressivity. Is aggressivity fighting in bars, getting ahead in business, being creative, being a football star, a Don Juan, a war hero, a professor? Or is it being a mother who pursues City Hall and all of its politicians until a stoplight is installed where her children have to cross the street on their way to school?

Sociobiologists do not provide the answers to these questions. Every person who reads their literature has her/his own impression of what is being discussed, and perhaps that is precisely where Sociobiology's wide appeal and acceptance lies. Its statements can be interpreted in accordance with any person's subjective experiences, expectations, frame of reference, or prejudices rather than needing to be measured or judged against generally accepted standards of meaning or definition. This omission of a definition of the behavioral units that are being "explained" makes for further difficulty when we try to understand how Socio-biologists relate behaviors to genes. For example, if aggressivity is genetic and biological, what is it that is being inherited? Is it a physiological state of high energy; is it overactive adrenal glands with high levels of adrenalin in the blood; is it high intelligence and creativity; is it good body coordination; is it being "too" short and "therefore" insecure; is it "maternalism?" Or, as another example, what exactly do genes "encode" when they encode for hypergamy in females or entrepreneurship in males? Would biological determinists simply have to agree that what is biologically based is the perception of hunger and the drive for survival, and that both hypergamy and the different forms that entrepreneurship takes are simply those among an infinite variety of behavioral strategies that human beings *learn* and *select* as solutions to the problems of hunger and survival in their particular ecological and cultural niche? Or do they really mean that all females inherit a gene or a cluster of genes that drive them to look for and, of course, scheme to marry a rich man? Would they concede the possibility that, rather than genes for "entrepreneurship," the more successful gatherer-hunters may have been distinguished from the rest by their greater inventiveness (of tools), better memory (for plants and fertile sites), quicker intelligence, more energy or speed, or by superior ecological circumstances? Surely to understand the evolution of complex behaviors, a multiplicity of such characteristics can be considered and perhaps profitably analyzed, but invoking a murky concept like entrepreneurship seems useless, in contrast, except perhaps as a means of justifying the inevitability of our economic system.

Anthropomorphizing: The Choice of Animal Models and Use of Language

Following close on the heels of the first, large problems of Sociobiological methodology that I have just discussed—its subjective and fuzzy conceptualizations and categorizations of human behavioral "traits" and social relationships—is the next great problem: anthropomorphizing, the substitution of human "equivalents" for real or postulated animal behaviors. In efforts to uncover the biological origins of human behavior, some investigators select an animal model that reflects their image of relationships presumed to exist in human society and then impose the language and concepts ordinarily used to describe human behavior upon their observations and interpretations of animal behaviors. The conclusions are inevitable, for the entire structure is a self-fulfilling prophecy. It involves a method, long in disrepute, of reading human motivation and intent into animal behavior. This makes for poor science because it cannot lead to an understanding of an animal species' behaviors or how the behaviors have come to solve the animal's problems of survival in its particular environment; it is also a circular and ineffectual way to approach human behavior even if one could understand human behavior by extrapolating from animals. (For reasons I discuss later, I do not believe one can.) If you initially interpret an animal's behavior in terms of what you believe about human behavior, you cannot then use your interpretation of *that animal's* behavior to explain something about human behavior.

Anthropomorphizing makes for a poor science of animal behavior for several reasons. The one I have discussed is that applying to animals assumptions that one has about human behavior or relationships structures and distorts the actual observations that investigators make as well as those they fail to make, and, in so doing, biases the course and outcome of the research. A second related reason is that the technique makes the assumption that simply because an animal and a human behavior *look* alike, they *are* the same. But the two behaviors could have a superficial similarity and at the same time have a totally different significance for the body economy and represent different solutions to two completely different sets of problems of survival in their respective ecological circumstances. To apply human terminology to animals not only totally ignores these distinctions, but in the process circumvents or cancels out all the relevant questions and investigations that could lead one to understand either the animal or the human behavior. Examples of some of these biasing concepts are the concepts of *dominance hierarchies*, *rape*, and *harem* to be discussed in the following pages.

The technique of describing animal behaviors in human terms was characteristic of primate studies in this country until the last decade or two and was especially incisively criticized and parodied by Ruth Herschberger in *Adam's Rib*, which was first published in 1948, but today is still fresh and apt in its wit and viewpoint. Herschberger describes the work of Robert Yerkes, a pioneer investigator in the field of primatology, and quotes a passage from his book, *Chimpanzees*:

> In the picture of behavior which is characteristic of femininity in the chimpanzee, the biological basis of prostitution of sexual function stands revealed. The mature and sexually experienced female trades upon her ability to satisfy the sexual urge of the male. (1943, p. 86)

By imagining how Josie (a female member of the world-renowned chimpanzee colony collected and studied by Yerkes in the 1920s and later) might view the situation, Herschberger criticizes Yerkes' concept of prostitution:

> Jack [the largest male chimp in the colony] and I can go through almost the same motions, but by the time it gets down on paper, it has one name when Jack does it, and another if it was me. For instance, when Jack was at the [food] chute, and I gestured in sexual invitation to him, and after his acquiescence obtained the chute, this was put down . . . as downright prostitution. Please note that on March 21, as well as on other occasions, Jack came up to me repeatedly at the chute and similarly gestured in sexual invitation. Doesn't this suggest that he was trying to get me away from the chute by carnal lure? Or was Jack just being (as everyone wants to think) an impulsive male? The experimenter took it as the latter. (1948, p. 11)

But that didn't end Josie's complaints:

> When Jack takes over the food chute, the report calls it his "natural dominance." When I do, it's "privilege"—conferred by him. If you humans could get enough perspective on your language, you'd find it as much fun as a zoo. While I'm up there lording it over the food chute, the investigator writes down "the male temporarily defers to her and allows her to act as if dominant over him." Can't I get any satisfaction out of life that isn't *allowed* me by some male chimp? Damn it! (p. 10)

Apes and Dominance Hierarchies

The behavioral category of dominance hierarchies was for decades a major organizing principle for investigators of primate social behavior. Assuming, presumably from their own perceptions of their world, and possibly from observations of caged primates, that primate species were naturally organized within male dominance hierarchies, they indeed saw male dominance hierarchies among the primate troops they observed whether they existed or not. An important function of the concept of dominance hierarchies, of particular relevance to Sociobiological theory, is that it was and is used to explain the evolution of male aggressivity and dominance, and therefore the inevitability of patriarchy. The theory is that the dominant (therefore presumably more aggressive and larger) males have more frequent access to the estrous females (those in heat) and thus pass on their "genes for aggressivity" and dominance. Now that the questions of dominance hierarchies and the relationships between an individual male's status within the group and his access to females have begun to be investigated by primatologists, anthropologists, and sociobiologists who are not motivated to justify the sexual status quo, important observations clearly contradict the stereotyped descriptions and the evolutionary formula that was derived from it (Lancaster, 1975; Leavitt, 1975; Leibowitz, 1975, 1978; Rowell, 1972, 1974). It has now been shown that dominance hierarchies are neither universal nor always male. In many primate species dominance hierarchies cannot be discerned and in our closest relatives, the chimpanzees, interactions involving dominance appear to form a small fraction of total behaviors. In some species dominance is matrilineal and males derive their status from their mothers. For example, rank order among Japanese macaques, rhesus macaques, and vervets runs from the mother through the older daughter to the younger one, and the rank of a male depends on that of his mother so long as he remains in her troop. Secondly, across primate species there is no correlation between dominance status in the group and sex, size, aggressiveness, leadership, territoriality, *or mating behavior*. In some carefully studied baboon and Japanese macaque troops, no evidence was found that dominant males have more frequent access to females than less dominant males (Eaton, 1974). The large silver-backed male gorilla may set troop movement, but he is mild-mannered and has no sexual prerogatives (Schaller, 1963). It has been suggested that some studies correlating mating frequency with dominance are weighed in favor of the dominant males who, being prominent, receive disproportionate observer attention, while the less dominant males wisely mate only when out of sight of the dominant males and human observers. Furthermore, estrous females usually are the ones who select mating partners; they are not passive recipients and they do not select only dominant males. Finally, when dominance interactions exist, they are usually situation dependent and change frequently. In some species and troops, rank among females appears to remain stable for long periods while rank among males may change with age and seniority in the troop. But in some species, whether males remain in a troop long enough to achieve seniority is determined by the females (Kolata, 1976; Pilbeam, 1973).

Models were chosen that fit stereotypic views of human relationships and social organization into male dominance hierarchies, while disregarding or ignoring animals whose behaviors failed to lend support to the stereotype. A favorite and highly popularized primate has been the savanna baboon, since early descriptions presented a familiar vignette: the large aggressive male who defends the troop and its territory, dominates the hierarchy of other males and all females, decides troop movements, and has first choice in food, sex and grooming. But this was a description of baboon life that had been observed in game parks and is a form of social organization that develops when predators are common and food availability is outside of the control of the baboons (Pilbeam, 1973). As the primatologist Thelma Rowell has shown, a wide range of life-styles exists among baboons in their natural habitats, and ecological factors are important in determining the social organization that any troop assumes. Among the population of forest baboons that Rowell observed for a period of five years (1972), the females and their young formed the stable core of the troop while the males moved periodically from troop to troop. It was the older females who decided when and in what direction the troop would move. Males did not establish rank ordering or hierarchies; they engaged in few aggressive encounters with other males and appeared largely to enjoy cooperative relations in their main task as lookouts for the troop. She concluded that "there is no evidence for any 'quality of dominance' either inherent or acquired by the animals which could influence the way in which rank relationships become structured" (1974, p. 151). Males did not defend the troop, since each member of the troop fled in response to danger, each being on its own, including the mothers with babies clinging to their fur. Rowell rarely saw encounters of any kind between troops, and they did not appear to be territorial. But when such generally peaceable primate troops are captured and/or fed by humans, aggressive encounters and hierarchies appear, clearly learned responses to environmental change.

In short, a reading of the recent literature on primate behavior reveals much richness and diversity of social arrangements and behaviors not only between primate species but also between troops within any particular species and within individual troops under differing ecological circumstances. As the primatologist Jane Lancaster has pointed out, "dominance is only one principle of social organization and even for the most dominance-oriented species, it is only one aspect of social life" (1975, p. 19). The elevation of the ideology of dominance hierarchies to a scientific principle underlying the social organization of primates did in fact structure and distort the observations that were made of primate behaviors and, consequently, also the course of primate research for many decades.

In a recent book, Sarah Blaffer Hrdy (1981) has written an extensive description of the innumerable varieties of sex differences and relationships between the sexes among primate species and an analysis of their possible significance. She emphasizes that while it is possible to support any proposition about primate or human characteristics by citing isolated examples, the meaningful approach is to look for patterns and find under what circumstances certain phenomena exist. For example, why or under what circumstances do males in polygynous species defer to females, who may "take priority at feeding sites and control social access to other group members" (p. 60), or what are the circumstances that explain females competing with each other, as well as with males, or, on the other hand, bonding together? Whatever the relationships may be of females to males in their troop—and indeed in some species they are subordinate under some circumstances—they do not conform, with a few exceptions, to the stereotype of them as unidimensional male-protected mothers. Hrdy's important point is that those who seek to explain women's subordinate status as an inevitable evolutionary consequence of genetic patterns laid down in and inherited from our primate ancestors, have to ignore a mass of contradictory evidence offered by modern female apes and monkeys who are, by and large, "highly competitive, socially involved and sexually assertive individuals" (p. 189). They protect territory, fight for their own or other mothers' young, take food from males, and bond with other females to fight aggressive males.

It is fortunate that some primatologists are replacing stereotypical notions with careful observations of monkeys and apes and the cultures that they evolve within their particular ecological niches. But just as primatologists obviously would not study chimpanzees if they wanted to understand orangutan behavior, it should be equally obvious that we shall never understand human behavior by studying baboons or by trying to hunt down some prototypical primate. Observations of other primates can provide valuable clues about the range of biological and social possibilities that existed for evolving hominids, just as do observations of modern gathering and hunting societies. More complete understanding of the evolution of modern human societies, of dominance hierarchies, and of relationships based on gender depend upon the careful accumulation of cross-cultural data and upon the reconstruction of the archeological/anthropological record of our own evolving species, as well as the continuing study and re-analysis of our recorded social history.

Flowers, Ducks and Rape

We can find a particularly extravagant use of human behavioral concepts and language in the descriptions of animals in Barash's second book, *The Whisperings Within*. He claims he does not want to be a "racy modern Aesop," but says he will, nonetheless, be telling many animal stories about "rape in ducks, adultery in bluebirds, prostitution in hummingbirds, divorce and lesbian pairing in gulls, even homosexual rape in parasitic worms" (p. 2). Noteworthy for its relevance to a key contemporary issue for women is Barash's view of the origins of rape.

Among Sociobiologists, Barash in particular sees rape rampant in nature. First he cites the work of Daniel Janzen, "one of our most creative ecologists," who has pointed out that even plants "perform courtship displays, rape, promiscuity, and fickleness just as do animals." Barash goes on to describe what he evidently considers to be rape in flowers:

> For example, plants with male flowers will "attempt" to achieve as many fertilizations as possible. How is this done? Among other things, they bombard female flowers with incredible amounts of pollen, and some even seem to have specially evolved capacities to rape female flowers, by growing a pollen tube which forces its way to the ovary within each female. (1979, p. 30)

So by defining the insertion of a pollen tube into a female flower as a rape, Barash begins to set the scene for the naturalness and—yes—the innocence of rape:

> Plants that commit rape . . . are following evolutionary strategies that maximize their fitness. And, clearly, in neither case do the actors know what they are doing, or why. We human beings like to think we are different. We introspect, we are confident that we know what we are doing, and why. But we may have to open our minds and admit the possibility that our need to maximize our fitness may be whispering somewhere deep within us and that, know it or not, most of the time we are heeding these whisperings. (p. 31)

Barash here strongly suggests that rapists are simply unwitting tools of a blind genetic drive; that rape is an unconscious urge for reproductive success and hence, biologically speaking, both advantageous and inevitable. But he seems unaware that there may be a different definition of rape; that most women see it as an act of violence expressing hatred, contempt, and fear of women and also as a weapon of social control that keeps women from asserting autonomy and freedom of movement, and forces them to depend on male "protectors." If *that* is the definition of rape, and I would say women have the right and the knowledge to decide that, then it is not relevant to flowers. And *to name what flowers do as "rape" is specifically to deny that rape is a sexual act of physical violence committed by men against women*, an act embodying and enforcing the political power wielded by men over women.

Later in the book, Barash turns to rape among the birds and bees, especially mallard ducks. He explains that mallard ducks pair up for breeding, leaving some males unmated since there are usually more males than females. He then describes how one male or a group of unmated males may copulate with a mated female without the normal preliminary courtship rituals that mated couples engage in and "despite her obvious and vigorous protest. If that's not rape, it is certainly very much like it" (p. 54). But first of all, he gives no indication whether this is a frequent or a rare occurrence nor does he describe the circumstances of the observation. Secondly, there is again the problem of language, in the use of the word *protest*. Courtship rituals are complex behaviors set in motion as a result of complex interactions between the hormonal and nervous sytems of the animal, usually the female, and certain environmental conditions, for example, season of year. The female's state stimulates the male and, in turn, sets in motion the courtship rituals between partners, which further sequentially prime the reproductive systems for biological readiness to mate, ovulate, and fertilize—an intricate, balanced interplay between sight, smell, the brain, hormones, and gonads.

Thus, we could accommodate Barash's description of resisted copulation within the concept of the female's being *biologically not primed* for mating at the time of the bachelor's intrusion, but to impute *rape* and *protest*—intent and motivation— to ducks is again to use words for some purpose other than the clarity and accuracy required of scientific description and analysis. And the next page provides us with a lead to his purpose:

> Rape in humans is by no means as simple, influenced as it is by an extremely complex overlay of cultural attitudes. Nevertheless mallard rape and bluebird adultery may have a degree of relevance to human behavior. Perhaps human rapists, in their own criminally misguided way, are doing the best they can to maximize their fitness. If so, they are not that different from the sexually excluded bachelor mallards. (p. 55)

So Barash completes his portrait of the pitiful rapist: a lonesome fellow, left out of the mainstream of socially acceptable ways to copulate and so spread his genes about, he must force himself upon an unwilling female for the purpose of ensuring their reproduction.

In these examples, then, Barash used the word *rape*, which has a specific connotation in human terms, to describe behavior of a plant and a bird. This serves two purposes for Sociobiology: to establish that rape is biological and hence *natural* and to defuse rape as an urgent political issue, which has at its heart a cultural tradition of misogyny and male violence directed against women.

Harems

Thus far in the discussion of methodology, the basic problem has been the projection of investigators' personal and cultural values and biases about human behavior in their society onto their observations and interpretations of animals' and other cultures' behaviors. Since what is involved in these anthropomorphic and ethnocentric descriptions is language, we see that words become burdened with heavy implications. Language can be used to mold reality to a particular "truth," to impose a particular perception of the world as reality. Sociobiologists use language to mold the truth when they say that courted females are *coy* or that insects have evolved "*rampant machismo*" (Wilson, 1975b, p. 320), or that *aggressivity* is a universal trait of males. When Barash and other Sociobiologists use the word *rape* to describe a male flower's act of pollinating a female flower, they appropriate the word in order to remove rape from its sociopolitical context of male violence against women, to make it an act of sexual desire and of reproductive *need*, and, finally, to claim for rape a biological basis and inevitability because of its universality in the animal world.

The traditional use of the word *harem* in primatology to describe a single-male troop of females is another example of biased language and androcentric fantasy that served to structure observations and conceptualizations concerning the social organization of such troops. In our culture, *harem* has a generally accepted connotation of a group of women who are dependent economically, socially, and presumably sexually on a powerful male whose bodily needs are their central concern and occupation.[1] When that word was then used to signify single-male troops of female primates and their offspring, it automatically carried with it the entire complex of meanings and assumptions stereotypically associated with humans. It was assumed that the male was of central importance, defending the troop, making decisions, having his choice of sex partners, and in return was groomed, fed, and sexed by his harem of dependent females. Language substituted for actual observations, but it served ideology and circular logic by "demonstrating" that human male dominance and polygyny are innate since they are rooted in our primate ancestors. While hierarchical organization around a central male exists for some primate species under some circumstances, for many species, the solitary male is peripheral, functions mainly as a stud, and remains only so long as the females want him (Lancaster, 1975).

The Omission of Unwelcome Animal Data

Another problem in Sociobiological writings is the omission of unwelcome data that confound the stereotype. For example, rather than being engaged by redwinged blackbirds that exhibit polygyny and hypergamy, Sociobiologists, in the true scientific spirit of inquiry, could find it challenging to try to understand the South American male rhea bird that incubates and tends the 50 or so eggs that are laid by several females in the nest he builds. Or they could find it fascinating to explore shared parenting by examining the phenomenon of "double clutching," a situation in which female shore birds produce two clutches of eggs in quick succession, one of which becomes her responsibility and the other the male's. Or there is the female South American jacana bird who has a territory where she keeps a "harem" of males. She fills with eggs the nest that each male builds in his own subterritory and leaves him to incubate them and tend the brood (Bonner, 1980). Many bonded sea bird pairs take turns sitting on the nest

---

[1] For a different and multidimensional view of harems and the Muslim women who inhabit them, see Ahmed (1982).

while the partner goes out to sea to bring back fish. Some penguins have an even more elaborate system whereby both partners fish together leaving the young in a huge crêche tended by a few adults. The emperor penguin father remains nearly immobile during the two months he incubates his offspring's egg in a fold of skin about his feet, while the mother hunts for food. Bonner notes that monogamy is the main mating system among animals in which both sexes share in parental care (p. 156), and I wonder why Sociobiologists do not use this phenomenon as a "natural" model for human social organization as much as they do examples of male promiscuity and female domesticity.

Other Problems with Language and Logic

There is another way in which writers can manipulate language and logic in order to reach a desired conclusion. This technique is to use words with different meanings as though they were equivalent. As previously described, Sociobiologists attribute mothers' major responsibility for child care to the greater maternal biological investment in conception, gestation and lactation. Two Sociobiologists explain the inevitability of the situation:

> For a woman, the successful raising of a single infant is essentially close to a full-time occupation for a couple of years, and continues to claim much attention and energy for several more years. For a man, it often means only a minor additional burden. To a limited extent, sexual roles can be modified in the direction of equalization of parental load, but even the most "liberated" husband cannot share pregnancy with his wife. In any case, most societies make no attempt to equalize parental care; they leave women holding the babies.
>
> Among most vertebrates, female involvement with offspring is obligatory whereas male involvement is more facultative. For example, . . . among orangutans, males on Sumatra typically associate with a female and her young, whereas on Borneo they defend territories and limit their interactions to other adult males. . . . Significantly, predators and interspecific competitors are more abundant on Sumatra. In short, biology dictates that females bear the offspring, although environmental conditions can exert a powerful influence on the extent of male parental investment. Males and females are selected for differing patterns of parental care, and there is no reason to exempt Homo sapiens from this generalization. . . . (Van Den Berghe and Barash, 1977, pp. 813-814)

The authors show in this example that important, presumably genetic characteristics like the nature and quantity of parental care are actually determined by environmental conditions—but only for the male, since they consider the female still biologically committed to parental care. But this is where slippery language and logic intrude because they themselves reduce the mother's necessary or obligatory involvement in parenting to only the *pregnancy* itself, yet they skip from that fact to the conclusion that the mother's involvement in *child care* is biologically obligatory without in any way demonstrating the fact. Clearly the time that animals spend nursing offspring is obligatory but in most species consumes but a fraction of the mother's day. Among some species, for example, the siamang great ape, tamarins and marmosets, many fathers carry and care for the young all day and return it to the mother only for nursing (Snowdon and Suomi, 1982). Among many primate species studied it has been observed that adult male behavior toward infants is highly flexible and influenced by the particular social circumstances within the troop in any period of time (Parke and Suomi, 1981). Thus, whatever biological influences exist, parenting behaviors by both females and males are molded by social and ecological factors and learning as well. For most animal species, the amount of time the females invest in care of the young is also facultative, also related to ecological conditions and tends to be the reciprocal of the father's investment even in the example presented in the paragraph quoted above. Certainly, for humans, where even breast feeding is not obligatory, the authors have presented no argument for the natural selection of "differing patterns of parental care."

Nonetheless, Sociobiologists have no doubts about what is biologically right, as Barash expresses it:

> Because men maximize their fitness differently from women, it is perfectly good biology that business and profession taste sweeter to them, while home and child care taste sweeter to women. (1979, p. 114)

Once again, as in their treatment of rape, Sociobiologists select for their attention an issue of particular vital and current concern to women and try to establish with faulty methodology the genetic origins of the social arrangements our society provides for child care. But in the same discussion quoted above, Barash goes far beyond expressing his biological opinion about the naturalness of the predominant social order that sees woman's proper place to be in the home. He warns that in the recent efforts to find "alternative lifestyles," it is child-care practices that are frequently at issue and "predictably there is a cost in disregarding biology." He cites a study that describes children reared in the counterculture as being neglected, deprived, and emotionally disturbed, and says that women seeking such "liberation" from total responsibility for child care are adopting a male biological strategy and denying their own. Thus, Sociobiology provides its public with an important sociopolitical theory and program: many aspects of modern civilization, however undesirable, are unavoidable, being expressions of our genetic inheritance; if we attempt to eliminate certain obvious social injustices, we tamper with evolution and risk incalculable harm, as Barash warns, "to everyone concerned." What this may mean we can only guess.

The Search for Evolutionary Behavioral Continuity: Culture in Animals

Throughout this critique of the methodology of biological determinism, one underlying problem has been the particular animals that are chosen as models for human behavior. The reason for Sociobiologists' citing of examples from a variety of animal species is, as I have mentioned, to establish universality and therefore evolutionary continuity. At the outset it can be said that there is no necessary correlation between universality (even if it *could* be demonstrated and it cannot) and evolutionary continuity, since what are being examined are present-day representatives of species that have evolved independently of each other for the last 15 million to about 500 million years. That is, according to the fossil evidence, the first hominid lines split off from the apes either about 15 or 5 million years ago and continued their own evolutionary course; the apes and monkeys diverged into their independent evolutionary lines about 40 to 50 million years ago; the first primates radiated off from other mammals about 70 or more million years ago; mammals, from the other land vertebrates about 325 million years ago; and over the previous 200 million years the various water and amphibious vertebrate species were evolving in their niches (Pilbeam, 1972). Thus, with independent lines of development for every species over the last millions to hundreds of millions of years, we do not know what, if any, evolutionary relationships similar behaviors of different present-day species have to each other. But certainly no one can seriously maintain that either the behaviors or the brains of present-day species represent a "recapitulation" of the evolutionary pathway that humans have followed. All that we can assume is that each species has evolved in relationship to the series of ecological niches within which it has survived, and today's array of forms and behaviors represents the varied outcomes of those historical relationships. Related to this point is the fact that the kind of faulty use of animal examples being discussed here involves the implicit assumption of a "chain of being" and "ascent" of humans over more primitive animal "precursors." But since contemporary animals are not our precursors, it is no more logical to look at chimpanzees or mice to gain insight into our behavior that it would be to look at our behavior to gain insight into theirs.

A faulty premise underlying some of the studies or observations of animals, particularly primates, either in the laboratory or in the wild, is that such study will reveal basic biological mechanisms of behavior that have evolved genetically and are "uncontaminated" by culture. There are two questionable assumptions in this premise. The first is that there is such an entity as "basic biological mechanisms" of human behavior that can be *revealed* by stripping off layers of culture; that is, that there is any definition of human behavior that can conceptually or in reality exclude culture. But that is an issue of such importance and complexity that it requires its own chapter, Chapter 3. The other erroneous assumption is that animals themselves have no culture affecting their "basic biological" or genetically influenced mechanisms; that their behaviors express only genes and no learning. In his fine review and analysis of the behaviors of animals, Bonner (1980) describes the various manifestations of the capacity for learning, teaching, and culture among vertebrates. Related to differences in relative size and complexity of the organization of the brain are differences in complexity and flexibility of behavioral responses to environmental challenges and the ability of animals to learn new and adaptive behaviors from one another. It is this transmission of information by behavioral means that Bonner defines as culture and that plays an important role in social behaviors and relationships among animals and in their adaptation to their environments. Thus, we cannot look to most animal behaviors as *instinctual* or *innate* and, therefore, as providing peepholes into the pure genetic core and *nature* of the human species.

Validation by Prediction

One of the methodological techniques by which some Sociobiologists attempt to provide scientific validity or substance to their speculation is by making predictions. One criterion of a theory's value is its ability to predict what we will find under particular circumstances if we go and make the observations or conduct the proper experiment. Sociobiologists, Barash in particular, constantly "prove" the validity and predictive values of their theories by "predicting" what they and everyone else already know to be demonstrated fact; for example:

> Sociobiological theory would predict that adults with the most to gain and the least to lose would be the most eager adopters, and certainly this is true in the United States where childless couples are the predominant adopters. (1977, p. 313)

More relevant to this book is Barash's opinion about depression, which he sees as a "cry for help." Since males are genetically selected to be the *providers* of resources and females are those who are provided *for*,

> . . . in all societies, depression is significantly more common in women than in men. Their biology makes it more likely that women should be the sex to attempt care-eliciting behaviors. Males are supposed to be the care providers. Depression is also frequently associated with marital strife, a finding consistent with the suggestion that depression represents an unconscious effort to mobilize concern, attention and resources, in this case from an unresponsive or insufficiently responsive husband. (1979, p. 217)

Then Barash proceeds once again to address directly issues raised by the women's movement in his observation that, while depression is more common among married than among unmarried women, the opposite is true for men:

The discovery that unmarried men are more likely to be depressed than are married men has been an important weapon for radical feminists, since it suggests that marriage itself is a male-designed phenomenon, tending to free men from depression while depressing women, presumably because of the emotionally stressful, sexist demands made upon married women in today's society. There may be much truth in this claim, but the male-female differences in depression associated with marriage also fit well with the sociobiological hypothesis. If men are the resource-providing sex and women are biologically predisposed to be resource receiving, and if depression is in fact a petition for resources (emotional, financial, etc.) it seems reasonable that unmarried men who showed depressive inclinations would be considered unattractive mates, while depressive tendencies in women would not be nearly as undesirable. (1979, pp. 217, 218)

We find in these passages a medley of methodological faults. First, there is the sarcastic dismissal of any suggestion that there may be a sociocultural context for depression among women, particularly among women who are married. Secondly, the explanation for depression is based upon acceptance of a sequence of unsubstantiated premises: "if men are the resource-providing sex," if women are "biologically predisposed to be resource receiving," "if depression is in fact a petition for resources," that depressed men are unattractive to women, and that depression in unmarried men is a cause rather than a result of their unmarried state. No one knows if any of these is true. Furthermore, other key Sociobiological premises posit quite the opposite—that women are the resource *providers* to their families, by *nature*, the nurturers, the givers. Even in an economic sense, so far as we know, women have historically always shared equally in providing material resources for their families through their labors both within and outside the home.

Barash than goes on to secure his argument by making a prediction: "We would also predict that if depression is a care-eliciting behavior, then it should be especially common following the birth of a child. . ." (1979, p. 218). As usual he claims a particular Sociobiological theory has been confirmed because it is able to "predict" a phenomenon that he, we, everyone already knows to exist; namely, postpartum depression.

If I were for the moment to accept Sociobiological premises, my predictions would be quite different from those proposed by Sociobiologists: Since women have a great biological investment in each pregnancy, which predisposes them to provide most of the parental care in order to protect optimally their genes in their offspring, I would predict:

1. A low incidence or absence of postpartum depression in women, since depression is *not* the optimal mental/physical state for the high energy requirements

of postpartum lactation and infant care. In fact, I would further predict that the infants of depressed mothers do not fare as well physically or emotionally as infants of non-depressed mothers.

2. A high incidence of postpartum depression in fathers because they are deprived of a considerable portion of the parental care formerly invested in them by their wives, who, despite their high energy levels and resource-giving capacities, have finite limits and must share their resources equally. The father's depression is, of course, care-eliciting behavior, an unconscious effort to mobilize concern, attention, and resources.

3. A low incidence of depression in women in general, since most of them are fulfilling their biological predispositions to be mothers and nurturers. As Barash has said, life tastes "sweet" to them; in fact, I would predict that most women are manic most of the time. Furthermore, they are sensible enough to realize the futility of engaging in care-eliciting behavior directed toward men whose biological predisposition is toward aggressivity, activity, and competitiveness rather than nurturance.

4. In general, a high incidence of depression among both married and unmarried men. The vast majority of the men in the world in fact have very few resources, are not leaders, and rarely have an opportunity to hunt or go to war. In the face of the fact that they *cannot* provide resources as they are supposed to, are *not* fulfilling their genetic and evolutionary destinies, all that is left for them to do, in despair and frustration, is to cry for help.

Aside from the amusement of this exercise, I have wanted to illustrate two important fundamental flaws that make Sociobiology a very flimsy superstructure. First, premises in science are ordinarily expected to represent a generally accepted statement of current knowledge or at least a statement with some supporting evidence. But Sociobiological premises themselves are arbitrary, subjective, and conjectural even though they are stated as *givens*. Secondly, given any set of premises, whether conjectural or supported by evidence, *any number* of logical predictions or hypotheses may follow, not just the one a Sociobiologist or any particular scientist chooses to propose. The logical next step then is to recognize the importance of challenging the hypotheses by subjecting them to experimentation or to further observations that may tend to support or exclude one or another of the possible alternative hypotheses.

Sociobiologists predict what is already known to be true, then offer that known fact as proof of the validity of the premises from which they claim to be making the prediction. This method precludes the need either to test the prediction or to question the premises on which it was based.

GENES AND BEHAVIOR: NATURE-NURTURE RECYCLED

Underlying the methodological problems in biological determinist theories of human behavior, the fundamental scientific issue is the role of genes and biology in determining characteristics and behaviors. This is an issue of central importance for the validity of Sociobiology, since this theory asserts that our behaviors and social relationships, our culture itself, have evolved through natural selection involving gene transmission of behavioral "traits." An opposed view is that our behaviors and culture represent evolutionary adaptions that have been transmitted through teaching and learning; that what has evolved biologically *and* culturally is the brain and its increasing capacity for innovation and learning; that culture has its own nongenetic evolutionary history. These opposing views, of course, signify that recurrent controversy, the genes/environment, nature/nurture, instinct/learning dichotomy with respect to human personality, behavior, and social organization. In order to discuss some of the issues involved in this dualism, it is important first to review some information about genes, their actions, and their interactions with the environment.

All of the cells of our bodies, including eggs and sperm, have within their nucleus 23 pairs of chromosomes (structures that carry the genes), one of each pair coming from our mother and one from our father. Before fertilization between an egg and a sperm, the egg had divided so that it has only one chromosome from each of the 23 pairs; that is, it has a total of 23 chromosomes. Since the distribution of the members of the pairs seems to be random, about half of the chromosomes in each egg have come from the mother and half from the father of the woman producing the egg. The same thing is true of the sperm. After fertilization (the union of one egg with one sperm) then, the fertilized egg has 46 chromosomes again which comprise 23 pairs, with again one member of each pair from the egg and one member from the sperm. Each gene on all the chromosomes has a match on its companion chromosome, and each such pair of genes are called alleles. Because of the random distribution of the members (maternal and paternal) of the 23 chromosomal pairs into the egg and sperm before fertilization, there are 2^{23} or 8,388,608 possible chromosomal pairings or different combinations possible in the offspring from a given pair of parents, which is why parents do not produce identical offspring (except for single-egg twins). Other chromosomal and genetic events, like crossover of chromosomal segments between members of a pair before final division, introduce even more genetic diversity into each offspring of any given pair of mates.

One of the 23 chromosomes is called the sex-chromosome, X or Y. In females, the two members of the pair of sex chromosomes are both X-chromosomes; in males, one is an X-chromosome and the other a Y-chromosome. If an egg is fertilized by an X sperm, a girl results because the cells in her body will have the XX pair; if fertilized by a Y sperm, a boy results because his cells will have the XY pair. This means that the boy's X-chromosome is always from the mother; the Y is from the father. Unlike all the other chromosomes, the Y does not have any matching genes for those on its paired X-chromosome. Thus far the only known functions of the Y-chromosome in normal development are to carry a gene for hairy ears and to influence the fetal biopotential glands to develop into testes rather than into ovaries. In the female XX fetus, the biopotential gonads develop into ovaries.

The effort of Sociobiologists to attribute human behaviors—even if they were more definable and predictable than the *altruism, entrepreneurship, coyness,* and *aggressivity* they try to explain—to genes runs into untold difficulties. First, the staggering number of unique genetic combinations from any pairing makes predictability and reproducibility virtually impossible. Secondly, the role that genes appear to play in the synthesis of proteins by cells in the developing organism places their influence at a level far removed, both conceptually and in reality, from the social behaviors and characteristics of the mature animal and human being coping with the specifics of its particular environmental demands. Explanatory principles for the effects and interactions of the genes, which are DNA molecules, at the cellular level are necessarily different from those for the actions and interactions of organisms at the environmental level. While each level, from the intracellular to the organismic to the ecological, is coherent, integrated, and at the same time interactive with other levels, explanations of how a gene works cannot be automatically extrapolated to explanations of how an organism functions in its environment.

Beyond that, however, there is simply no evidence whatsoever that patterns of behaviors are inherited in simple and predictable ways as the theories of Sociobiologists and other biological determinists would require. In her important critique of theories of genetic reductionism and their use by hereditarianists and genetic engineers, Ruth Hubbard (1982) examines the historical and scientific development of the modern accepted concepts of genes as irreducible and separate *things* that *determine* events; that is, that genes have particular discrete analyzable and measurable effects that can be separated out of the *processes* of biological development in which they participate. This thinking evolved quite naturally from the rather ancient conviction that traits and characteristics are inherited through their transmission by particles from generation to generation, and it lends support to the reductionist idea of the primacy of the genes as agents that impart an immutable specificity in the developmental process and by themselves determine events. But as Hubbard says,

> Genes (DNA) impart specificity, but so do other molecules (e.g., RNA, proteins, and even carbohydrates and lipids), and so do many *processes* that occur within organisms and in the interactions in which organisms engage with their environments. (1982, p. 65)

Even at the level of cellular protein synthesis (the developmental process in which genes are involved), let alone at the level of behaviors, genetic specification cannot be separately analyzed. The main action of each gene appears to be to specify, through the sequence of elements (bases) within its own molecular structure, the sequence of elements (amino acids) within a particular protein molecule. But how the very long and intricate protein molecule folds up, that is, its three-dimensional configuration, critically affects its function; and the pattern of folding is *not* determined by the gene alone but is also "a consequence of the environment in which the molecule finds itself" (Lewin, 1981, p. 43). Thus, it is not possible, Hubbard writes, "to conclude that DNA controls or programs the many different ways in which proteins participate in the structure and functioning of organisms, not to speak of the many more complex characters of individuals and of species" (1982, p. 71).

Not only can a complex behavior pattern or a characteristic not be linked to a gene or a gene cluster, there is not even any simple cause and effect relationship between a particular gene and a particular anatomical feature; for example, between a gene and eye color or body size. Any gene's action or expression is affected, first of all, by its interactions with many other genes, including its allele on the paired chromosome, as well as with a myriad other intracellular factors, and the nature of these interactions is not at all clear. The next factor that complicates genetic effects on body structure is the uterine environment of the fetus. It is there that maternal as well as other environmental influences interact with genetic influences in affecting the fetus' body form. That is, fetuses develop within a maternal physiological milieu including salts, fluids, proteins, fats, carbohydrates, oxygen, acid-base balance, hormones, and so on, which are at the same time the milieu within which genes' actions occur that guide the fetus' growth and development. Genes' actions occur only within such an environmental milieu and are affected by it. In short, what genes do is only *one part* of the developmental process.

Since we tend to take for granted (or ignore) the normal physiological milieu as an essential part of development, it is easier to recognize the influence of environmental milieu on genetic expression if we consider *external* environmental factors that affect fetal development in humans through their disruptive effects on the maternal milieu. The mother's diet, drug ingestion (for example, thalidomide, DES, alcohol), virus infections (such as herpes and German measles), stress, and other known factors may have serious effects on the physical characteristics of the developing fetus. In some way all of these environmental factors have the capacity to induce abnormalities in the environmental milieu of the fetus, and it is the *interactions* between genetic factors and disturbed internal environmental factors that result in altered fetal development. There is no way to tease apart genetic and environmental factors in human development or to know where genetic effects end and environmental ones begin; in fact, this is a meaningless way to view the problem since from conception the relationships between the gene's protein synthesizing activity and the fetus' maternal environment are interdependent. As Lappé has said, "Genes and environments do not simply 'add up' to produce a whole. The manner in which nature and nurture interact to cause biological organisms to flourish or decline is an extraordinarily complex problem" (1979, p. 192).

Since our main subject is behavior, a critical element in this discussion of the developing fetus is the brain. The brain, after all, mediates behavior, and it attains its normal development and functional potential as mind *only* in interaction with its environment. Even though genes are involved in the embryonic differentiation of the various nerve cell types and in the spatial organization of nerve cells (neurons) within the fetal brain, the final form, size, and connections between different neurons and therefore the brain's proper functioning also depend on the maternal environmental milieu and on input from the external world.

Most of the information we have concerning the interactional effects of genes and environment on the development of the brain comes from research on experimental animals or from pathology in humans. In most animals and humans, a significant amount of neuronal growth and the development of functional, connecting networks among neurons occurs after birth as well as before. It has been found that malnutrition throughout the period of postnatal development of rat pups results in a decrease in both the number and the size of neurons in the brain. If the pups were also malnourished *in utero*, they can suffer as much as a 60 percent reduction in brain cell number, as compared with controls, by the time of weaning. Human infants dying of malnutrition during the first year of life also have smaller than normal brains with a reduced number and size of neurons (Winick, 1975). On the other hand, experimental exposure of young laboratory rodents to enriched sensory environments of various types appears to result in an increased volume of the cortex, the outer cellular layers of the brain, and increased surface area of the branching processes of neurons, the site where the majority of functional connections (synapses) with other neurons occurs (Rosenzweig, Bennett, and Diamond, 1972). Experimental work in the visual system has shown that in young animals deprived of light and visual stimulation from birth, some of the neurons processing vision fail to develop properly, anatomically and functionally (Hirsch and Leventhal, 1978). What this means is that for the neurons in developing animals to grow and function properly, they require not only normal genetic influences but the appropriate environmental input. Primate and human babies are born with their eyes open and apparently able to "see" the outside world. But for a period of two or so years a process of maturation or "fine tuning" of the visual system occurs in which the genetically influenced neuronal growth and connectivity interact with and are modified by inputs from the environment—an interaction of genetic effects, neuronal fine structure, experience, and learning.

With increasing sophistication of conceptualization and the equipment available to make scientific observations (for example, recording of electrophysiological responses of bird embryos within the shell), increasing knowledge is gained about the influence of prenatal and early postnatal environment and learning in the determination even of the kinds of behaviors in birds and mammals that previously were called *instincts* and thought to be entirely genetically programmed and not learned from others. An important example of this is the behavior of newly hatched mallard ducklings, which immediately and selectively respond to their own mother's call and follow her. This phenomenon results in fact from a developmental learning process occurring while the duckling is still in the shell. It hears and responds to its mother's call and to its siblings in their shells as early as five days before hatching. Its ability to respond to its own mother's call upon hatching depends upon the amount of auditory input from its mother and siblings and by its own responsive vocalizations while still in the shell (Brown, 1975). Thus, the structure and functioning of the duckling's brain and, therefore, behavior, is influenced by environmental input *along with* the input of genetic factors. This work and other similar findings have led J. L. Brown, in his monumental book, *The Evolution of Behavior* (1975) to write,

> The overall development of social preferences in neonates can be clearly seen from these studies to be the result of several different kinds of experiences in certain normal sequences, each building on the preceding combination of physiological-anatomical maturation and experience. Studies designed to illuminate only experiential or only genetic factors in development of social experience can never, because of their own one-sided design, give a full understanding of the factors guiding development. (p. 651-652)

Furthermore, Brown states categorically that *no* behavior can be attributed entirely to genetic factors or to environmental factors since every behavior must develop in an environment and its development must be influenced by genetic factors.

In the examples above, I have been referring mainly to environmental effects that act directly on the prenatal and early postnatal development of the structure and functioning of the nerve cells of the brain, the most fundamental level at which behavioral changes can be analyzed. But it is important to see that beyond that level of interacting genetic and environmental influences on structure, the effect of *learning*—whether it is the learning by birds of their specific songs and dialects or the more complexly variable learned behaviors of primates—is but a further extension of the process of environmental interaction with internal biological processes. The developing organism from the time of conception represents and reflects ongoing processes of interaction between its genes' actions, its own developing biological mechanisms and parts, and its maternal milieu, which reflects the external world. Each of the elements of this developing whole is constantly changing and recreated by virtue of its interactions with the other changing elements and the emerging whole. At every moment the fetus represents a new stage of the cumulative (but not simply additive) effects of all the preceding and constantly changing interacting processes. At the time of birth, new conditions impinge upon the organism and the course of its further development: the external world is experienced directly without the intervention and the transforming effects of the mother's body. The external world-experience and learning continue to influence the course of growth and development of the structure and functioning of the body, including the brain, throughout life.

SUMMARY AND CONCLUSION

Sociobiology, the modern version of biological determinist theories of human behavior, attempts to validate the belief that genes determine behaviors and that social relationships and cultures have evolved through the genetic transmission of behavioral traits and characteristics. Of central importance in Sociobiological theory, in keeping with the biological determinist tradition, are its efforts to explain in terms of *biology* the origins of the gender-differentiated roles and positions held by women and by men in modern as well as past civilizations. In so doing, Sociobiologists attempt to assign *natural* causes to phenomena of social origin. It is in part because Sociobiologists specifically address the very social issues that the women's movement has highlighted that Sociobiology functions as a political theory and program. Sociobiologists reinforce ancient stereotypes of women as coy, passive, dependent, maternal, and nurturant and base these temperaments in our genes. At the same time, and despite their liberal protestations, they explain and justify the existence of women's social and physical oppression by asserting the genetic origins, and hence inevitability, of rape, the sexual double standard, the relegation of women to the private world of home and motherhood, and other forms of the exploitation of women. Furthermore, its use of shoddy methodology and incorrect logic to support insupportable claims suggests a motive force other than the dispassionate pursuit of knowledge.

I have demonstrated a number of basic conceptual and methodological flaws in the work of Sociobiologists, which include faulty logic; unsupported assumptions and premises; inappropriate use of language; lack of definitions of the behaviors being explained; and ethnocentric, androcentric, and anthropocentric biases underlying the questions that are asked, the language used, the selection of animal models, and the interpretation of data. The more fundamental scientific problem, however, is the dichotomy that is drawn between genetic and environmental determinants of behavior. From the time of conception genes do *not* act in isolation from their environment, and even fairly stereotypical behaviors in animals, with few exceptions, represent interactions between experience or learning and biological mechanisms. What has evolved in response to environmental challenge is the brain and its capacities for learning and culture, not behaviors themselves. Behaviors are the *products* of the brain's functioning in interaction with the external world, and the innumerable patterns of social behaviors, relationships, and organization that characterize human societies have evolved through cultural transmission within specific historical contexts.

REFERENCES

Ahmed, L. Western ethnocentrism and perceptions of the harem. *Feminist Studies*, 1982, *8*, 521-534.
Barash, D. *Sociobiology and behavior*. New York: Elsevier, 1977.

Barash, D. *The whisperings within*. New York: Harper & Row, 1979.

Bonner, J. T. *The evolution of culture in animals*. Princeton: Princeton University Press, 1980.

Brown, J. L. *The evolution of behavior*. New York: W. W. Norton, 1975.

Dawkins, R. *The selfish gene*. New York: Oxford University Press, 1976.

Eaton, G. G. Male dominance and aggression in Japanese macaque reproduction. In W. Montagna and W. Sadler (Eds.), *Reproductive behavior*. New York: Plenum, 1974.

Herschberger, R. *Adam's rib*. New York: Harper & Row, 1970.

Hirsch, H. V. B., and Leventhal, A. G. Functional modification of the developing visual system. In M. Jacobson (Ed.), *Handbook of sensory physiology*, 1978, *9*. *Development of sensory systems*. New York: Springer-Verlag.

Howell, N. Sociobiological hypotheses explored. *Science*, 1979, *206*, 1294-1295.

Hrdy, S. B. *The woman that never evolved*. Cambridge: Harvard Univesity Press, 1981.

Hubbard, R. From termite to human behavior. *Psychology Today*, 1978, *12*, 124-134.

Hubbard, R. The theory and practice of genetic reductionism—from Mendel's laws to genetic engineering. In S. Rose (Ed.), *Towards a liberatory biology*. London: Allison and Busby, 1982.

Kolata, G. B. Primate behavior: sex and the dominant male. *Science*, 1976, *191*, 55-56.

Lancaster, J. B. *Primate behavior and the emergence of human culture*. New York: Holt, Rinehart & Winston, 1975.

Lappé, M. *Genetic politics*. New York: Simon & Schuster, 1979.

Leavitt, R. R. *Peaceable primates and gentle people: Anthropological approaches to women's studies*. New York: Harper & Row, 1975.

Leibowitz, L. *Perspectives in the anthropology of women*. In R. Reiter (Ed.). New York: Monthly Review Press, 1975.

Leibowitz, L. *Females, males, families: A biosocial approach*. North Scituate, MA: Duxbury Press, 1978.

Lewin, R. Seeds of change in embryonic development. *Science*, 1981, *214*, 42-44.

Lewontin, R. C. Sociobiology—a caricature of Darwinism. *Journal of Philosophy of Science*, 1976, *2*, 21-31.

Midgley, M. Gene-juggling. In A. Montagu (Ed.), *Sociobiology examined*. Oxford: Oxford University Press, 1980. (a)

Midgley, M. Rival fatalism: the hollowness of the sociobiology debate. In A. Montagu (Ed.), *Sociobiology examined*. Oxford: Oxford University Press, 1980. (b)

Parke, R. D., and Suomi, S. J. Adult male-infant relationships: human and nonhuman primate evidence. In K. Immelmann, G. Barlow, L. Petrinovich and M. Main (Eds.), *Early development in animals and man*. New York: Cambridge University Press, 1981.

Pilbeam, D. *The ascent of man*. New York: Macmillan, 1972.

Pilbeam, D. An idea we could live without: the naked ape. In A. Montagu (Ed.), *Man and aggression*. Oxford: Oxford University Press, 1973.

Rosenzweig, M. R., Bennett, E. L., and Diamond, M. C. Brain changes in response to experience. *Scientific American*, 1972, *226*, 22-30.

Rowell, T. *Social behavior of monkeys*. Baltimore: Penguin, 1972.

Rowell, T. The concept of social dominance. *Behavioral Biology*, 1974, *11*, 131-154.

Schaller, G. *The mountain gorilla: ecology and behavior*. Chicago: University of Chicago Press, 1963.

Snowdon, C. T., and Suomi, S. J. Paternal behavior in primates. In H. E. Fitzgerald, J. S. Mullins and P. Gage (Eds.), *Child nurturance*, 1982, New York: Plenum.

Van Den Berghe, P. L., and Barash, D. P. Inclusive fitness and human family structure. *American Anthropologist*, 1977, *79*, 809-823.

Wilson, E. O. Human decency is animal. *New York Times Magazine*, 1975, Oct. 12, 38-50. (a)

Wilson, E. O. *Sociobiology: The new synthesis*. Cambridge, MA: Harvard University Press, 1975. (b)

Wilson, E. O. *On human nature*. Cambridge, MA: Harvard University Press, 1978.

Winick, M. Nutritional disorders during brain development. In D. B. Tower (Ed.), *The clinical neurosciences*, 1975, New York: Raven Press, 1975.

Woolf, V. *Three guineas*. New York: Harcourt Brace & World, 1938.

Yerkes, R. M. *Chimpanzees*. New Haven: Yale University Press, 1943.

Chapter 3
The Brain and Human "Nature"

> As long as there are entrenched social and political distinctions between sexes, races or classes, there will be forms of science whose main function is to rationalize and legitimize these distinctions.
>
> Elizabeth Fee, 1979, p. 433.

In many ways and for many reasons, the question "What really is a woman?" has haunted writers and philosopher-scientists since the beginning of written history. Today, from under the weight and confusion of the judgements, opinions, and definitions of literature, history, sociology, psychology, anthropology, and that final arbiter of Truth, natural science, women themselves are asking that question in a new way. Traditional thought would have us believe there is a female *nature*, which logically means there must also be a male *nature*, unless it is assumed, as generally seems to be the case, that *male nature* is indeed synonymous with *human nature*.

As we have seen, it is a premise in Sociobiological and other contemporary biological determinist theories that there is indeed a female and male nature underlying and explaining all social phenomena. Biological nature is invoked as an ultimate explanation especially for those social phenomena that, in their inhumanity, transcend rational justification: sexual and social oppression, economic and political exploitation, slavery, racism, war. Nature becomes confused with history, biology with politics. This ideological confusion is important because ideology has the power to strip the oppressed of hope or ability to be freed, and it divides them from each other into their individual and subjective sloughs of assigned inferiority and subordination, just as it unites the namers and definers in their unassailable superiority.

We find the writings of scientists of western Europe and America in the 1860s and later reflecting the concerns of a society fearing serious disruptions by both the women's rights and antislavery movements. As Elizabeth Fee has chronicled, the French craniologist, F. Pruner, wrote in 1866: "The Negro resembles the female in his love for children, his family, and his cabin" and "the black man is to the white man what woman is to man in general, a loving being and a being of pleasure" (1979, p. 424). Anthropologists and craniologists alike found the biological basis for these endearing and loving natures in similarly undeveloped brains, as described by James Hunt, President of the London Anthropological Society, in 1863: "there is no doubt that the Negro's brain bears a great resemblance to a European female or child's brain and thus approaches the ape far more than the European, while the Negress approaches the ape still nearer" (Fee, 1979, p. 421). It was a consistent concern throughout the last half of the nineteenth century to explain how women and men are *naturally* fitted for the different jobs they have. "The Victorian woman's ideal social characteristics—nurturance, intuitive morality, domesticity, passivity, and affection—were all assumed to have a deeply rooted biological basis" (Smith-Rosenberg and Rosenberg, 1973, p. 334). Physicians and scientists commonly agreed that woman was both the "product and prisoner" (p. 335) of her reproductive system, and that work and higher education alike would only damage her reproductive capacity and threaten the future of the race—warnings similar to those of "modern" Sociobiologists. It was clear she belonged in the home, as male writers tirelessly asserted. Thus, physician William Holcombe wrote in 1869 about women,

> Mentally, socially, spiritually, she is more interior than man. She herself is an interior part of man, and her love and life are always something interior and incomprehensible to him. . . . Woman is to deal with domestic affections and uses, not with philosophies and sciences. . . . She is priest, not king. The house, the chamber and the closet, are the centres of her social life and power, as surely as the sun is the centre of the solar system. (Smith-Rosenberg and Rosenberg, 1973, p. 337)

A striking feature, of course, of such poetic pronouncements about ideal womanhood by physicians and others in nineteenth-century America and England is their class- and race-bound nature, since the writers had to pretend ignorance that the majority of women *were* workers—as slaves, as laborers in the mills and sweat shops, and as domestic workers in their own and in middle- and upper-class homes.

The ultimate explanation for these natural temperamental and intellectual differences lay in the different structure of the female and male brains. During the last half of the nineteenth century, neuroanatomists believed that the frontal lobes of the human brain accounted for the highest mental and intellectual human functions. Scientists then reported that the frontal lobes of men were more highly developed than those of women, who had relatively larger parietal lobes. Near the turn of the century, newer calculations of neuroanatomists pointed to the parietal lobes, rather then the frontal lobes, as the seat of the intellect. It did not take long for the leading anatomists of the period to "discover" that women's parietal lobes were *not* really larger and their frontal lobes smaller than men's, as had been thought, but quite the reverse:

> The frontal region is not, as has been supposed smaller in woman, but rather larger relatively . . . . (furthermore) a preponderance of the frontal region does not imply intellectual superiority . . . the parietal region is really the more important. (Shields, 1975, p. 742)

In the following decades, however, with continual failures to find any reliable index for the structural inferiority of the female or the "Negro" brain, craniology and brain measurements went out of style. But the lack of that "scientific" validation did not stop the flow of writings about physiological or anatomical bases for the *nature* of woman that so fortunately and admirably fits her for the tasks of society that we find her performing. Right up to the present, as Janet Thomas (1977) has documented, psychologists can state, for example, that women's tactile sensitivity "may contribute to their greater manual dexterity and early in life direct them towards activities which require manual skills such as sewing, knitting, embroidery, dental laboratory work, and microscopic research in biology and biochemistry"; also, they excel "in the perception of details in tasks which require frequent shifts of attention, such as typing, filing, checking lists for accuracy and other clerical skills" (p. 331). We have already seen that Socio-biologists, too, find a most felicitous congruence between women's biological natures and their social functions insofar as "home and child care taste sweeter to women" while "business and profession taste sweeter" to men (Barash, 1979, p. 114). There can be little argument with Kate Millett's observation that " . . . the most fundamental of society's arbitrary follies . . . [is] its view of sex as a caste structure ratified by nature" (1970, p. 19).

After craniology failed to provide explanations for the social position of women and blacks, there developed in the twentieth century a parallel industry of intelligence testing that was to provide the new approach to uncovering the innate sources of the inferior position of blacks (and others) in American society. Stephen Jay Gould (1981) has brought together the rather sordid record of the prejudiced views, biased assumptions and methodologies, or fraudulence that characterized the work of some of the most eminent scientists of their day who devoted their careers to the "mismeasure" of the human brain and intelligence (see also Billig, 1979; Hirsch, 1981). The IQ test was designed by Alfred Binet in France at the turn of the century as a tool for identifying children with specific learning disabilities in order to improve their cognitive abilities by means of special education. Imported into the United States and popularized, beginning about 1912, by H. H. Goddard, and subsequently by L. M. Terman and R. M. Yerkes, the IQ test became the means for generating data to support hereditarian theories of intelligence and for categorizing groups of people (classes, "races," nationalities) on the basis of their "innate" and immutable intelligence. Studies and writings by American and British scientists and psychologists on "race," intelligence, and IQ have been a core element in the scientific support of racist theories. The popularization of scientific studies that purport to prove the innateness of particular social characteristics of women and blacks (or Jews or lesbians or Poles) makes it possible, as Gould has said, for millions of people to suspect "that their social prejudices are scientific facts after all" (1981, p. 28).

Biological determinists believe that genetically based behavioral and biological patterns or predispositions constitute our innate natures; that individual and social behaviors are expressions of genetically (and/or hormonally) determined mechanisms. My alternative thesis is that human behaviors are the products of our brains-minds-bodies responding to their environments; that the brain-mind itself, like the rest of our body, has evolved genetically *and* in dynamic interaction with its environment; that all development and behavior must be seen as the product of continuous interactions between biological and environmental influences from the time of conception; and that the capacity of the brain to be modified by environment and experience, to *learn*, to acquire language, and to *invent* has freed human behaviors from stereotypical or predetermined responses to biological factors, though not, unfortunately, to cultural forces. I would contend, in fact, and will attempt to demonstrate that we have more built-in biological capacity for behavioral flexibility than our cultural training allows us to exploit.

It is not my intent to deny the obvious, the influence of the biological (genetic, hormonal) components of human behavior, but rather to view biology as potential, as capacity and not as static entity. Biology itself is socially influenced and defined; it changes and develops in interaction with and response to our minds and environment, as our behaviors do. Biology can be said[1] to define possibilities but not determine them; it is never irrelevent but it is also not determinant. For each person, brain-body-mind-behaviors-environment form a complex entity the parts of which are inextricable from each other; the parts and the whole are ceaselessly interacting and changing and carry within themselves the entire history of their interactions.

In order to support the alternative thesis I outlined above, this chapter describes significant phenomena in the evolutionary and embryological development of the brain. The reconstruction of the evolutionary development of the human brain from fossil evidence and from the comparative study of mammalian brains suggests a sequence of interacting biological and environmental phenomena in our hominid evolutionary history that resulted in a brain with an enormous capacity to respond structurally and functionally to its environment, providing us with the capacities to learn, invent, remember, symbolize, make choices; to have self-awareness, beliefs, convictions, intent and motivation; and to transmit cultures. Similarly, during fetal and postnatal development, the brain and its nerve cells are exquisitely sensitive structurally and functionally to input from the external world. In this chapter I shall argue that the notion that there lurks an immutable core of *instinct* or *nature* beneath and outside of these dynamic, constantly changing and interacting relationships between our brain, body and environment, beneath and outside of culture and learning is mystical, undemonstrable, and scientifically useless in that it makes impossible any valid explanation of human cultural evolution, behaviors, and social institutions. Instead, the cultures we have created, rather than our biology, impose limitations on our minds and development, construct

---

[1] I am indebted to Zillah Eisenstein for this way of expressing my position.

definitions of *woman* and *man*, of male and female, and produce a science that helps to explain and justify differences of ideological, social, political, and economic origins as natural and biological.

HUMAN EVOLUTION WITH SPECIAL REFERENCE TO THE BRAIN

The following version of the course of early hominid evolution has been constructed from the available fossil evidence as it has been interpreted by some investigators (Isaac and Leakey, 1979; Leakey and Lewin, 1977; Pilbeam, 1972; Simons, 1964, 1977; Washburn 1960). Over 15 million years ago in Southern Eurasia and possibly Africa a stock of arboreal apes became adapted to ground living and to foraging for small, tough plant foods like nuts, roots, and seeds. Such a move may have occurred in those areas where there was a recession of tropical forest cover and the development of forest fringe areas and woodland-savanna environments, an environmental evolution which is indicated by paleoecological evidence. This earliest hominoid (ape-human common ancestor) gave rise both to the large ground apes of Southern Eurasia and Africa and to the earliest known primates with distinct hominid features, *Ramapithecus*, *Sivapithecus* and possibly other contemporaries. About two dozen *Ramapithecus* jaws and teeth have been found dating to the period from 14 or 15 million to about 8 or 9 million years ago. It is believed that *Ramapithecus*, *Sivapithecus* or perhaps some contemporary relatives whose remains have not yet been found were ancestral to *Australopithecus* and its contemporary *Homo* lines, such as *Homo habilis*, which led to modern humans, *Homo sapiens*, though a fossil gap of about 4 million years exists between the latest *Ramapithecus* specimen and the earliest australopithecine fossils of 4 million years ago.

The move from trees to ground is a critical stage in human evolution, since it accelerated selection pressures for bipedal upright posture and locomotion, which freed the hands for grasping rather than walking. In describing the following series of interacting events it is important to keep two things in mind: that the time scale of development is measured in millions of years—from about 15 to about 3 million years ago; and that developmental processes are interactional, interdependent. Among archeologists, paleontologists, paleoneurologists, and paleoanthropologists there are differences of opinion about exact dating of specimens, sequences, and "causality," but all appear to agree regarding the particular phenomena that were important in human cultural evolution.

As the paleoanthropologists Adrienne Zihlman and Lynda Brunker emphasize (1979), locomotor and feeding adaptations are structurally and functionally intertwined, and this has been a crucial concept in the reconstruction of hominid evolution from fossil remains. Bipedal locomotion was a process initiated by life in the trees, and it allowed the development of mechanisms necessary for the emancipation of the hands (Napier, 1962). Part of the adaptation from tree to ground living by the earliest ape-humans over a span of millions of years was toward bipedal upright posture and locomotion, which would, among other things, facilitate the gathering, catching, and carrying of food. That is, when ecological conditions, such as recession of forests, necessitated moving from the trees to the ground in search of food, those species of primates that had skeletal features facilitating upright posture and manual dexterity would have been better able to survive to maturity and to reproduce. While no fossil remains of the pelvis and hindlimbs of *Ramapithecus* or contemporaries have yet been found, abundant archeological evidence from fossil remains of foot, ankle, and pelvis and also from footprints reveal that hominids (*Australopithecus* and earliest *homo* species) were fully upright and bipedal by 3.5 to 4 million years ago and had a gait similar to that of modern humans (Zihlman and Bunker, 1979). Pressures for uprightness probably also came from the need to watch for predators and perhaps to frighten them off by brandishing branches (like modern chimpanzees), since foraging in open woodland-grassland-savanna country does not provide the cover and automatic protection of elevation from ground stalking carnivores that primates swinging through the forest canopy enjoy. The increasing use of the hands and visual system would have favored the evolution of those brains of a size and organization that could accommodate the increased use and need for distance vision and more refined motor skills. At the same time it seems probable that their greater visibility, and therefore vulnerability, as upright bipeds in open grasslands would also have stimulated some degree of social organization and communication, both made possible by the increasing brain capacity for conceptualization and symbolization.

Another important development accompanying ground living and bipedal posture was the evolution of the hands. Since the ground foraging would involve the gathering (picking, grasping, and digging) of small seeds, plants, and insects, those individuals or species with the appropriate structural capabilities of the hands would have been at a selective advantage; that is, they could gather more food and ensure their own survival to reproductive maturity and that of their offspring. The main evolutionary change involved the thumb, which increased in length and mobility, enabling it to rotate and sweep across the palm and effect a precision grip between thumb tip and the tip of each of the other four fingers. This greatly expands the capacity of the hand for precise manipulations as compared with the hands of apes, which grasp either with all the fingers curled into the palm or with the short thumb pressed against the side of the index finger. This expansion of hand size and use would also increase an important source of sensory input to the brain. This increase in sensory input would be used to best advantage by those brains with expanded sensory and motor areas, which, in turn, would have an increased functional ability to utilize the more highly differentiated hands.

With increased manual dexterity and increased intellectual capacity provided by the growing, reorganizing brain, early hominids began extending their food-obtaining capabilities by using stones and branches as tools. Eventually, with increasing intelligence, they learned to modify natural objects like stones and sticks into tools, which have been found in association with australopithecine and other hominid fossil remains dating back to 3.5 to 4 million years ago. The appearance of the stone tools suggests that they could have been used for scraping, chopping, and cutting.

Increasing motor skills and sensory input; increasing complexity of tool use, food gathering, processing, and sharing; increasing range of locomotion afforded by the evolution of a fully upright posture and by the ability to carry objects, such as food, tools, and babies; and the simultaneous and interdependent increase in brain size and reorganization would have facilitated increasing amounts of social interaction and communication culminating in acquisition of language. Language could only have developed when the slow evolutionary increase in brain size and neuronal numbers and the functional reorganization of the brain provided the capacity for symbolization and abstraction. The acquisition of language would then have effected another major jolt to cultural evolution, since language provides the capacity for social interaction and planning at a qualitatively new level of complexity.

Another element in this story concerns the paradoxical evolution of larger brains and skulls at the same time that the pelvis and the birth canal were becoming narrower as part of the evolution of upright bipedal locomotion. The evolutionary solution to this dilemma was that human fetuses were born at a stage of greater immaturity than other primates, that is, with a relatively smaller size of head, which permits passage through the birth canal. Some consequences of this fact are, first, that the human brain at birth is many years from its full growth and development, thus lengthening its period of highest susceptibility to modification by experience and learning as compared with other mammals; and, secondly, that human infants are completely helpless and dependent upon others for survival for many years during which learning and cultural molding, for better or worse, can take place. Prolonged infant dependency possibly also served as another pressure for increasing social interaction and communication.

EVOLUTIONARY DEVELOPMENT OF THE HUMAN BRAIN

Much information about the evolution of hominid brain size and shape has been gained from the study and measurement of fossil skulls and the endocranial casts (molds of the interior of skulls) that were formed naturally or that were made from fossil skulls (Holloway, 1968, 1974, 1975, 1978; Pilbeam, 1972;

Tobias, 1971). There is presently no information about the brain of *Ramapithecus*, but australopithecine and *Homo habilis* brains show the hominid pattern of neurological organization in their shape and proportions (Holloway, 1974). The sizes of these early hominid brains of 3 to 4 million years ago range from about 425 to 550 cc. in volume for *Australopithecus* and 600 to 650 cc. for *Homo habilis*, the approximate ranges of today's chimpanzee and gorilla brains. The australopithecine brain, however, was larger than its contemporaneous chimpanzee brain both absolutely and also relative to body size (it appears that the two species had similar body weights) (Holloway, 1975). The australopithecine body weight also appears to have been far less than that of the modern gorilla or its ancestor. For these reasons, Holloway (1974) has concluded on the basis of various estimations and calculations that the brain of *Australopithecus* had a ratio of brain size to body size (encephalization) that is closer to that of humans (1:45) than that of the great apes (1:200 for gorilla), and that, therefore, a significant amount of growth and reorganization of the hominid brain had occurred by 3 to 4 million years ago. The significance of this has been noted by Holloway: since encephalization "must reflect patterns of postnatal growth timing between the brain and body," selection pressures for this prolonged growth of the brain must have "great significance toward understanding the role of social behavior and 'intelligence' in hominid evolution" (1976, p. 342). The fact that *Australopithecus* was a bipedal upright locomotor with a much more advanced tool culture than that of modern chimpanzees suggests such a correlation between a relatively large brain, learning, and social organization.

It was at that period, beginning three million years ago, that the hominid brain underwent a burst of growth that did not begin to level off until the Neanderthal period between 100,000 and 35,000 years ago (Fig. 3.1). This increase in size, even when correlated with body weight, which was also increasing in the hominid lines, is of a different order of magnitude from that of other primates. Thus, when the hominid brain was beginning its precipitous growth, its possessor had already fashioned a simple toolmaking and social culture which was distinguishable from and advanced beyond that of other primates. It was a brain that underwent explosive growth and development over the next three million years within the context of the increasingly complex cultures that its hominid possessors were creating. Hominids' own culture became an increasingly significant part of the environment shaping the course of hominid evolution and can be considered, as Geertz (1973) and Holloway (1974, 1975) have emphasized, an essential condition for human evolution.

While some archeologists and paleontologists believe that *Australopithecus* and contemporaries may have used language, others date the period of the transition of the hominid brain to fully human capacities, which would include language, to the Neanderthal Mousterian cultures (Isaac, 1976; Jaynes, 1976; Marshack, 1976). They point out that even advanced toolmaking and other subsistence skills do not require syntactical language when other forms of visual, vocal, and tactile signals are available. Rather, the existence of language can be

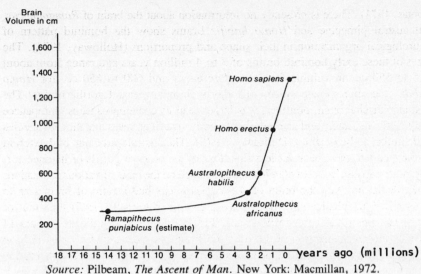

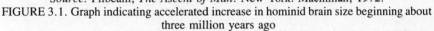

Source: Pilbeam, *The Ascent of Man*. New York: Macmillan, 1972.
FIGURE 3.1. Graph indicating accelerated increase in hominid brain size beginning about three million years ago

more convincingly argued when there is evidence of ritual behaviors and representational art that require complex symbolization and abstraction in order to represent the unseen and the unknowable. Such evidence appears in the archeological record at the end of the Mousterian cultures (that is, about 35,000 to 30,000 years ago) in the form of sculpture, representational art, personal ornamentation, and burial offerings (Marshack, 1976). It was the same period of about 40,000 to 30,000 years ago that witnessed both an explosive development of more complex tools than those present in the preceding millions of years and also a levelling off of the brain growth spurt at approximately its contemporary size and proportions.

It appears, then, that bipedal posture and locomotion, freedom of hands and use of tools, environmental pressures, social interaction, and communication in combination and interaction with a markedly enlarging and reorganizing brain characterized the emergence and evolution of *Homo sapiens*.

We are then left with the need to interpret the significance of the extraordinary growth in size of the brain, since size alone tells us nothing beyond an increase in some parameters, for example, in the number of neurons, that can support the level of cognitive functioning that distinguishes human behaviors: complex symbolization and language, long-term memory storage and associations, insight and planning, habitual inventiveness, creativity, abstraction, conscious self-awareness, intent and motivation, flexibility of choices and adaptability. To whatever degree any of these are present in other species, they are, as a whole, characteristic only of human brain-mind functioning.

Since any discussion of brain growth and organization must include a consideration of neurons, the primary structural units of brain function, it is necessary to digress briefly to describe neurons. Neurons have many different sizes and shapes, but, with a few exceptions, all have a characteristic and unique common structure (Fig. 3.2). Like other cells, neurons have a central cell body with a nucleus and cytoplasm, but unlike the cells of most organs, they have many cytoplasmic extensions known as *processes* radiating out from the cell body. All but one of the processes are dendrites that branch successively, like a tree, into ever thinner branches the farther they are from the cell body. The dendrites are covered with tiny spines and, together with the cell body, constitute the principal receiving surface for input from other neurons. A single slender process, the axon, leaves the cell body and forms specialized contacts called *synapses* with the dendrites and cell bodies of other neurons. It is at the synapses that information derived from the external world, usually in the form of chemical substances, called neurotransmitters, are transferred between neurons, most often from the axon of one neuron to the dendrites and cell bodies, sometimes also to the axons, of other neurons. A neuron may receive messages from as many as a thousand or more neurons and in turn transmit messages to as many as a thousand neurons, or even 5000 as calculated for the visual system (Holloway, 1968). There are estimated to be more than 50 billion neurons in the human brain.

Within any species, cranial capacity or brain size is extremely variable, and also size differences cannot be correlated with particular behaviors. Among

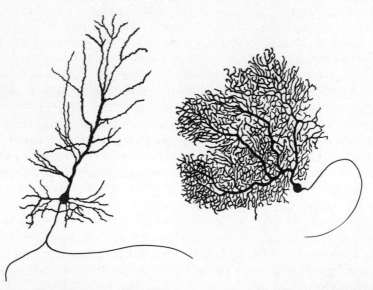

FIGURE 3.2. Drawings of two different types of neurons. These show the rich dendritic arborizations and the tiny spines that are sites of synaptic contacts with other neurons. The single smooth process extending from the cell toward the bottom of the page is the axon, carrying information to other neurons

humans no known correlation exists between brain size (within normal limits) and intelligence; high levels of creativity or intellectual functioning have been associated with brains of 1100–1200 cc. volume (Anatole France and Walt Whitman) or 2200 cc. (Lord Byron and Ivan Turgenev). Conversely, mental retardation is not correlated with small brain size except in microcephaly. From an evolutionary point of view, we only know that an increase in brain size accompanied an increase in behavioral adaptability requiring cerebral functions that are called intelligence, memory, insight, conceptualization, symbolization, inventiveness, etc. Important processes of internal reorganization probably occurred incorporating the increase in the number, size, and complexity of neurons that is assumed to have accompanied and accounted for the steady increase in brain size (Holloway, 1968; Pilbeam, 1972; Tobias, 1971).

Unfortunately, cranial fossils, while indicating brain size, shape, and proportions, offer no clues to the internal structure or organization of early hominid brains, to the number, size, distribution, or connectivity of the neurons. At the present time, the best source of insight into the nature of the organizational changes that the early hominid brain may have undergone to acquire its present human form is the comparative study of the structure and organization of brains of different species. We cannot view present-day species of monkeys and apes as representing an evolutionary sequence leading to *Homo sapiens*, since all mammalian species, monkeys, apes, and hominids have each had their own evolutionary course over the past millions of years; that is, we cannot make the assumption that the modern chimpanzee brain is like the brain of an early hominid, since both lines independently evolved from a common hominoid ancestor. But we can derive some degree of confidence in the comparative method from the fact that there is a certain steady progression in the levels of growth and organization of certain important features of the brain among species from fish through mammals and from tarsiers and monkeys through apes to humans that parallels the progression in levels of variability, complexity, and flexibility of the behavioral repertoires among these species.

Among vertebrates the basic structure and organization of the brain as well as the physiological mechanisms of neuronal functioning are similar, though certain areas facilitating particular functions are more highly developed in some species; for example, touch in raccoons (Welker, Johnson, and Pubols, 1964) and vision-flight in birds. The part of the brain that has undergone the most dramatic evolutionary expansion in proportion to the rest of the brain is the cerebral cortex, the outer surface layers of nerve cells, in particular the major portion of the cortex known as the neocortex. It is the "avalanching enlargement" of the neocortex that is a major aspect of mammalian evolution, that distinguishes primates from other mammals and humans from other primates, and that correlates best with evolutionary achievement (Mountcastle, 1977).

In comparing the cerebral cortex of representatives of the major classes of vertebrates, the relative increase in expansion of the cortex from fishes to primates is obvious and is shown in Figure 3.3. Within the mammalian order, another

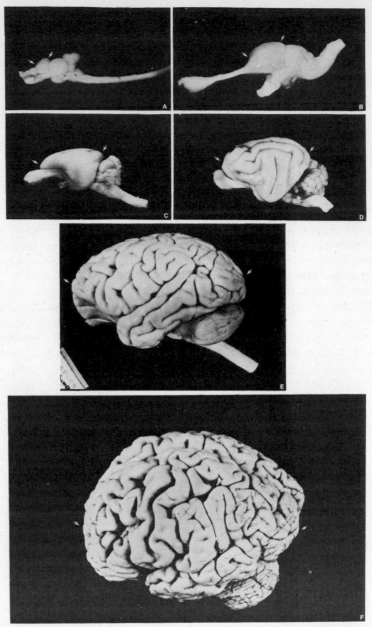

FIGURE 3.3. Photographs of brains to show the increase in size of the cerebral hemispheres (and, therefore, cerebral cortex) relative to the rest of the brain and the increase in folding or fissuration (and, therefore, extent and volume) of the cerebral cortex as one goes from animals of limited behavioral flexibility to those of more complex, learned behaviors. The arrows indicate the rostral end (on the left) and the caudal end (on the right) of the cerebral hemispheres. **A**, fish; **B**, lizard; **C**, rabbit; **D**, cat; **E**, chimpanzee; **F**, human. These are not shown at the same scale of magnification. The lizard and fish are shown at about five-sixths of the actual size; the rabbit and cat, at one-half of the actual size; and the chimpanzee and human at about one-third of the actual size

sequence of increases in cortical volume or area and complexity of organization and functioning can be discerned: the cortical surface of the cerebral hemispheres, which is smooth in the rabbit and the mouse, becomes convoluted in carnivores and increasingly convoluted in primates (Fig. 3.3). The convolutions, however they evolved or develop embryologically, permit a large increase in the total volume of the neocortex, in proportion to the underlying brain stem, within a skull that evolutionarily could not have increased indefinitely in size and weight in order to accommodate an enlarging brain and still get through the birth canal of the pelvis. The family of insectivores is considered to be ancestral to primates, and since contemporary insectivores (for example, tree shrews) are believed to have evolved very little from their ancestors, their brains have been used to calculate an index of evolutionary development for different brain structures in primates. This "progression index" calculated for the neocortex is 156 for humans, 60 for chimpanzees, and 40 for old-world monkeys, as compared with the index of 1 for insectivores (Mountcastle, 1977).

The neocortex ultimately receives and processes all of the modalities of stimuli from the external world, as well as from our own bodies, and in interaction with neuronal units and systems in other parts of the brain, provides for conscious perception and awareness and our responses to such perceptions. It has been shown that the basic functional and structural units of the mammalian neocortex are adjacent columns of interconnected neurons. The column "is a complex processing and distributing unit that links a number of inputs to several outputs" (Mountcastle, 1977, p. 38). While the columns in comparable cortical areas are similar and constant in numbers of neurons (about 110) in mice, cats, monkeys, and humans alike, the difference as one goes from mice to humans is in the tremendous increase in the total number of columns and the accompanying reorganization and amplification of cortical connections and information processing that they provide. It has been estimated that the human neocortex contains about 600 million minicolumns and about 50 billion neurons (Mountcastle, 1977) as compared with about 5.5 billion neurons in the chimpanzee (Holloway, 1968). When one considers that every neuron is in synaptic contact with about 2000 or more other neurons, the magnitude of the increased functional complexity introduced by the addition of even a few billion neocortical neurons is enormous.

Extensive neurophysiological cortical mapping experiments comparing, for example, primitive insectivores such as the hedgehog, which has less neocortex than any living mammal, with monkeys suggest that neocortical evolutionary growth has been accompanied by a multiplication of parallel and interconnected neuronal circuits (Merzenich and Kaas, 1980). This multiplication cannot be viewed as simple redundancy, but rather as an "avalanching" elaboration of the processing of incoming information, an increase in the complexity and magnitude of "re-entrant" signaling that associates current sensory input with stored information (memory and prior experience), and the vast multiplication of associated alternative pathways and switching points for processing both input and output. While neuroscientists are far from understanding the mechanisms of, for example, consciousness and memory, it seems clear that the tremendous enlargement of the neocortex in humans and the associated multiplication of interconnecting neuronal circuits laid the basis for the unique characteristics of human mind-brain functions, much flexibility in neuronal circuits (and therefore in behavioral and cognitive responses), abstraction, long-term memory storage and retrieval, inventiveness, etc. It is a cortex that, with the rest of the brain, permits an infinitely rich behavioral plasticity and frees us, if we choose, from stereotyped behavior patterns. Furthermore, the human cortex constructs and transmits the body of ideas and values that constitute our culture, liberates our human history from many prehuman modes of behavior, and provides the context within which our distinctly human behaviors and social relationships develop.

I would, in fact, argue that rather than our biology determining responses and therefore limiting the range and flexibility of our behavioral repertoires, it is our cultural milieu, created by our inventiveness and flexibility, that, paradoxically and ironically, limits and contains our full potential for flexibility and creativity in behaviors and forms of social organization and relationships.

To summarize evolutionary factors considered of importance in brain development: Evolutionary selection pressures in the earliest hominoid-hominid lines were for increasingly larger brains, but the selection was not for size alone. With increases in size came changes in internal structure—larger neurons, more complex connectivity, a greatly expanded neocortex, and internal reorganization—which permitted the development of more complex functional operations of the brain and, consequently, more complex and flexible behavioral patterns in response to environmental demands. The selective advantage of the enlarging brain was in the constantly expanding behavioral repertoire which it made possible. This expanding repertoire represented not only a quantitative surge over that of hominoid ancestors and relatives but a qualitative leap that included symbolization and inventiveness. A number of factors, not the least of which was the acquisition of language, led to increased social organization and cooperation. Expanding behavioral flexibility and increasing social cooperation together equipped increasing numbers of evolving hominids with the ability to survive to child-bearing age and to reproduce within their changing ecological niches.

FETAL DEVELOPMENT OF THE BRAIN

Having traced the evolutionary course of the developmnent of the size and complexity of the human brain within the limitations of present knowledge, I would like now to discuss some aspects of the fetal development of the brain in order to demonstrate its structural and functional plasticity in response to environmental influences. Theories of the evolutionary and genetic transmission of human behaviors or their determination by other biological factors, such as hormones, appear less tenable when we see that the actual structure of the fetal and postnatal brain, its development, and its functioning are affected by environmental input and learning.

A host of genetic, biological, and environmental factors influence a developmental sequencing in time and space of neuronal origin, differentiation, migration, and final destination as well as the initial outgrowth and the pattern and direction of dendritic and axonal processes. This sequencing shapes the basic patterns of cellular relationships within the brain though not necessarily, as I shall discuss later, the final patterns of interneuronal connectivity and functioning. This temporal-spatial patterning characterizes neurogenesis across vertebrate orders and results in a similar basic organization of all vertebrate brains into distinct regions and cell groupings, circuits, and systems, some of which are recognizably homologous from one species to another or from one animal to another.

After the migrating neurons have reached their destinations within the embryonic brain, the major prenatal portion of dendritic and axonal growth occurs. The neurons begin to make synaptic contacts with other neurons, sometimes traveling long and intricate pathways to do so. It is still not known what specific factors intrinsic to the brain are responsible for the course taken by growing axons or for effecting cellular recognition in the formation of functional synapses between appropriate neurons, though it is a question that inspires extensive experimental investigation (see Cotman, 1978; Jacobson, 1978; Lund, 1978, for reviews of the field of developmental neurobiology). As already noted in the previous chapter, it is known that a variety of environmental factors can adversely affect the normal prenatal growth and development of neurons, their dendrites and axons and, therefore, their synaptic connections, such as maternal malnutrition, certain drugs, virus infections, and hormonal disturbances, particularly of the thyroid and adrenal cortex. Such environmentally induced developmental defects in neuronal structure may result, of course, in detectable functional deficits in behaviors or cognitive abilities.

A significant implication of these pathological situations, which represent a distortion of the normal or physiological maternal milieu, is that neuronal growth and connectivity *ordinarily* require a particular environmental range or set of conditions for normal development to occur. If malnutrition, for example, retards or distorts neuronal growth, then it means that neurons *normally* require the presence in their environment of a certain minimum level of particular substances in order to develop without any structural or apparent functional deficits. The important point here is that normal development of neurons and the brain not only is guided by genetic influences but also requires interaction with a range of particular environmental influences.

POSTNATAL DEVELOPMENT OF THE BRAIN

Critical to any consideration of the environmental impact on the developing brain is the fact that in mammals a significant part of brain growth and development occurs after birth, even though no new neurons are formed (except for two known areas in the brain, cerebellum and olfactory bulbs). The major part of this development occurs as a result of the growth in size and complexity of neurons and of their dendritic and axonal ramifications, and, therefore, in the extent and complexity of synaptic connections among neurons. This growth provides for more alternative pathways or switching points, more modulations of responses, and, consequently, increased complexity and flexibility of behaviors. In the cortex of rodents and cats, there is a tenfold or greater increase in neuronal connectivity in the month following birth (Jacobson, 1978).

The primate brain is relatively more immature at birth than most other mammals, and the human brain is the most immature. It more than doubles in size within a year after birth and almost doubles again by the age of four years, when it is close to adult size. Thus, the human brain quadruples in size from the neonatal period to adult status, while in other primates it doubles in size during the comparable period. The major expansion in the dendritic and synaptic network takes place in the first two years of life, though growth continues to adulthood (Schadé and van Groeningen, 1961).

Since the primate brain undergoes its major growth spurt following birth, this means that a significant amount of growth occurs under the influence of and in functional interaction with input from the external world. In fact, research on developing animals has shown that these critical processes of growth and formation of synapses *require* input from the external world for normal brain development and function to occur. For example, without input of light and visual stimuli to one or both eyes of cats and monkeys, neurons processing visual information fail to develop normal dendrites and spines and normal connections (Hirsch and Leventhal, 1978; Hubel and Wiesel, 1970; Wiesel and Hubel, 1963a, 1963b, 1974). It was also found that the functioning of the adult visual system could be altered by exposing young animals to an abnormal visual environment. For example, by rearing kittens in an environment of either horizontal or vertical stripes, the visual system becomes preferentially attuned correspondingly to either horizontal or vertical stripes (Hirsch and Spinelli, 1970). Similarly, the auditory system depends upon environmental stimulation for normal development. Auditory neurons remain structurally and functionally immature in mice reared with partial or complete sound deprivation, and profound structural changes in auditory neurons were found in a child born with sensorineural deafness (Trune, 1982; Webster and Webster, 1977, 1979). Finally, in yet a third function and a uniquely human one, language, it appears that adequate environmental stimulation is needed during a critical postnatal period for normal neuronal development to occur (Walker, 1981). Without exposure to a sociolinguistic environment, language does not develop, and the normal acquisition of language cannot occur, so far as is known, after puberty; that is, around the age of 12 years. The critical period of language acquisition, from the age of 2 to 12 years, coincides with the period during which the brain acquires anatomical and functional maturity. It is during the critical periods of development for the different systems thus far studied that the "functional validation" (Walker, 1981) of developing synapses occurs through environmental input, as a means by which neurons acquire normal anatomical connections and subsequent function.

Conversely, it has been shown, as noted in Chapter 2, that early exposure of rats to an enriched environment results in a thicker cortex with larger neurons having more complex dendritic branching, more spines and increased connectivity. Other studies have also demonstrated that the pattern of developing neuronal connections can be modified both by experimental manipulations and by environmental influences (Cotman, 1978; Goldman and Rakic, 1979; Jacobson, 1978; Kalil and Reh, 1979; Lund, 1978). This structural and functional plasticity of the brain is most marked in young animals and human infants but continues into adult life (Goldberger and Murray, 1974; Murray and Goldberger, 1974; Raisman, 1969; Rose, Malis, Kruger, and Baker, 1960).

While it seems clear that experience is critical for establishing normal synaptic connections in the developing brain, it is not known what biological processes account for this extraordinary developmental plasticity of the brain. One explanation involves the observation that in all species of mammalian brains studied, many more neurons are produced early in fetal development than finally survive, and they make a considerable number of temporary connections (Jacobson, 1978; Lund, 1978). The reduction in number of neurons occurs by neuronal death in the late fetal and early postnatal period. Those neurons remain which have made functional synaptic contacts, or "sustaining" connections, with other neurons; or, conversely, neurons that do not establish functional connections degenerate. At least one factor in determining whether or not certain neurons survive, that is, whether or not they form sustaining connections with other neurons, is functional reinforcement in the form of experience or environmental input. For a variety of reasons that may be unnecessary to describe here, it seems reasonable to speculate that the sensory input from the environment sets off a chain of metabolic effects that influence the formation and maintenance of sustained synaptic connections between neurons within particular functional systems (Bleier, 1969; Hamburger and Oppenheim, 1982; Zelená, 1964).

LEARNING AND THE DEVELOPING BRAIN

Thus far I have examined some of the evolutionary and ontogenetic evidence that appears relevant to an understanding of the morphological development of a human brain that exhibits enormous behavioral plasticity. I shall now explore the behavioral manifestations of the susceptibility of the developing brain to environmental influences. Some research on animal behaviors emphasizes that, even among vertebrate species with relatively limited behavioral repertoires, experience and learning play a significant role in the development of normal brain function and behavior. This work calls into question the behavioral category of *instincts*, which upon probing with ever finer and more sophisticated investigative tools and concepts, shrinks in the scope and numbers of behaviors it can include. One such example of a seemingly instinctive behavior is the ability of the newly hatched duckling to recognize and follow its own mother. In Chapter 2 I described the work showing that prehatching exposure to the mother's, siblings', and its own vocalizations was necessary for the normal development of the duckling's ability to recognize its mother's call. In some way normal neuronal functioning and connectivity in the auditory system are disrupted if the duckling's developing brain is deprived of any of these particular environmental inputs.

While it appears that there are species where some behavioral mechanisms seem to be innate, that is, not learned, the more complex the structure of the central nervous system becomes, the more behavioral options, that is, plasticity, the brain provides the animal in its responses to the environment. While genetic and biological factors determine that a bird sings rather than barks, specific bird songs are usually learned. One of the few examples among birds or mammals where a specific behavior occurs in the apparent absence of learning is provided by some birds that are brood parasites (J. L. Brown, 1975). The eggs are laid in nests of foster parents (of another species) who raise the young. Even when apparently isolated from their own parents, the newly hatched birds sing only the simple stereotyped song of their species. There are other brood parasites, however, that learn the song of their foster parents. Most birds will not develop their species' characteristic songs if raised in isolation and will sing only imperfectly. Most birds learn not only their species' specific songs but also local dialects from their conspecifics. Birds that pair bond learn to recognize their mates at a great distance, and some pairs engage in antiphonal duetting. In some species in which only the male sings, the development both of normal song and of the group of neurons in the brain responsible for singing are dependent both upon exposure to the bird's own androgens (sex hormones) during a critical period of development and upon auditory input, that is, learning, from conspecifics. The interaction of genetic, biological, and experimental or learning influences on behavior is seen in the migration pattern of indigo buntings (Bonner, 1980). This bird, which migrates at night, first learns the patterns of stars in the northern sky during its nesting period; its own hormones affect whether it flies north or south; and then it learns specific flight routes from older birds.

In considering human infants, Sherwood Washburn in his critique of Sociobiological extrapolations from ape to human behaviors, points out that "learning is the crucial factor in the two basic abilities that distinguish human beings from all other primates: the ability to walk on two legs (bipedalism) and human speech"

(1978, p. 73). While there is a biological basis for walking, just as there is a part of the brain mainly responsible for language, human beings do not "instinctively" walk. They must learn to walk, just as they must learn any language they speak. Washburn goes on to point out that just because certain behaviors have a biological base, it does not mean that special genes for those behaviors are involved. For example, the arms and legs of primates make swimming possible, but apes and most humans do not swim. Humans who learn to swim use arms and legs that evolved for different purposes but obviously no special genes have been required for swimming.

The examples above indicate the importance of learning, even for behaviors that appear stereotyped and have been considered to be "instinctive." The importance of early experience for normal development of both the brain and its product, behavior, has been shown in most vertebrate species where the question has been investigated. To genetically influenced mechanisms necessary for survival, the capacity to learn introduces a flexibility in behavioral responses that enhances adaptability to environmental change and challenge. The effects of early experience are the greatest in those mammalian species where a major part of growth and development of the brain occurs after birth, as one might logically expect. In fact, one could also say that it is precisely this correlation which has evolved most dramatically in the hominid line; that is, selection pressures were for a larger and consequently reorganized brain that could accommodate and enable the increasingly complex behavior patterns made possible by bipedalism and increased use of hands and eyes. *Because* of the large size of the brain relative to the birth canal, it was born earlier, when it was smaller, and, therefore, at a level of immaturity that would then require a long period of growth and development to achieve mature size and function. That function is to receive, process, and store information from the outside world and to guide behavioral responses to that information; and it develops during the brain's long postnatal growth period in interaction with and response to input from the external world.

Across vertebrate species, a brain of increasing complexity has evolved providing for an increase in the flexibility of behavioral responses from single, relatively stereotyped patterns to a multitude of possible alternative responses that are learned and invented. Genes could not, as Sociobiologists imply, encode the brain for all the behaviors required of a species that inhabits every possible terrestrial environmental niche. Instead, cultural evolution provides a non-genetic mode for adaptive behavior in humans. Because it became possible to transmit, accumulate, and even invent new information providing for adaptation and survival without any *direct* instruction from the genes, as Bonner has emphasized, "changes that might have taken hundreds of thousands of years could now occur in weeks or days, or even hours" (1980, p. 194). A look at all civilization around us makes abundantly clear both the dynamism and inventiveness of the human response to our environmental challenges and also the enormous variability among peoples in those responses.

It is because of the developmental plasticity of the brain and because humans learn so quickly and easily that we become adapted so thoroughly to the dichotomized cultures we are born into and we learn to accept, as *natural*, our proper place. Most of us are taught in minute detail, sometimes subtly and sometimes with sledgehammer force, from birth what it means to be either a boy or girl. We are each presented with a range of acceptable behaviors and characteristics that is different from and exclusive of the *other* range, both of which reflect, we are told, the way the world is divided. We learn, and we learn well, how it is appropriate for us to look, walk, think, feel, behave with others, think about ourselves, hope and want for ourselves. We learn we are to be either physically, intellectually, and emotionally tough or physically, intellectually, and emotionally soft and dependent. We know we must be *either* brave, assertive, aggressive, dominant, inquisitive, argumentative, acquisitive, appropriating, intrusive, and masterful *or* sweet, quiet, lovely, loving, helpful, giving, unobtrusive, submissive, compliant, and receptive. The maintenance of these stereotypes is the predominant characteristic of every aspect of our culture, and it is science's special contribution to demonstrate the biological basis for this dichotomization of human potential. It tells us, for example, how it is that males are *innately* superior to females in mathematics, which itself requires being brave (taking chances), assertive, aggressive, inquisitive, argumentative and masterful, and knowing that this society *will reward* you for those skills.

THE SEARCH FOR INNATE LAWS OF HUMAN BEHAVIORS

Were it not for the biological determinist insistence on genetic and biological primacy in human behaviors and characteristics, it would seem redundant in the extreme for anyone to detail or explain the obvious dependence of human beings on learning processes. It is that very dependence that makes human beings so awesomely vulnerable to their experiences in the early years of their existence, experiences that we *know* mold personalities, characteristics, patterns of behavioral and emotional responses, peculiarities and uniqueness, beliefs, values, fears, expectations, self-concept, madnesses, longings. We may not know *how*, but we know experience *does* mold and shape and, for better *and* worse, we bear and express its effects throughout our lives. But despite the overwhelming body of evidence from psychology, anthropology, and our own perceptions documenting both the primacy of experience and learning in human development and also the limitless variability of behavioral patterns among and within cultures, there persists a strong trend in a variety of fields to attempt to explain human behaviors by uncovering *basic* units of universal behaviors isolatable in a psychology or biology laboratory.

This positivist view, that the methodologies of the natural sciences are applicable to the study of social events and processes, has likewise dominated the human social sciences for a number of years, with mainstream psychology viewing the experimental method as *the* scientific way to study and understand human behavior (Parlee, 1979). The method is directed toward finding and elucidating universal *laws* of behavior by lifting behaviors out of the context within which they occur and subjecting them to scrutiny under "controlled" laboratory conditions. The aim of the research, whether on rodents or humans, is that such discovered laws be free of the constraints of any particular context and therefore applicable to all.

Goldfoot (1983), whose work with monkeys has shown the possibilities of shaping what have been considered to be "basic biological mechanisms"—reproductive behaviors—by manipulating the social environment, suggests that it may be more desirable to consider social factors as part of the research design rather than as "noise" to be factored out. Since "social contributions are important mediators of sexually dimorphic behavior," he emphasizes that it is necessary to observe animals in many different social environments of rearing and testing (p. 27).

In his critique of context-stripping methods in the behavioral and social sciences, Mishler (1979) has described alternative approaches to studying contextually grounded, meaningful behavior and social interactions. These include methods drawn from ecological psychology, phenomenological research, sociolinguistics, and ethnomethodology, where the study of *situated* meaning is central. Aside from the basic methodological difficulty that even the laboratory itself is *not* a pure, neutral, context-free setting but introduces its own set of contextual variables that are usually ignored, Mishler points to the paradox "that we all know that human action and experience are context dependent and can only be understood within their contexts"; and yet

> The other side of the paradox is that this ordinary and commonsense understanding of meaning as context dependent has been excluded from the main tradition of theory and research in the social and psychological sciences. . . . As theorists and researchers, we tend to behave as if context were the enemy of understanding rather than the resource for understanding which it is in our everyday lives. (1979, p. 2)

Mary Brown Parlee, in her review of the field of psychology (1979), observes that feminist scholarship in psychology appears to have had less of a significant impact on mainstream thinking than has feminist research in other disciplines and offers the explanation that it is because feminist research poses a challenge to the basic commitment to the experimental context-stripping methods by which mainstream psychology defines itself. She believes that feminist research at its best, while also evaluating its results by the usual scholarly criteria of reliability, logical inference, consistency, and so on, is characterized by "the investigator's continual testing of the plausibility of the work against her own experience" (p. 130). In psychology, she points out, feminists would rather find the best possible version of the truth about the subject than adhere strictly to a particular method. In analyzing mainstream psychology's resistance to the vigorous criticism of its context-stripping methods by both feminist psychologists and traditional social psychologists she asks, what function is served by "psychology's unswerving commitment to a particular method as defining the field?" (p. 131). She approaches the answer by describing feminist research on conversational interactions that focus on the means through which power is created in social interactions: for example, men interrupt women more than women do men; women follow up on conversational topics introduced by men and work harder to keep conversations going. She cites these subtle processes as showing how power is created and maintained on a day-to-day-basis in the most taken for granted ways. Context-stripping methods, however, cannot reveal interactional systems that reflect socially structured power relations.

> Insistence on context-stripping methods as the only valid ones, then, benefits those who do not want public (scientific) examination of the way relations at the individual level are embedded in and reflect social roles and the institutions in which they are located. . . . One might further argue that context-stripping methods not only discourage investigation of micropolitical interactions, but by providing an alternative formulation of the phenomenon they actively obscure or falsify what experience tells us is really going on. . . . Women's psychology is 'explained' by reference to impersonal processes (genes, hormones, reinforcement contingencies) rather than being seen as the meaningful result of interaction with other people who intend, want, or desire to produce particular behaviors and experiences in the women. (Parlee, 1979, p. 132)

Parlee then makes the telling observation that "psychology's commitment to context-stripping methods is a commitment to making the political personal" (pp. 132-133).

This is precisely analogous to the methodology of biological determinists who make the political biological, the historical natural. What is implied by the search in animals for basic biological or genetic mechanisms for human behaviors and social relationships is that human behaviors can be separated from the cultural context within which they develop and occur. Sociobiologists' explanations of human behaviors and social phenomena strip those events of all cultural context and meaning, and make of them simple and logical manifestations of individual biological *natures*. Such Sociobiologists see war as the collective result of individual male innate aggressivity and conformity; and racism, nationalism and capitalist competition (all!) as a natural aversion to those, who as non-kin, do not carry any of our genes.

Then on the level of individual human behaviors and characteristics, biological determinist theory in essence denies the unique qualities of the human brain. Since behavior is an expression of brain function, the concept of instinctive behaviors and characteristics constituting a human *nature* assumes a genetic programming in the brain of evolved behavior patterns. An understanding of the brain, its development, and functioning negates such a concept. Context-stripping methods deprive human behaviors of meaning and each individual of the unique history of her *particular* nature.

THE INDIVIDUALITY OF HUMAN NATURE
AND THE ENFORCEMENT OF SOCIAL CONFORMITY

Knowledge of who we are, our femaleness or our maleness, of who we are to be, and knowledge of others' expectations of us is reflected back upon us from the moment we are born. That knowledge and those expectations are transmitted directly to our bodies in the ways our bodies are handled and in the tones of the voices that impinge upon an auditory system in the infant that can recognize meaning that is not verbal. And finally, when we become visually and verbally cognitive, culture fully enters our consciousness. Our earliest identity was our perception of who or what others perceived us to be. Our individual *natures* began to *form* from the time of our earliest perceptions, experiences, and learnings of the world and our interactions with the people around us. Even before acquiring language, but particularly afterward, we store fantastic amounts of information derived from all of our experiences; information in the form of memories, associations, values, beliefs, expectations. That set of experiences and associations is necessarily unique for each person and influences how she interacts with the world, how she perceives herself, whom she loves. Each person brings to a particular behavioral response or personality characteristic her unique and continually changing set of past and present circumstances, experiences, motivations, and emotions as well as anatomical and physiological qualities. In short, there is no universal or individual *innate* nature or behavior that exists beneath or outside of the cultural context of each person's life and history.

This stress on the uniqueness of each person's development is not, however, to deny that the culture and ideology of every social order act as a mold on that heterogeneous multipotential base of personhood, enforcing and ensuring, with a fair degree of success, a *conformity that becomes known as human nature.* Thus we have the paradox of a brain, structurally and functionally capable of permitting a nearly limitless variety of behavioral responses, being constrained in the full range of its possible expression by the cultures it has itself produced. That the conformity which every culture achieves does not benefit from *genes* for conformity, as E. O. Wilson proposed (1975, p. 562), is suggested by the tremendous expenditure of effort necessary for the dominant culture to ensure conformity: through force and violence, laws, and ideological indoctrination.

It is the rule of force that has allowed the shooting or jailing of war-deserters and nonconformists, the lynching and murder of blacks who were not obligingly inferior and obsequious, and myriad other violences committed against the bodies and minds of women and men. As I will discuss in detail in Chapter 7, these violences against women flourish within and because of a cultural context that insists it is women's *nature* to be primarily committed to, dependent upon, and identified with men, and that consequently permits, requires, and acknowledges the rightful and unquestioning access to and ownership of women's bodies by men: oggling, touching, and verbal assault at any time; rape and marital rape; mass rape of women as the spoils of warfare; woman-battering, child sexual abuse and incest; control of abortion and contraception with the consequent killing of women by illegal abortions and experimentation with contraceptive pills and devices; involuntary sterilization; unnecessary hysterectomies; clitoridectomies and other horrors of genital mutilations; footbinding; the beating, murder or gang rape of women who commit adultery; the hospitalization, drugging, and lobotomization of women who deviate from prescribed roles; forced feeding of jailed suffragists; witch-burning; pornography and its role in encouraging violence and brutality against women as an acceptable feature of heterosexual relationships. By such physical means, it is ensured that woman's *nature* conforms to patriarchal needs and expectations.

It has been the law that enforces women's economic and social conformity and dependence on men through its control of the conditions of childbirth, motherhood, marriage, divorce, property, employment, welfare, and education. It has protected the rights of universities to exclude women as students and teachers officially until the last 100 years or so and unofficially until the 1970s; of professions and trades to refuse admittance to women; of husbands to beat wives and to own their bodies, their children, and their property; of society to outlaw contraception and abortion. It has been the law that, without question until recently, protected the rights of employers and supervisors to underpay women workers and to fire women who would not accept sexual assaults as part of their jobs. It is the law that punishes prostitutes but protects their pimps, procurers, and patrons. By such legal means, it is ensured that woman's *nature* conforms to patriarchal needs and expectations.

And finally, it has been ideology that enforces conformity through the myths of a female nature and a male nature. But, as both Simone DeBeauvoir (1953) and Monique Wittig (1980) have written, one is not born a woman. New explorations by symbolic and cultural anthropologists (Ortner and Whitehead, 1981) have begun to show that, in any culture, the categories and meanings of "women" and "men" are cultural or symbolic constructions rather than reflections of biological "givens." What women and men are seen to be or represent, what gender is or means, what relations exist between women and men are "largely products of social and cultural processes" (p. 1).

The very emphasis on the biological factor *within* different cultural traditions is variable; some cultures claim that male-female differences are almost entirely biologically grounded, whereas others give biological differences, or supposed biological differences, very little emphasis. (Ortner and Whitehead, 1981, p. 1)

And in our Western industrialized and scientifically "advanced" countries, century upon century of being told that woman's value and definition are her biological ability to bear children has made of *woman* that particular social construct. It is because *woman's nature* has been defined biologically to *be* a mother and wife that the rest of the social construct of woman "naturally" follows: nurturing, passive, dependent, weak, intuitive, non-intellectual, and asexual (but nonetheless obligatorily heterosexual). The category *woman*, like that of *man*, is a cultural category, not eternal (Wittig, 1980). The distinction of human characteristics as feminine or masculine, based on "nature," obscures the social, political, and economic origins of the differences between the sexes and of women's subordination as a class. Dominant cultures create confusion about what is *given* and what is *consequence*. To the seemingly ingenuous question, "Why is it that women do the things they do?" (that is, why are they in a subordinate position to men?) comes the obvious answer: "By jove, it is in their very nature to do so." Woman's nature is seen to be the *given*; her roles and functions are the results. In fact, the situation is quite the reverse. Patriarchal social orders need and assign rigidly set and subordinate functions or roles for women, which, in turn, require and mold certain characteristics and behaviors: patience (called "passivity"), compliance, eagerness to please, sensitivity to feelings of others, and understanding, loving, caring, nurturing behaviors. These characteristics are often essential for survival. In a social order that requires women to gain and maintain male approval, women become exquisitely sensitive to the most subtle nuances and clues indicating disapproval and, in general, to others' feelings and thoughts (hence, women's "intuition"). Women, assigned the care, loving and nurturing of children, develop caring, loving, nurturing "natures." Many women, of course, do not conform, often at great cost to their energies, creativity, productivity, sanity, or health. Certainly the last thing society desires of its women has been intellectuality or independence. In short, the roles or functions are actually the *given*; women's *natures*, the social consequence. The *natural woman* is a cultural invention that insures the loyalty and bondage of women to the roles and functions the patriarchal social order has assigned her.

I do not mean for a moment to devalue the many ways that women are; in fact, I celebrate them. But it is important to recognize they are not biological or inevitable. And yet, it might be asked, how is it that a veritable empire of research—in psychology, anthropology, sociology, biology—rests on the presumption of innate sex differences in behaviors, cognitive functions, and characteristics of temperament? I have already given much of my answer to the question. As both Kate Millett and Monique Wittig have also analyzed, control and power are supported through both violence and ideology. An important part of the ideology is the constitution of sex differences, which reflects

> . . . the formation of human personality along stereotyped lines of sex category ('masculine' and 'feminine'), based on the needs and values of the dominant group and dictated by what its members cherish in themselves and find convenient in subordinates: aggression, intelligence, force, and efficacy in the male; passivity, ignorance, docility, 'virtue', and ineffectuality in the female. (Millett, 1970, p. 26)

Constituting a difference is an act of power and requires social dominance to be successful. As Wittig has written: "Men are not different, whites are not different, nor are the masters. But the blacks, as well as the slaves, are" (1980, p. 108).

SUMMARY AND CONCLUSIONS

An evolutionary sequence of interacting events resulted in a brain that enabled the emergence of toolmaking, language, and complex social interactions which themselves, in turn, influenced the course of the evolution of the human brain and intelligence. The capacities for symbolization, language, and conceptualization permit many of the unique aspects of human intelligence: the communication of thought, long-term memory storage and immediate recall, insight, foresight, planning, abstract thought, creativity and inventiveness, and a seemingly limitless capacity to learn. Just as the evolution of the brain has resulted in an enormous increase in the numbers of neurons and therefore in the numbers and complexity of higher order interactions among the neurons, so has the parallel and consequent evolution of the capacity for culture resulted in an enormous increase in the numbers and complexity of behavioral responses of individuals to, and interactions with, their environment, an environment that includes the very cultures that their brains have created.

The full development of the capacities of the brain depends upon its normal fetal growth and organization, which occurs as a sequence of complex interactions among genetic, biological, and environmental influences from the time of conception. The very structure of neurons and their interconnections are affected by environmental input both before and after birth. In all mammals a significant proportion of the brain's growth and organization occurs after birth, a period of rapid learning. It has become increasingly clear over the past decade or two that even animal behaviors formerly assumed to be innate or "instinctive" are influenced by learning before and after birth. In primates, the brain is particularly immature at birth and, consequently, structurally and functionally susceptible for many years and, to a lesser degree, throughout life, to environmental modification through sensory experience and learning. Human beings have by far the most extended period of postnatal development, the brain quadrupling in size from birth to the age of four years and reaching full structural and physiological maturity only around puberty. This circumstance is the key to understanding what critically differentiates humans from other primates and also to understanding the meaninglessness of biology-learning dichotomies. The effect of the extended period of postnatal development is the augmentation of the influence of the environment on the brain, and this occurs through the shaping and modification of the functional connections of various neuronal systems.

Visual input affects the number, size, and synaptic patterns of neurons processing visual information, and auditory input similarly affects auditory neurons during development. It also seems quite likely that the development of symbolic language itself, a unique human characteristic, depends upon the effects of the linguistic environment upon certain neurons during the critical period of language acquisition. Thus, while the basic neural organization of the brain is significantly genetically influenced, the ultimate pattern of synaptic connections and therefore brain functions is significantly shaped by the effects of environmental input on neuronal activity.

Paradoxically, it is the very culture that on the one hand has provided a powerful adaptive force for the exuberant evolutionary course of human behaviors and social organization, freeing our human history from the otherwise slow evolutionary course of the pre-human modes of behavior, that on the other directs, molds, and constrains the extraordinary potential our brains offer for a seemingly limitless flexibility of behaviors and relationships. This is not to say, however, that culture and learning are any more narrowly deterministic than are genes. Each of us is exposed to a unique set of environmental-social circumstances and interacts with them in uniquely creative ways. Every person does not, after all, conform to the stereotypical expectations that the dominant culture holds for the social category of which she is a member. Our intelligence and ingenuity ensure that neither genes nor culture can necessarily produce the lumbering robots Sociobiologists would have us believe we are.

The cultures of patriarchal societies have developed an ideology or a concept of *woman* and her *nature* within a political context in which women are an oppressed class, just as theories of the nature of the slave and more contemporary racial beliefs and theories have served important economic, social, and political functions for dominant classes. The constructed nature of woman is seen to suit her admirably for the tasks that our society has in fact required of her: the care, loving, and nurturing of its men and children.

The distinctions of human temperaments and personality into feminine and masculine have always been *creations*, and in our patriarchal cultures are a part of the ideology that attempts to make what are in fact social and political distinctions appear to be natural and biological. These presumably natural, biological differences between the sexes then provide the explanation and justification for the differences in social roles and for relationships of dominance and subordination.

It is not unreasonable to believe, in Kate Millett's words, that "sexual caste supersedes all other forms of inegalitarianism: racial, political or economic," and that the basic unit of oppression and exploitation is that between the sexes (1970, p. 20), though I recognize there are other valid speculations about the history of oppression, as I discuss in Chapter 6.

It is rather striking that women are *defined*, and seen as *constrained*, by our biology, while the biology of men presumably fits them to fill *every* role, except, of course, that of mothering and nurturing. The brain, however, knows no such distinctions. Limitations are placed on the fullest exploitation of its rich potential for thought, creativities, innovation, humaneness, and emotional expression not by hormones or mystical *natures* but by poverty of environment, experience, and opportunity and by the ideological constraints imposed, both crudely and subtly, by any individual, class, or social order that cannot permit autonomy in "others."

In attempting to discard the concepts of instincts, innateness, or biological predispositions in human behaviors, I may seem to be discarding biology altogether. Rather, my hope and intent is the discarding of the controversy and dichotomy between nature and nurture or biology and learning because the dichotomy is impossible, unresolvable, and scientifically meaningless. It is a controversy that serves to obscure social and political origins of inequality and to undermine change and, furthermore, cannot lead to an understanding of human behaviors. All factors affecting and determining human behaviors and relationships not only interact with each other in effecting responses but in the process change each other so one cannot separate out and measure proportions of influence.

What can be considered the unique *nature* of humans is our capacities to learn, to exercise choice among alternative behaviors, to be self-conscious and intentional, and to use written and spoken language. But what we *do* with those capacities, our behaviors and characteristics, whether we are altruistic or aggressive or nurturing or analytical (and so on) are *learned*, just as we learn to go to war, to want babies, to parent, to be obedient, to be competitive, to dominate, or create. Our potential for creativity is a nearly limitless resource. We are able to put 64,000 bits of information on one computer chip that is too small to hold between the fingers, but we devote only a tiny fraction of that ingenuity to ensure freedom from hunger and oppression, diseases of poverty, or war. It is within our human/biological capacities to liberate the human mind and behaviors from the cultural molds that confine them and only serve the best interests of a minority.

REFERENCES

Barash, D. *The whisperings within*. New York: Harper & Row, 1979.

Billig, M. *Psychology, racism and facism*. Birmingham: A. F. & R. Publications, 1979.

Bleier, R. Retrograde transsynaptic cellular degeneration in mammillary and ventral tegmental nuclei following limbic decortication in rabbits of various ages. *Brain research*, 1969, *15*, 365-393.

Bonner, J. T. *The evolution of culture in animals.* Princeton: Princeton University Press, 1980.

Brown, J. L. *The evolution of behavior.* New York: W. W. Norton, 1975.

Cotman, C. (Ed.) *Neuronal plasticity.* New York: Raven Press, 1978.

DeBeauvoir, S. *The second sex,* New York: Alfred A. Knopf, 1953.

Fee, E. Nineteenth century craniology: the study of the female skull. *Bulletin of the History of Medicine,* 1979, *53,* 415-433.

Geertz, C. *The interpretation of cultures.* New York: Basic Books, 1973.

Goldberger, M., and Murray, M. Restitution of function and collateral sprouting in cat spinal cord: deafferented animal. *Journal of Comparative Neurology,* 1974, *158,* 37-54.

Goldfoot, D. On measuring behavioral sex differences in social contexts. In N. Adler and D. Pfaff (Eds.), *Neurobiology of reproduction.* New York: Plenum, 1983.

Goldman, P. S., and Rakic, P. Impact of the outside world upon the developing primate brain. *Bulletin of the Menninger Clinic,* 1979, *43,* 20-28.

Gould, S. J. *The mismeasure of man.* New York: W.W. Norton, 1981.

Hamburger, V., and Oppenheim, R. Naturally occurring neuronal death in vertebrates. *Neuroscience Commentaries,* 1982, *1,* 39-55.

Hirsch, H. V. B., and Leventhal, A. G. Functional modification of the developing visual system. In M. Jacobson (Ed.), *Handbook of sensory physiology,* 1978, *9. Development of sensory systems.* New York: Springer-Verlag.

Hirsch, H. V. B., and Spinelli, D. N. Visual experience modifies distribution of horizontally and vertically oriented receptive fields in cats. *Science,* 1970, *168,* 869-871.

Hirsch, J. To unfrock the charlatans. *SAGE race relations abstracts,* 1981, *6,* 1-65.

Holloway, R. The evolution of the primate brain: some aspects of quantitative relations. *Brain Research,* 1968, *7,* 121-172.

Holloway, R. The casts of fossil hominid brains. *Scientific American,* 1974, *231,* 106-115.

Holloway, R. *The role of human social behavior in the evolution of the brain.* New York: American Museum of Natural History, 1975.

Holloway, R. Paleoneurological evidence for language origins. *Annals of New York Academy of Sciences,* 1976, *280,* 330-348.

Holloway, R. Problems of brain endocast interpretation and African hominid evolution. In C. Jolly (Ed.), *Early hominids of Africa.* London: Duckworth, 1978.

Hubel, D., and Wiesel, T. The period of susceptibility to the physiological effects of unilateral eye closure in kittens. *Journal of Physiology,* 1970, *206,* 419-436.

Isaac, G. Stages of cultural elaboration in the Pleistocene: possible archeological indicators of the development of language capabilities. *Annals of the New York Academy of Sciences,* 1976, *280,* 275-288.

Isaac, G., and Leakey, R. E. F. (Eds.) *Human ancestors.* San Francisco: W. H. Freeman and Co., 1979.

Jacobson, M. *Developmental neurobiology.* New York: Plenum, 1978.

Jaynes, J. The evolution of language in the late pleistocene. *Annals of the New York Academy of Sciences,* 1976, *280,* 321-325.

Kalil, K., and Reh, T. Regrowth of severed axons in the neonatal central nervous system: establishment of normal connections. *Science,* 1979, *205,* 1158-1161.

Leakey, R., and Lewin, R. *Origins*. New York: E. P. Dutton, 1977.

Lund, R. D. *Development and plasticity of the brain: an introduction*. Oxford: Oxford University Press, 1978.

Marshack, A. Some implications of the Paleolithic symbolic evidence for the origin of language. *Annals of the New York Academy of Sciences*, 1976, *280*, 289-311.

Merzenich, M., and Kaas, J. Principles of organization of sensory-perceptual systems in mammals. *Progress in Psychobiology and Physiological Psychology*, 1980, *9*, 1-42.

Millett, K. *Sexual politics*. New York: Doubleday, 1970.

Mishler, E. G. Meaning in context: is there any other kind? *Harvard Educational Review*, 1979, *49*, 1-19.

Mountcastle, V. B. An organizing principle for cerebral function: the unit module and the distributed system. In G. Edelman and V. Mountcastle (Eds.), *The mindful brain*. Cambridge: MIT Press, 1977.

Murray, M. and Goldberger, M. Restitution of function and collateral sprouting in cat spinal cord—partially hemisected animal. *Journal of Comparative Neurology*, 1974, *158*, 19-36.

Napier, J. The evolution of the hand. *Scientific American*, 1962, *207*, 56-62.

Ortner, S. B., and Whitehead, H. *Sexual meanings: the cultural construction of gender and sexuality*. Cambridge: Cambridge University Press, 1981.

Parlee, M. B. Psychology and women. *Signs*, 1979, *5*, 121-133.

Pilbeam, D. *The ascent of man*. New York: Macmillan Co., 1972.

Raisman, G. Neuronal plasticity in the septal nuclei of the adult rat. *Brain Research*, 1969, *14*, 25-48.

Rose, J. E., Malis, L. I., Kruger, L., and Baker, C. P. Effects of heavy, ionizing, monoenergetic particles on the cerebral cortex. II. Histological appearance of laminar lesions and growth of nerve fibers after laminar destructions. *Journal of Comparative Neurology*, 1960, *115*, 243-296.

Schadé, J. P., and Groeningen, W. P. van. Structural organization of the cerebral cortex. *Acta Anatomica (Basel)*, 1961, *47*, 74-111.

Shields, S. Functionalism, Darwinism, and the psychology of women. A study in social myth. *American Psychologist*, 1975, *30*, 739-754.

Simons, E. L. The early relatives of man. *Scientific American*, 1964, *211*, 52-62.

Simons, E. L. Ramapithecus. *Scientific American*, 1977, *236*, 28-35.

Smith-Rosenberg, C., and Rosenberg, C. The female animal: medical and biological views of woman and her role in nineteenth-century America. *Journal of American History*, 1973, *59*, 332-356.

Thomas, J. Adam and Eve revisited—the making of a myth or the reflection of reality? *Human Development*, 1977, *20*, 326-351.

Tobias, P. V. *The brain in hominid evolution*. New York: Columbia University Press, 1971.

Trune, D. Influence of neonatal cochlear removal on the development of mouse cochlear nucleus. I. Number, size and density of its neurons. *Journal of Comparative Neurology*, 1982, *209*, 409-424.

Walker, L. The ontogeny of the neural substrate for language. *Journal of Human Evolution*, 1981, *20*, 429-441.

Washburn, S. L. Tools and human evolution. *Scientific American*, 1960, *203*, 63-75.

Washburn, S. L. What we can't learn about people from apes. *Human Nature*, 1978, *Nov.*, 70-75.

Webster, D., and Webster, M. Neonatal sound deprivation affects brain stem auditory nuclei. *Archives of Otolaryngology*, 1977, *103*, 392-396.

Webster, D., and Webster, M. Effects of neonatal conductive hearing loss on brain stem auditory nuclei. *Annals of Otolaryngology*, 1979, *88*, 684-688.

Welker, W. I., Johnson, J. I., Jr., and Pubols, B. H., Jr. Some morphological and physiological characteristics of the somatic sensory system in raccoons. *American Zoology*, 1964, *4*, 75-94.

Wiesel, T., and Hubel, D. Effects of visual deprivation on morphology and physiology of cells in the cat's lateral geniculate body. *Journal of Neurophysiology*, 1963, *26*, 978-993. (a)

Wiesel, T., and Hubel, D. Single-cell responses in striate cortex of kittens deprived of vision in one eye. *Journal of Neurophysiology*, 1963, *26*, 1003-1017. (b)

Wiesel, T., and Hubel, D. Ordered arrangement of orientation columns in monkeys lacking visual experience. *Journal of Comparative Neurology*, 1974, *158*, 307-318.

Wilson, E. O. *Sociobiology: the new synthesis*. Cambridge: Harvard University Press, 1975.

Wittig, M. One is not born a woman. *Feminist Issues*, 1980, *1*, 1103-1111.

Zelená, J. Development, degeneration and regeneration of receptor organs. In M. Singer and J. P. Schadé (Eds.), *Progress in brain research*, 1964, *13. Mechanisms of neural regeneration*. New York: Elsevier, 1964.

Zihlman, A., and Brunker, L. Hominid bipedalism: then and now. *Yearbook of Physical Anthropology*, 1979, *22*, 132-162.

Chapter 4
Hormones, the Brain, and Sex Differences

We are told that the social gap between the sexes is narrowing, but I can only report that having, in the second half of the 20th century, experienced life in both roles, there seems to me no aspect of existence, no moment of the day, no contact, no arrangement, no response, which is not different for men and for women. . . . And if others' responses shifted, so did my own. The more I was treated as a woman, the more woman I became. . . . I discovered that even now men prefer women to be less able, less talkative and certainly less self-centered than they are themselves; so I generally obliged them.

Jan Morris, 1974, pp. 148-149.

Masculine/feminine, male/female are the categories which serve to conceal the fact that social differences always belong to an economic, political, ideological order.

Monique Wittig, 1982, p. 64.

The detection and measurement of presumed sex differences in behaviors, temperaments, and abilities have constituted a major research area in the social sciences over the past few decades.[1] That same period has seen the spectacular growth of an area of biological research also devoted to the investigation of sex differences: the effects of hormones on the developing brain and on subsequent adult behaviors. These different disciplinary approaches to the study of presumed sex differences in humans are integrally related, since much of the work in the relevant biological disciplines—reproductive endocrinology and neuroendocrinology—has been based in the laboratories of comparative and physiological psychologists.

---

[1] Throughout this chapter I have used the term *sex differences* since that is the name by which this area of biological and social science research is known. In actuality, what is at issue are gender differences; that is, different sets of social attributions–characteristics, behaviors, appearance, dress, expectations, roles, etc.–made to individuals according to their gender assignment at birth. As discussed in Chapter 3, gender is, in fact, a social construction or accomplishment, and gender attributions differ across cultures. Science, however, in the form of gender-difference and gender-role (sex-difference and sex-role) research, views these gender attributions as *natural* categories for which biological explanations are appropriate and even necessary. The critical question of gender has been sensitively and radically explored by Kessler and McKenna (1978).

Beginning with efforts to understand the hormonal mechanisms underlying ovarian cyclic function (i.e., menstrual cyclicity in primates or estrous cyclicity in rodents), it was found in the 1950s that cyclic regulation of the ovaries by hormones from the pituitary gland in the rat was mediated through the brain, specifically the hypothalamus. There followed, logically enough, investigations of mating behaviors in rats and other small laboratory animals—guinea pigs, mice, and hamsters—through hormonal manipulations, such as castration at birth and/or administration of the so-called sex hormones, estrogens and androgens, which are secreted in both sexes by ovaries, testes, and adrenal glands. The hypothesis was that since these hormones directly influence hypothalamic neurons in their regulation of estrous cyclicity, they may also be responsible for related sex-differentiated behaviors, such as patterns and postures of mating activity, through their actions on the brain. Indeed, it proved to be the case that such hormonal manipulations affected mating behaviors in rodents, though often in contradictory and unanticipated ways. It was also found that hypothalamic neurons have receptors for and are directly responsive to administered estrogens, androgens, and progestins.

As one might anticipate, this work provided a conceptual model for investigating other apparently sex-differentiated behaviors or characteristics in rodents and other species and for wide-ranging theorizing about the hormonal and neural bases for human sex differences in such characteristics as aggressivity, intelligence, and sexuality. The reasoning starts with the observation that women do not share equally with men in positions of leadership, authority, or power and are far from equally represented in industry, business, the university, the arts, engineering, science and other professions, government, sports, and crafts. The suspicion follows, then, that perhaps this situation has less to do with ideologies and institutions, with sex-role stereotyping and channeling from babyhood on, or with conscious and unconscious, legal and illegal discrimination against women in educational and employment opportunities than with women's innate inability to perform equally with men, either because of our naturally nurturant, passive, noncompetitive, and unambitious temperaments or because of biological limitations on the capacities and skills required to achieve in our kind of society. The hypotheses (widely seen as established facts) are that women's lack of androgens may account for their lack of aggressivity and drive for achievement, and that either hormones or genes or both (or their lack) have influenced the development of a brain less able to conceptualize visuospatial relations that are basic to mathematical and perhaps other intellectual skills and, therefore, to success in engineering and the sciences and many other fields as well.

Like Sociobiology and evolutionary theory, the research area of brain-hormone interactions has had an important influence on the thinking and theorizing in other disciplines, such as psychology and sociology. Some conclusions have been accepted as unavoidable truth (because "scientific") in most psychology texts and by some feminist writers, and have received prominent coverage in the popular press: *New York Times* (December 19, 1978), *Boston Globe* (September 9, 1979 and May 5, 1981), *Newsweek* (May 18, 1981, with a circulation of a quarter of a million), and *Reader's Digest* (September, 1981, with a circulation of over 31 million in 16 languages), to name but the few with which I am familiar. *Newsweek* assigned seven reporters to assemble the data for their six-page article, called "Just How the Sexes Differ," from research centers in New York, Boston, Chicago, San Francisco, and Los Angeles, but devoted only the last three-quarter page to indicating the serious criticisms that three researchers had of the work described in the other five and one-quarter pages. In view of the extraordinary complexity of the issues, the many unresolved contradictory experimental results, and the vast gaps in knowledge that presently still characterize this area despite great progress over the past 20 years, one wonders at the uncritical speed and near unanimity with which the theory of androgen determination of brain organization and, therefore, behavior has been accepted from the beginning. Without doubt, however, the subsequent leap from rodents to humans and the popularization of the notion that gender inequalities in status and power rest upon *in utero* hormonally determined differences in temperament and ability reflect and reinforce the ideology that presents as "natural" and "essential" that which is social and political. The sociologist Steven Goldberg unabashedly makes the connection in his book, *The Inevitability of Patriarchy* (1973):

> . . . human biology precludes the possibility of a human social system whose authority structure is not dominated by males, and in which male aggression is not manifested in dominance and attainment of position, of status and power. (p. 78)

In this chapter I shall review some of the scientific background for such a statement and show how it cannot justifiably be used to explain aggressivity or intellectual and cognitive differences in humans.

EXPERIMENTAL BACKGROUND

Findings in the fields of neuroendocrinology and reproductive endocrinology, which explore the functional relationships between hormones and the brain and the effects of those interactions on the functioning of other organs and on behaviors, have become influential in science over the past decade. The part of the brain primarily involved in the regulation of the endocrine (hormonal) system is the hypothalamus, situated in the middle of the base of the brain, and connected anatomically as well as functionally with the pituitary gland. Neurons of the hypothalamus function like neurons in the rest of the brain, transmitting and receiving messages across synapses with other neurons, and also like endocrine cells, since they produce hormones, known as *releasing factors* or *hormones*, which regulate the hormonal output from the pituitary gland (specifically, the part known as the anterior pituitary). The pituitary is the body's principal endocrine organ, regulating by its hormones the hormonal output from the other endocrine glands in the body, including ovaries, testes, thyroid, breast, and adrenals. The output of each of the hormones from the anterior pituitary is influenced not only by a specific hypothalamic releasing hormone, but also, to varying degrees depending on the species of animal or the particular hormonal system, by the levels in the blood of the hormones produced by the endocrine glands that the pituitary regulates—a type of direct feedback system. The hormonal feedback systems are roughly analogous to the system by which thermostats regulate heat production by furnaces: high levels of environmental temperature turn off the furnace and falling levels turn it back on. Like the pituitary itself, the hypothalamus may also be influenced in its hormonal regulation of pituitary functioning by the level in the blood of the various hormones from the endocrine glands that the pituitary regulates. This means that the responsible hypothalamic neurons are sensitive not only to synaptic input from other neurons but also to direct humoral effects of particular hormones from the ovaries or testes, thyroid, adrenals, and the pituitary itself, which reach the hypothalamus through the blood vascular system. Thus, specifically, in the regulation of the ovaries, the hypothalamus secretes follicle-stimulating hormone-releasing factor (FSH-RF) and luteinizing hormone-releasing factor (LH-RF) (either separately or as one large molecule that acts differentially), which stimulate the release of FSH and LH respectively from the anterior pituitary. These pituitary hormones, called gonadotrophins, regulate the maturation each month of one ovarian follicle, the production of estrogen by that follicle, the release of the egg from the follicle (ovulation), and the secretion of progestins by the follicle both before and, in largest amounts, after ovulation, when the follicle becomes transformed into the corpus luteum. In turn, the secreted estrogen and progesterone bring about the familiar cyclic changes of the lining of the uterus, the endometrium, which ordinarily culminate in menstruation, and they also influence hypothalamic neurons and the anterior pituitary, as well as other organs.

Most of the experimental work on ovarian regulation has been done on the rat and suggests the following relationships in humans (Fig. 4.1): At the beginning of the estrous cycle, hypothalamic FSH-RF stimulates the release of FSH by the anterior pituitary. FSH stimulates ovarian production of estrogen and the rising levels of estrogen in the blood suppress further production of FSH-RF by the hypothalamus (negative feedback) and stimulates increasing production of LH-RF (positive feedback), culminating in a marked surge of pituitary release of LH which triggers ovulation; that is, release of the egg from the follicle. The subsequent increasing levels of progesterone produced by the corpus luteum feed back on the hypothalamus suppressing LH-RF production. By the end of the cycle (approximately two weeks after ovulation in humans), the levels of FSH and LH have fallen so low as a result of the suppressive effects of estrogen and progesterone on the hypothalamus or pituitary that they no longer sustain ovarian production of estrogen and progesterone. Consequently, estrogen and progesterone fall to levels in the blood sufficiently low that the hypothalamus is turned on; that is, stimulated to increase its production and release of FSH-RF, and the menstrual cycle begins all over again. (The shutdown of production of estrogen and progesterone also results in menstruation, the shedding of the uterine lining

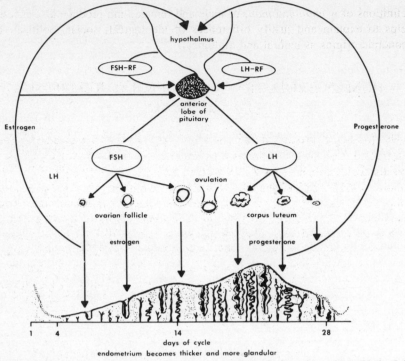

Source: Modified from Silverstein, *Human anatomy and physiology*. New York: John
Wiley & Sons, 1980.

FIGURE 4.1. A diagrammatic representation of the human menstrual cycle, showing
hormonal feedback relationships among hypothalamus, anterior pituitary, and ovaries.

as a result of the loss of support of the two hormones.) This ovarian-pituitary-
hypothalamic cyclicity is affected variously in different species of mammals by
a number of extrinsic and intrinsic factors, such as diet, stress, environmental
temperature, diurnal and seasonal environmental light and dark cycles, and others.

Males, too, have FSH-RF and LH-RF production by the hypothalamus and
FSH and LH production by the pituitary, all of which regulate the production
of androgens by the testes. (For completeness, it may be noted here that the
ovaries, testes, and adrenal glands all produce progestins, androgens, and estrogens,
though in different relative quantities, in females and males of all species.) The
main difference between females and males is that the secretion of these hypothalamic and pituitary hormones is considered to be constant (or tonic) in
males rather than cyclic, though there are fluctuations in levels, and some diurnal
as well as larger interval cyclicity has been reported in males in a variety of
species, including humans (Kihlstrom, 1971; Ramey, 1972). The differences in
patterns of cyclicity between females and males have been shown by measuring
blood levels of the hormones in various species, though information in this area
is far from complete. Most of the information, however, concerning the mechanisms
of the regulation of cyclicity in females comes from investigations of rodents.

In adult female rats, injections of estrogen will result in the typical LH-RF and LH surge that triggers ovulation, but such an LH surge cannot be stimulated in adult male rats by the administration of estrogen. This cyclicity of hypothalamic-pituitary-ovarian functioning that produces the LH surge and ovulation appears to be a property of the response patterns of the hypothalamus rather than of the pituitary or ovaries; that is, certain hypothalamic neurons will turn the production of releasing factors on or off in response to varying blood levels of estrogens and progestins. Thus, the question arose: How does the female rodent's hypothalamus differ from the male's?

Studies in rodents suggested that the presence of androgens produced by the testes of the fetal and newborn male suppresses or blocks the ability of hypothalamic neurons to respond cyclically and therefore to regulate pituitary and gonadal cyclic functions. Thus, if a male rat is deprived of androgens at birth by castration, his pattern of hypothalamic release of FSH-RF/LH-RF and pituitary release of FSH and LH can be made to be cyclic by the administration of estrogen. An LH surge can be produced, and ovaries transplanted into the male will undergo cyclic changes and ovulation (Harris, 1964). This will not occur if removal of the testes is performed later than five to seven days after birth. If, on the other hand, a newborn female rat is given a single injection of one of the androgens, testosterone, she will not have cyclic ovulation at maturity, presumably because of the effects of testosterone on hypothalamic neurons. It is for these reasons that it is said that androgens have an "organizing" effect on the fetal brain, and that a basically "female" brain develops in females or males in the absence of circulating androgens (Harris and Levine, 1965; Phoenix, Goy, Gerall, and Young, 1959).

GENERALIZATIONS TO HUMAN BEHAVIOR

I have gone into this detail because of the unwarranted extrapolations to human behavior (and civilization itself) that have been made from these observations in the laboratory rat. This work has been generally interpreted, reasonably enough for the rat, as demonstrating that androgens have an "organizing" effect on the developing brain and a critical role in sexual differentiation of the brain with respect to cyclicity of gonadal function in the adult. While similar results have been obtained in other rodents, they have not been in primates, as I will discuss below. This work has had an extraordinary influence both within and outside the fields of neuroendocrinology and reproductive physiology. Within these fields, the studies of the late 1950s and early 1960s provided the stimulus for a flowering of research on the interactions between the sex hormones and the brain and for the development of new experimental approaches to the investigation of the cellular mechanisms involved in behavioral responses of experimental animals. The early work was also important because it became the model for a more generalized theory that androgens have an organizing effect on the developing brain in determining other sex-differentiated adult behaviors and characteristics such as mating behavior and aggressivity; that is, the hypothesis was that if androgens directly and irreversibly "masculinize" the brain with respect to reproductive cyclicity, they may account for other "masculinizing" effects on the brain and behavior. The theory thus became generalized not only to behaviors that are more complex than the hormonal regulation of estrous cyclicity, but also to species beyond the rodents who were the original models. It has provided the conceptual framework for theories and beliefs about the sexual differentiation of human brains and, consequently, of our social roles and behaviors. Though such extrapolations are not usually made by the biologists doing the research, they are made by some, and they have also been uncritically and widely applied by social scientists and natural scientists in other fields. The effects of androgens on the developing fetal human brain have been claimed to include aggressivity and dominance, intelligence, tomboyism, lesbianism, and male gender identity. It is the absence of the effects of androgens on the developing female brain that accounts for the "feminine" counterparts: passivity, compliance, and, bluntly speaking, inferiority. A further extension of this theorizing is that "inadequate" amounts of androgens in the developing male fetus will inadequately "masculinize" the fetal male brain, with the subsequent development of such nonconforming adult male behaviors and characteristics as homosexuality and confused gender identity.

I shall next examine some research findings that seriously confound the simplicity of the original rodent model and the validity of extrapolations to primates. Then I will discuss faulty assumptions and methodologies in studies that explore hormonal and other biological influences on such human characteristics as aggressivity, intelligence, and mathematical ability.

FLAWS IN THE ANIMAL MODEL

As I have indicated, the first difficulty encountered by a generalized theory of the organizing effects of androgens on the developing brain and subsequent behavior is with the rodent model that gave rise to the theory. While it seems clear that fetal androgens somehow abolish the capacity of the hypothalamus to initiate the cyclic release of LH in response to estrogens and progesterone in the rat, it does not do so in guinea pigs or primates. An important study done with adult male rhesus monkeys demonstrated that estrogen elicited LH surges that "closely resembled, in both duration and magnitude, the spontaneous preovulatory LH surge observed during the normal menstrual cycle of female rhesus monkeys" (Karsch, Dierschke, and Knobil, 1973). Similar results have been found in guinea pigs (Byne, Terasawa, Bleier, and Goy, 1983). It has also been found that estrogens will elicit an LH surge in men similar to that in women, though of smaller magnitude (Kulin and Reiter, 1976). Furthermore, androgens do not suppress cyclicity and ovulation, menstruation, or pregnancy in human or nonhuman primate females exposed as fetuses to high levels of circulating androgens from the early gestational period (Goy and Resko, 1972; Karsch *et al.*, 1973; Valdés, del Castillo, Gutiérrez, Larrea, Medina, and Pérez-Palacios, 1979). Thus, there is no evidence in primates that androgens have an "organizing" affect on the fetal brain as they appear to have in rodents, and more recent work even suggests that the feedback effect in the regulation of ovarian cyclicity by estrogens is on the pituitary itself in primates rather than on hypothalamic neurons (Knobil, Plant, Wildt, Belchetz, and Marshall, 1980), as has been assumed.

Almost simultaneously with the work on cyclicity, observations were made of the effect of the same hormonal manipulations on mating behavior, the subject contributing probably the largest body of data and contradictory results in this area of research. By and large, however, experimental results in rats suggested to investigators that androgens were essential for the expression of mounting behaviors in males (or treated females) and for the suppression in males (or treated females) of the stereotypical female mating posture of lordosis (arched back and raised hindquarters). These experimental findings led to the generally accepted theory that androgens "masculinize" brains for adult male mating behaviors and that the absence of androgens with the presence of estrogens results in "feminized" brains and female mating behaviors. It has appeared logical that so fundamental and biologically necessary a behavior as sex-associated mating postures be hormonally determined—in all species. And yet, Goldfoot, Wallen, Neff, McBrair, and Goy (1983) have found that the social conditions of rearing rhesus monkeys dramatically affect their mating behaviors. In the absence of any hormonal manipulations, isosexual rearing of females significantly augments mounting and suppresses presenting, while the isosexual rearing of males results in suppression of mounting and the augmenting of presenting. Thus, while prenatal and postnatal hormones influence mating behaviors, the nature of the animals' interactions with their peers is also a critical factor in the shaping of the expression of these gender-associated behaviors.

CONFOUNDING VARIABLES IN HORMONE-BEHAVIOR RESEARCH

Even in the rat, however, the matter of sex differences is not so simply reduced to the presence of androgen effects on the fetal male brain. Systematic measurements in the laboratory rat have shown that androgens circulate in females as well as males during the fetal and immediate postnatal periods during which the rodent brain is undergoing differentiation and organization, and that the eighteenth fetal day is the only time when levels are higher in males than in females (MacLusky and Naftolin, 1981). In addition, newborn female *and* male rats have high levels of estrogens (probably mainly of maternal origin) for two days, then the levels fall until approximately the ninth day, when the levels begin to increase in both sexes to levels that exceed those seen in mature females, with the usual peak around day ten or eleven (Döhler and Wuttke, 1975). It is also known that estrogen levels are very high in primates during pregnancy (Resko, Ploem, and Stadelman, 1975) and that the fetal ovaries along with the placenta contribute estrogens to the fetal circulation, at least in rhesus monkeys. Thus, it appears that both female and male brains develop in a milieu rich in estrogens, progestins, and androgens, with differences in levels appearing at particular days or periods. What the significance of this may be for brain growth and differentiation is only beginning to be investigated (Shapiro, Goldman, Bongiovanni, and Marino, 1976; Toran-Allerand, 1978).

Next, it is difficult to isolate the effects of estrogens, progestins and androgens from each other, since both females and males of all species produce all three of these groups of hormones; that is, the ovaries, testes and adrenal glands all produce the three families of hormones. In general, males produce more androgens than females and females more estrogens and progestins than males, though the levels in any individual fluctuate daily and under different physiological circumstances, and the physiological ranges for the two sexes overlap (Table 4.1). Furthermore, there are many different forms of estrogens, progestins, and androgens, all closely related to each other in chemical structure (Fig. 4.2). They all have as their basic structure the four carbon rings of cholesterol (which is the common characteristic of hormones in the class known as steroids), with the main difference among them being in one or two of the side chains having oxygen (O) or hydrogen (H). In various body tissues of both sexes, cholesterol is normally metabolized to progesterone, which is metabolized to testosterone, the major androgen, which is metabolized to estradiol, the major estrogen. There are many other circulating metabolic forms of the three steroids, each with unique physiological effects, present in varying levels in females and males, with constant conversions from some forms to others (Fig. 4.2). On theoretical grounds alone, then, one would

Table 4.1. Normal range of steroid hormones in plasma in humans.

HORMONE	UNITS	MALE	CYCLING FEMALE
Androstenedione	ng/ml	0.2–3.4	0.3–4.2
Estradiol	pg/ml	32–99	0–421
17-OH-Progesterone	ng/ml	0.23–2.0	0–2.34
Progesterone	ng/ml	0.05–0.22	0–12.6
Prolactin	ng/ml	0–13	0–20
Testosterone	n/gml	2.1–10.9	0.08–0.8

Source: University of Wisconsin Hospital Laboratories, 1979.
ng = nanograms; pg = picograms; ml = milliliter

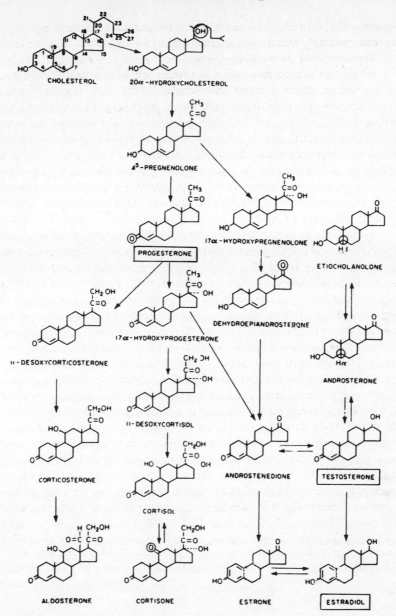

FIGURE 4.2. Metabolic pathways of steroid hormones. The gonadal steroid hormones are synthesized from cholesterol, the parent steroid. (See top left. A steroid is a molecule with this characteristic configuration of four carbon (C) rings. Each number indicates the position of a carbon atom.) Cholesterol is transformed to progesterone; progesterone to androgens, including testosterone; and androgens to estrogens, including estradiol. Note the minor structural differences among these forms, usually in one side arm.

suspect that the effects produced by the injection of a particular hormone may not be due to the actions of that hormone but to one of its metabolically converted forms. In addition, there is great variability in the amounts of the various metabolic forms of each of the three families of sex hormones among different species, as well as within any individual, and among individuals within a species, depending not only on sex but also age, environmental conditions, time of day, particular physiological states, and the particular resting metabolic state that may be characteristic of any individual. For example, women, sheep, goats, guinea pigs, and rats have high levels of estrogens toward the end of gestation, but rabbits and hamsters do not. Rabbits, however, have a ten-fold higher ovarian production of testosterone than of estrogen during pregnancy (Hilliard, Scaramuzzi, Penardi, and Sawyer, 1973).

But aside from the individual and species variability that is *known*, an astonishing amount of basic information does not exist to provide a sound basis for extrapolations from experimental data from one species to another with respect to relatively simple issues let alone the leaps that are made to complex human behaviors. Overpeck, Colson, Hohmann, Applestine, and Reilly (1978) surveyed the literature to find accurate measurements of the concentrations of circulating steroid hormones in normal male and female humans, chimpanzees, rhesus monkeys, rats, mice, and hamsters. Such data would be important, one would think, to provide baseline information for the interpretation of experimental results that involve hormonal manipulations in popular laboratory species. The authors found that few reports include data for both sexes, for different age groups, or for more than one species. Aside from the question, then, of the inadequacy of the data base, there is the further issue that in order to compare levels in the two sexes or in different species, it is necessary to use the results of studies done in different laboratories. The variability in measurements between laboratories, even for relatively uncomplicated determinations using simple techniques, is notorious, but hormonal assays are intricate. Overpeck *et al.* (1978) found the data for humans to be fairly complete, but reported a significant lack of information for other species.

> It is understandable why so little work with the chimpanzee has been completed, yet this primate is thought by some to represent the endocrine model most similar to humans. . . . The lack of data from rats and mice is not so understandable. It is remarkable that so many of these rodents have been employed in such a variety of physiological, pharmacological, and toxicological studies with exogenous hormones while so little has been established concerning normal plasma relationships. (p. 786-787)

Other workers in the field of hormones and behavior have also cautioned against making generalized conclusions without taking into account the varying effects of hormones on the neuroendocrine systems of different species and the varying results depending on dosage, mode of administration, and period of treatment (Etreby, Gräf, Günzel, Neumann, 1979).

MORPHOLOGICAL SEX DIFFERENCES IN THE BRAIN

In the search for "a clear signature of sexual differentiation" (Gorski, 1979, p. 114), several laboratories have reported morphological sex differences in the brain. One set of differences characterizes a group of neurons involved in vocalizations of songbirds, canaries, and zebra finches, species in which males but not females normally sing. The group of neurons and the neurons themselves are larger in males, and the size can be affected by castration in males or by androgen injections into females (DeVoogd and Nottebohm, 1981; Gurney, 1981; Gurney and Konishi, 1980; Nottebohm and Arnold, 1976). Females injected with estrogens or androgens soon after hatching also learn, like the males, to sing. This work represents the only clear-cut example of a direct association between a sexual dimorphism of the brain and a particular known behavior. It is also important to note that while the presence of androgen is a necessary element in the song of these species, it is not a sufficient influence, since the male bird must also learn the stereotyped song pattern from other male birds in order to be able to sing.

The other set of morphological sex differences has been found in rodents and affects neurons in the part of the hypothalamus (medial preoptic and anterior areas) that is associated with the regulation of estrous cyclicity and stereotyped mating postures. Differences have been found in the patterns and numbers of synapses on the dendritic tree (Greenough, Carter, Steerman, and DeVoogd, 1977: Raisman and Field, 1971, 1973), which appear to be influenced by the presence or absence of androgens. Differences have also been described in the patterns of distribution and packing density of neurons within the same area (Bleier, Byne, and Siggelkow, 1982; Gorski, Gordon, Shryne, and Southam, 1978) and in the size of the neurons (Gorski, Harlan, Jacobson, Shryne, and Southam, 1980). Since the investigator in whose laboratory this difference was first described has been influential as a pioneering investigator in the area of reproductive neuroendocrinology, it is instructive to read the introductory paragraph of his widely quoted paper describing the hypothalamic morphological sex difference.

The concept of the sexual differentiation of brain function is now well established, particularly with regard to the regulation of gonadotropin secretion, male and female sexual behavior, the regulation of food intake and body weight and aggressive behavior. In brief, this concept assumes that those functions recognized as 'masculine' in the adult are at least partially a result of the action of testicular hormones on the developing brain, which is undifferentiated and/or inherently female. Although this concept of a permanent or organizational action of the hormonal environment on neuronal differentiation and development is of considerable importance to both neuroendocrinology and neuroscience in general, the mechanism of this effect is poorly understood. (Gorski *et al.*, 1978, p. 334)

Regardless of the authors' intent, there is little doubt of the implications of this paragraph—that sex differences in behaviors of humans, since the rat is not specified, are based in hormonally directed sex differences in brain development. Appearing in a widely read scientific journal, its influence on the thinking of neuroscientists and other scientist-academicians, both as scientists and as influential people in a culture that values the scientific word, is incalculable, particularly since it fits into a coherent popular ideology. In addition, it misrepresents the conclusions of the authors of the paper cited on aggressive behavior (by Quadagno, Briscoe, and Quadagno, 1977), who have serious reservations concerning the validity of any correlations between hormones during brain development and aggressive behaviors in any primate species including humans.

As shown in Chapter 3, the effort to find anatomical differences in the brains of females and males has a long tradition as an explanation for observed differences in social roles and status. The finding of a morphological sex difference in a part of the brain regulating a clearly sex-differentiated function, such as estrous cyclicity in rats or singing in certain birds, does not, however, warrant extrapolations to other species or to more complex behaviors.

BRAIN LATERALIZATION

Another form that the search for morphological-functional sexual differentiation in the brain has taken is the study of differences in lateralization of function between the two hemispheres of the brain. It is generally believed that certain cognitive functions are asymmetrically represented in the cortex of the two hemispheres and that, for most individuals, the left hemisphere is specialized for language functions and the right for nonverbal perception and visuospatial functions. Starting with the very questionable assumption that there are true, probably "innate" sex differences in verbal and spatial abilities, efforts have been made to find sex differences in the degree of lateralization or specialization to one or the other hemisphere. There is an immediate logical problem that is ignored in such studies: since verbal functions are necessarily linked with analytical skills (left hemisphere) and the visuospatial abilities are linked with both artistic, mathematical-engineering, and "intuitive" functions (right hemisphere), it is not at all clear what the implications would be even if sex differences in the degree of hemispheric specialization of function were to be found. That is, girls and women are considered to be more verbal (left hemisphere) but less analytical (left hemisphere) and more "intuitive" (right hemisphere) but less visuospatially skilled (right hemisphere); and men are considered to be "naturally" gifted in visual-spatial (right hemisphere) and analytical (left hemisphere) cognition but not in intuitive, holistic, gestalt thinking (right hemisphere). But that conceptual difficulty is further confounded by the actual research, all by highly reputable investigators. One research group finds that women are *less* lateralized than men (i.e., verbal and spatial functions are equally represented in both hemispheres) and concludes that the reason girls and women are inferior in visuospatial tasks is because such tasks require hemispheric specialization, as is presumably the case in males. But they conclude that visuospatial tasks must require hemispheric specialization *because* women are not hemispherically specialized and are inferior. Another group finds that women are *more* lateralized (left hemisphere more specialized for verbal and the right for visuospatial tasks) and concludes that they are, therefore, inferior in visuospatial tasks because such tasks must require equal bilateral representation. They allow, however, that women are superior in verbal skills, since these, unlike visuospatial skills, must require hemispheric specialization. A third group finds no convincing sex differences in cognitive abilities or hemispheric lateralization, and yet a fourth (Hardyck, Tzeng, and Wang, 1978) questions the basic assumption that there is any lateralization of cognitive functions at all, quite apart from the issue of sex differences. (For reviews, see Star, 1979; McGlone, 1980.)

Aside from the obvious inconclusiveness, ambiguity, arbitrariness, illogic, and inadequacy of these results and the methodological problems these flaws imply, the fact remains that the basic question these studies purport to be answering is a false issue. There are no clear-cut sex differences in either verbal or visuospatial abilities. All females do not score better than all males in verbal tests, nor do all males score better than all females in visuospatial tests nor do the majority of either sex performs better than the majority of the other. Rather, the mean or average score of the entire group of girls tested is compared with that of boys, and there may be small difference in the two mean *group* scores. In short, comparable populations of females and males have the same range of test scores, the same range of abilities; and in some test situations the mean or average scores of the two groups may not differ at all or may differ, but only by a few percentage points (Fennema and Sherman, 1977; Sherman and Fennema, 1978). It is perfectly obvious that there are some girls or women who are more logical and analytical and better in mathematics and visuospatial skills than most boys or men and some boys or men who are more verbally skilled than most girls or women. This is not a promising situation for the investigation of "innate" or biological sex differences underlying cognitive functioning, and one wonders at the failure in logical and analytical thinking that has made this so popular a research question. The work of Julia Sherman and Elizabeth Fennema (1978) also contests the frequently aired but unsupported conjecture that visuospatial skills are genetically sex-linked.

OTHER GENERAL PROBLEMS
IN SEX-DIFFERENCE RESEARCH

There are a number of serious problems in the study of any group differences that emerge with added force in studies purporting to show sex-related differences.

SG–D*

Prominent among these is the one introduced in the discussion above concerning verbal and visuospatial abilities. The "sex difference" investigated is a small *statistical* difference between entire groups when it exists and it does not distinguish between the two groups. That is, the two sexes are not different. Knowing a particular score will not predict whether the subject is female or male nor will knowing the gender of the subject predict her or his score. In her recent critique of sex-difference research, Jacklin (1981) described a study that pooled and analyzed the results of 26 studies of verbal skills, representing 85,619 scores for 67,000 children, in the attempt to measure the predictive power of sex. Sex differences in verbal ability accounted for only 1 percent of the variance in these studies. A similar analysis of the scores of 292,574 children found that sex accounts for only 4 percent of the variance in scores for quantitative abilities.

Jacklin also gives the example of rough-and-tumble play, a popular measure of sex differences in primates and human infants and a presumed indicator of aggressivity. One study reported that 15 to 20 percent of the boys scored higher than any of the girls. But an equally important focus for interpreting this study is the fact that the remaining 80 to 85 percent of the boys are indistinguishable from 80 to 85 percent of the girls. A somewhat related issue is that, by and large, *only* positive findings of sex differences are reported and published in the scientific literature, and many of them are faulty or of dubious significance. There is, however, no field of "sex similarities." Jacklin argues that the fewer the variables that are confounded with sex, the smaller are the percentages of variance.

> Thus, paradoxically the better the sex-related research, the less useful sex is as an explanatory variable. In the best controlled sex-related research, sex may account for no variance at all. (1981, p. 271)

Despite the problems, however, the fascination with sex differences has resulted in a vast literature on aggressivity, intelligence, gender identity, sexuality, and other presumed sex-differentiated behaviors upon which it is necessary to comment. My discussion will highlight major flaws in studies using animals and humans. Other aspects of this work have been criticized in detail elsewhere (Bleier, 1976, 1979; Fausto-Sterling, in press; Fried, 1979; Salzman, 1979; for extended reviews of sex-differences research, see Maccoby and Jacklin, 1974; Parsons 1980; Sherman, 1978; Wittig and Petersen, 1979).

AGGRESSIVITY

One area of investigation of hormone-brain interactions has been the relationship between androgens and "aggressivity," an interest in this subject deriving no doubt from a general awareness of three social phenomena: that men run everything, commit most of the violent crimes, and wage war on each other. Starting, presumably, with the assumption that "aggressiveness" is an androgen-determined male characteristic, early studies demonstrated that male rats were less aggressive (that is, fought less) as adults if they were castrated at birth (Conner and Levine, 1969) and that female mice given androgens at birth were more aggressive following androgen injections as adults (Edwards, 1969). A multitude of such studies, primarily using rodents, has appeared over the past decade. One clue to the social assumptions implicit in this area of research lies in the use of the word "aggressiveness" itself. The actual phenomenon being measured is *fighting behavior* between two animals and not necessarily attack behavior or the actual initiation of fighting by one of the animals. But almost without exception, the titles of the papers, their results, and conclusions use the term *aggression* or *aggressivity* as the behavior being investigated, rather than the phenomenon actually observed, *fighting encounters*, in caged animals. The conclusion is drawn that aggressivity, rather than fighting behavior, is androgen-dependent. A particular and specific measure of one sort of aggressivity has been made synonymous with aggressivity in general. But the term *aggressivity* means many different things to different people; it is not value-free, objective, or uniquely defined, and when used with reference to people, it is not synonymous only with fighting behavior. In primate research, the word has often been used synonymously with dominance. With respect to humans, I believe the inordinate amount of scientific and popular interest in a biological basis for sex differences in "aggressivity" does not have to do with explaining why women so seldom fight in bars, but rather with explaining differences in achievement in the public world. In such a context, the word is invested with qualities that remain unexpressed and un-specified, such as assertiveness, independence, intelligence, creativity and imag-ination, which are usually associated with men who are leaders; that is, aggressive. So, by means of semantic flim-flam, such animal experiments are used to "prove" that men are naturally, hence inevitably, dominant or superior to women because of hormonal differences. Thus, however exemplary the work itself may be, it lends itself to misuse and misinterpretation when it uses language in ways that are both imprecise and laden with ill-defined anthropomorphic values and meanings.

This basic rodent model for "aggression" is flawed by problems other than its definitions and measures. Even in rats and mice and other animals whose cultural effects are probably less significant than they are for primates, environmental factors cannot be ignored. Caged animals in the artificial setting of animal rooms and laboratories are a different breed from their wild sisters and brothers. It is uncertain whether male field mice and rats often aggress upon each other. Fighting behaviors can and will be elicited in any species or sex given the appropriate stimulus. The normally noncombative female rabbit may be ferocious in defense of her young. Female hamsters, gerbils, and vervet monkeys fight more than the males of the species. Some workers in this area (Floody and Pfaff, 1974) emphasize the importance of the context dependence of aggressive behaviors. They point out that whatever the hormonal state of a given individual or species, a particular stimulus may consistently arouse fighting behaviors; conversely, given a particular hormonal condition, the animal's actual fighting behavior will be determined by a complex of other factors that must be considered in interpreting the results. Such factors include the possible social and ecological functions of the aggressive behavior; species and strain of the animal; its prior history; the characteristics of the opponent; and the system of measurement and definitions or criteria of aggressivity used to evaluate the behaviors.

As discussed in Chapter 2, studies in various primate species have failed to establish a consistent relationship between maleness, aggressivity, and dominance. In many species, aggressive behaviors are rarely seen. Dominance hierarchies may not exist; when they do, they may be based on female rankings and are usually not associated with aggressivity; and, finally, dominant males do not have privileged mating access to females in heat, who may prefer and select non-dominant males as mating partners. Most significant of all is the enormous plasticity and variations in behavioral responses that characterize primates as individuals and as species.

The primate laboratory research that is inevitably referred to in discussions of behavioral sex differences concerns the prenatally androgenized female rhesus monkeys (their mothers were injected with testosterone during pregnancy), who exhibit a level of "rough-and-tumble play" that is midway between that of the average untreated female and the average male during their youth (Goy and Phoenix, 1971). Too easy acceptance of these observations as evidence for the "masculinization" of the brain and behavior does not take into account several possible relevant factors and alternative interpretations. First, as already noted with respect to rats, the situation is an extremely abnormal one for evaluating mechanisms of normal behavior, since these baby monkeys were born and raised as caged captives to mothers who were also raised and usually born in captivity. Secondly, the androgenized females were born with masculinized genitalia, and androgens also affect muscle and bone growth and development differently than estrogens. It is surely possible that the sensory input from the enlarged penis-like clitoris and from the muscles and bones has an effect on the nature and frequency of the bodily contacts these laboratory animals have with their playmates. Finally, the parents' attitudes and behaviors toward their offspring may differ with the sex; that is, with the external genitalia and hormonal (olfactory?) or other characteristics of their offspring. Mother rats, for example, have been found to interact differently with female and male pups during the first 18 postpartum days (Moore and Morelli, 1979). A study of rhesus monkeys found that "the mother plays a role in prompting the greater independence and activity that is typical of males" (Mitchell and Brandt, 1970). Parke and Suomi (1981) have reviewed studies of human fathers and the adult males of a variety of nonhuman primate species showing their greater involvement with male than with female offspring: more physical contact, visual attention, vocalization, play initiation, and rough-and-tumble play. The differences exist from early infancy and become more pronounced as the infants get older. Human mothers and, in particular, fathers have been observed to treat sons and daughters differently both physically and verbally as well as to have a completely different gender-stereotyped set of adjectives with which they describe the appearance, character, and behavior of their newborn baby girls and boys whom they have only observed from behind a glass window in a nursery (Rubin, Provenzano, and Luria, 1974). Observers react in particular ways to babies who have been designated as boys and in different ways to babies designated as girls, regardless of what sex they really are. In short, such differences in behaviors toward babies depending on their sex are largely automatic and often unconscious. Wherever we look on the cognitive scale, whether the subject is a rat, a rhesus monkey, or a human baby, it is naive to believe that we are ever seeing some "pure" biological expression of behavior, when subtle or obvious molding forces are at play from birth.

AGGRESSIVITY IN HUMANS: "TOMBOYISM"

Despite the lack of consistent evidence from animal studies, there has been a persistent effort to link aggression, or some arbitrarily chosen equivalent, in boys and men to the effect of androgens and, by inference, to link passivity in women (that is, their relative lack of social and political achievement) to the absence of the androgen influence on their developing brains. The important book by Eleanor Maccoby and Carol Jacklin (1974), which reviews the massive psychological research literature on sex-related differences, concludes that aggressivity is one of the few areas in which sex differences have been really demonstrated, yet they ignore the large number of studies that find *no* sex-related difference in aggressivity in children (Fausto-Sterling, in press; Salzman, 1979). They use the studies purporting to demonstrate male aggressivity to support the hypotheses of biologically based sex differences in aggressive behaviors, yet many of these studies are seriously flawed. Fausto-Sterling (in press) reviews the few studies attempting to link aggressive or hostile behaviors with testosterone levels in the blood. Not only did half of these studies reach opposite conclusions from the other half, they also used varying and arbitrary definitions and measures of aggressiveness, such as being in jail, escaping from jail, being depressed, or using particular word associations on psychological tests. In addition, studies attempting to establish a causal relationship between testosterone and aggressivity or other characteristics equated with aggressivity do not take into account that, first, testosterone levels may be a *consequence* of behaviors and moods and, secondly, testosterone is but one component in a complex system of hormones including cortisone and adrenalin which interact under conditions, for example, of physical or psychological stress.

In order to investigate the possible effects of hormones on the developing human brain, two populations of girls exposed as fetuses to high levels of androgens have been studied (Ehrhardt and Baker, 1974; Ehrhardt, Epstein, and Money, 1968; Ehrhardt and Money, 1967; Money and Ehrhardt, 1972). In some, the mothers had received progestins (which are converted in the body to testosterone) during pregnancy; in others, the fetal adrenal glands had produced abnormal amounts of androgens (called adrenogential syndrome or AGS). These baby girls were born with masculinized genitalia, usually resembling a penis and scrotum closely enough that the girls were considered to be boys for a while and, in all but one case, requiring plastic surgery; namely, clitoridectomy, conversion of the scrotum to labia and fashioning of a vagina, since the labia had fused in the midline forming a scrotum, as normally occurs in males. Among the patient populations studied, the authors found a higher level of "tomboyism" in the subjects than in normal controls matched for age, sex, IQ, and father's occupation (Ehrhardt and Money, 1967; Ehrhardt, Epstein, and Money, 1968) or than in unaffected sisters in AGS families (Ehrhardt and Baker, 1974). They, and others, have interpreted the tomboyism as reflecting "masculinization" of the developing brain. By tomboyism the authors mean: intense energy expenditure; preference for boys as playmates, for boys' toys, outdoor play and athletics; little interest in dolls or in infant care; preference for functional clothes (pants rather than dresses); few or no fantasies about marriage, pregnancy, and motherhood; and an interest in career equal to or greater than that in marriage. Tomboyism is seen in these studies as a measure of aggressivity, induced by androgens. But since increased fighting behaviors were not observed, the investigators suggested that the masculinization applied to brain pathways ". . . that mediate dominance assertion" rather than outright aggression, and also inhibited "pathways that should eventually subserve maternal behavior" (Money and Ehrhardt, 1972, p. 103). That such "pathways" exist either in humans or animals is a product only of the authors' imaginations.

These studies have been widely and uncritically cited in the scientific and popular literature in support of the belief in the hormonal determination of human temperament and behavior despite a number of remarkable weaknesses. The first published report (Ehrhardt and Money, 1967) studied exactly ten girls with progestin-induced fetal androgenization, and the second (Ehrhardt, Epstein, and Money, 1968) studied 15 with AGS. Yet on the basis of these *same 25 patients*, in the face of the admittedly inconclusive nature of their findings and the possibility, acknowledged in these first papers, that other than biological factors may be involved, Ehrhardt and Money wrote a number of subsequent articles, chapters, and a book in which they became ever more assertive that the results *established* the behavioral effects of fetally androgenized brains. In their first paper Ehrhardt and Money (1967) raise the "question of whether tomboyishness may not be a frequent characteristic in the development of middle-class suburban and rural girls who have both the space and tradition of the outdoor life" (p. 96). They conclude, "It will require more than ten cases and better control of at least the socioeconomic variable before one can answer with confidence the question of the extent to which prenatal hormones can affect subsequent behavior" (p. 98). In their second paper, they wrote:

> It is not possible to estimate on the basis of present data, whether individual differences in degrees of tomboyism may have reflected differences in parental attitude. Each parent knew of the child's genital masculinization at birth. This knowledge may have insidiously influenced their expectancies and reactions regarding the child's behavioral development and interests, but in a way not the same from parent to parent. (Ehrhardt, Epstein and Money, 1968, p. 166)

And yet in their book four years later, with the same data from the same 25 patients, they wrote, "The most likely hypothesis to explain the various features of tomboyism in fetally masculinized genetic females is that their tomboyism is a sequel to a masculinizing effect on the fetal brain" (Money and Ehrhardt, 1972, p. 103).

Then there followed a later study on a new population of 17 female patients with AGS in Buffalo (Ehrhardt and Baker, 1974), which added no new techniques or dimensions of psychological or sociological analysis except that siblings were also studied, and the authors concluded that the findings "corroborated" the previous studies. "The consistency of results in both earlier and more recent studies suggests strongly that it is the fetal exposure to androgens that contribute to the typical profile of behavior exhibited by AGS females" (p. 48). But by 1979, the same studies do not only "suggest strongly" that fetal androgens affect adult behaviors but they have come to show that the "effects of prenatal androgens *have been established* [emphasis added] for the sex-dimorphic behaviour clusters" described in the previous papers (Ehrhardt and Meyer-Bahlburg, 1979, p. 41).

The flaws in the studies are numerous. The investigators, who are psychologists, have never considered as relevant the effect on a girl child's emotional and psychic life of having a penis and scrotum for the first year or 3½ or even 7½ or more years of their lives (their ages when the clitoridectomy and plastic repairs were done), nor the effects of *then* having them removed. In most cases, further vaginal surgery was necessary at the time of adolescence. Yet Money's own work had long ago suggested that gender identity is established along with language during the first two years of life. But for these children, the question is, Which gender identity? Surely the ambiguity of their situation in this extremely gender-polarized society would have some effect on their preferences, choices, or identifications in play, playmates, clothes, and attitudes toward eventual or possible motherhood and career. It evidently did not seem significant to the authors in their first study of 10 girls (Ehrhardt and Money, 1967) that the only girl who preferred dolls, showed no preference for outdoor play or boys' toys or clothes, and did not consider herself a tomboy was the *only* one without masculinized genitalia. Nor do the authors consider that the intense medical, surgical, and psychological scrutiny and interventions that the patients have undergone since birth, all centered on their genitalia, could have affected their behaviors and attitudes.

In all the studies the investigators too easily dismiss parental attitudes and the rest of the social-familial environment, accepting the mothers' word that they had no ambivalence about the child's gender and treated the affected daughters no differently from their other daughters. Yet many of them did not have other daughters for comparison, nor did Ehrhardt and Money (1967) themselves study the siblings. They did, however, record that one mother considered herself a tomboy as a child and reported that *both* her daughters, the patient and her unaffected sister, were tomboys. In addition they noted that it "was anecdotally evident, however, that some of the sisters of index cases were tomboyish . . ." (p. 96). So, with one definitely recorded case of tomboyism in a sister and a mother along with informally noted tomboyism in "some" (number unspecified) of the remaining normal sisters of the patient population of *nine* tomboys (some of whom had *no* sisters), it is difficult to avoid the interpretation that tomboyism was a common social characteristic among the females, nonpatients as well as patients, in this small sample of families, rather than being induced by exposure of the developing brain to excess androgen.

Only in the Buffalo study (Ehrhardt and Baker, 1974) were data collected directly from unaffected siblings in order to assess familial or social influences in "tomboy" behaviors. While the authors claim significant differences in their findings, their conclusions are not supported by their data for several reasons. First, their patient population included 17 girls and 10 boys with AGS, and the eleven unaffected sisters constituting the comparison control group came from the families of the *entire* group of 27 patients. Only *some* (number unspecified) of the eleven girls with whom the 17 AGS female patients were compared were their own sisters; the rest (an unspecified number) were sisters of the male AGS patients and, therefore, were not the female patients' own family controls. In short, they were irrelevant controls (though, in any case, the *only* really relevant controls would be girls who were not exposed to high levels of androgens as fetuses, but who, for some reason, were born with masculinized genitalia and subjected to the same medical and surgical care as the patients). Second, the authors state that six patients underwent surgical correction in the first year of life; seven between one and three years of age; and four, "later in life." Thus, if we generously exclude the six operated on during year one, about *60 percent* of the patients had a penis and scrotum during the period when sex and gender awareness and identity are established. In comparing the female AGS and the sibling "control" group, Ehrhardt and Baker found statistically significant differences between the two groups in the incidence of most of the measures for tomboyism they used (though no differences were found in fight initiation and career aspirations), but their charts show that the "tomboy" characteristics with the statistical differences were present in only about *60 percent* of the AGS female patients. Since these two 60 percent figures are calculations that I have made from the authors' data, and since the authors did not discuss the possible relationship between their behavioral measures, such as clothes or playmate preferences, and consciousness of masculinized genitalia and the social aura of boyhood, we are left to wonder whether the 60 percent with "tomboy" behaviors are the 60 percent with masculinized genitalia. Their own data strongly suggest, however, that the behaviors represent a flexible adjustment by the patients and their parents to a very ambiguous situation: having a boy's genitalia and being told you are a girl. Gender must seem a fragile and arbitrary construct if it depends upon plastic surgery.

There are many other problems in these studies having to do with the inadequacy of the controls, the questionnaires, the interviewing process, the language, and the underlying assumptions, but since these are discussed in detail elsewhere (Fausto-Sterling, in press; Fried, 1979) and I have already indicated some of the major flaws, there is no need to go into further detail here. It may complete my argument about the use these studies and their interpretations have served to quote the Sociobiologist Barash's discussion of the studies of Ehrhardt and Money:

It is recognized increasingly that there are real differences between little boys and little girls, behavioral differences that begin early in life and that derive at least in part from our biology. For example, boys tend to be more active and more aggressive than girls. Girls accidentally exposed to testosterone, the male sex hormone, while still in their mother's uterus were found to be "masculinized" as children. They often developed into tomboys, favoring rough-and-tumble outdoor play, and were generally more active than other, "normal" girls, even though their parents seemingly did not treat them any differently. In fact, the parents of such children were so disturbed by their daughters' "boylike" behavior that the children were brought to a doctor—the basis of the discovery of the testosterone exposure. (1979, p. 59)

It is important to know that the "fact" in the last sentence is a total fabrication. No babies or children were brought in for behavioral problems; rather, they were originally recognized as having a medical, an anatomical, problem. The study of behavior or of tomboyism was generated years later by Ehrhardt and Money, who had access to this large population of patients who had been diagnosed at, or were being followed in, the pediatric endocrinology clinic of the Johns Hopkins Hospital because of masculinized genitalia, *not* "masculinized" behavior.

INTELLIGENCE AND MATHEMATICAL ABILITY

In closely parallel studies, Money's group measured the IQ score of girls exposed fetally to high levels of androgens. The history of this work is as interesting as that on aggressivity, without even touching the issue of IQ scores themselves and what they measure. The first study (Money and Lewis, 1966) tested 70 girls with the adrenogenital syndrome (AGS) and found the mean IQ to be 109.9 with a range from 38 to 154. In contrast to the presumed normal IQ distribution curve of the general population with a mean of 100, 60 percent of the patients rather than the expected 25 percent scored higher than 110. The authors discounted any socioeconomic or intellectual factors that might have selected for a particular population of families that had access to sophisticated medical care in a major teaching and research medical center. They did, however, compare the IQ score of ten nonaffected siblings from seven families and, allowing for the small sample size, found "no appreciable difference between the two groups" (p. 371), that is, between the androgen-exposed and non-exposed. They further observed,

> The finding of an excess of high IQs is quite clear-cut. The interpretation of this finding would be more clear-cut had the sibling comparison yielded more definitive results. (p. 371)

Despite that observation they nonetheless concluded,

> There is a good possibility, therefore, that the present findings represent . . . a valid characteristic of the adrenogenital syndrome, namely that it does tend to be associated with above-average IQ. One possible explanation is that elevated androgen, characteristic of the syndrome, may in some way be responsible. (p. 372)

The next study (Ehrhardt and Money, 1967) examined the IQ in daughters born with masculinized genitalia of mothers treated with progestin during pregnancy. The mean IQ of these ten girls was 125. All six of the IQ scores over 130 were scored by daughters of college-educated fathers (mothers' education was evidently not considered relevant). As in the previous study, the authors discounted socioeconomic factors, however, referring to the first study as corroboration of the biological implications of the findings in this one. Siblings were not examined for IQ. On the basis of the same flawed and flimsy evidence from the two studies and 80 girls, these authors repeated their conclusions about the enhancing effects of androgens on IQ with ever increasing unconditional certainty over the next six years:

> It is, of course, still too early to make any sweeping generalizations from these findings. But Katharina Dalton's work, taken together with our own, strongly suggests that androgens . . . given prenatally, do produce an increase in intelligence. . . . (Money, 1971, p. 289)

> The clinical data on human females indicate elevated IQ and some behavioral masculinization, without gender-identity disorders, subsequent to prenatal exposure to androgenic substances. (Walker and Money, 1972, p. 119)

Finally, in 1974 with a new collaborator and in a new setting, Ehrhardt published a study of 27 patients with AGS and their families. The mean IQ of the 17 AGS females and of 11 unaffected sisters of AGS patients was 113; the mean IQ of ten AGS males was 111 and that of 16 unaffected brothers was 109. The conclusion seemed obvious, eight years after the first study: the modestly elevated IQs in these families have nothing to do with prenatal exposure of the brain to excess androgens.

In the 1980s the controversy about sex-differentiated cognitive differences rose into overnight prominence in the form of a study that suggested to the news media that some truly new and unexpected scientific discovery had been revealed. Days before the report in *Science*, the official journal of the largest professional science organization in the country, the newspapers announced that Johns Hopkins researchers found that boys are "inherently" better than girls in mathematical reasoning (*New York Times*, Dec. 7, 1980). *Time* magazine carried the story the same week the study appeared and quoted one of its authors, Camilla Benbow, as saying that many women "can't bring themselves to accept sexual difference in aptitude. But the difference in math is a fact. The best way to help girls is to accept it and go from there" (Dec. 15, 1980, p. 57). *Newsweek* of the same date asked in its story headline, "Do Males have a Math Gene?"

The study of Camilla Benbow and Julian Stanley (1980) tested about 10,000 students, mainly seventh and eighth graders who were in the upper 3 percent of students in math ability as judged by the College Board Scholastic Aptitude Test (SAT). The students are part of a larger project called the Study of Mathematically Precocious Youth. The mean score for boys in the math SAT was higher than for girls tested during the eight years of the study, and the highest score every year was made by a boy. It is significant that in the last two years, 1978 and 1979, however, the highest score by a boy was 790 and by a girl, 760, the smallest and least significant difference since the beginning of the study in 1972. (It is highly doubtful that this closing math gap reflects a change in the female *gene* pool for math.) The authors' conclusion was: "We favor the hypothesis that sex differences in achievement in and attitude toward mathematics result from superior male mathematical ability, which may in turn be related to greater male ability in spatial tasks" (p. 1264). The context of the article clearly implied a genetic sex difference.

Since up to the time of testing the girls and boys did not differ in the number of math courses taken, the authors did not seriously consider any other possible social or environmental factors, though they did suggest that their "data are consistent with numerous alternative hypotheses," which they did not explore. (It is important to note that no press reports carried that cautionary statement.) Nor did they think it important to take into account that the subjects were volunteers, despite the evidence that gifted boys are more likely to volunteer to take tests than are gifted girls (Jacklin, 1981). But as two professors of mathematics, Alice Schafer and Mary Gray, wrote in the lead editorial in *Science* five weeks after the Benbow and Stanley article appeared, in criticism of the Benbow and

Stanley hypothesis, "Anyone who thinks that seventh graders are free from environmental influences can hardly be living in the real world." Who helps with the math homework, the kinds of toys and games girls and boys are given, and the expectations of parents and teachers are of critical importance. Mathematically gifted boys can confidently expect to use and be rewarded for their skills in math, science, and engineering and will thus be highly motivated to excel, but it has been well documented that, by and large, parents, school counselors, and teachers have traditionally discouraged even talented girls from seriously pursuing mathematics and science skills or, equally damagingly, simply ignored them (Beckwith and Durkin, 1980; Brophy and Good, 1970; Delefes and Jackson, 1972; Ernest, 1976; Leinhardt *et al.*, 1979). One study found that "42 percent of girls interested in careers in mathematics or science reported being discouraged by counselors from taking courses in advanced mathematics" (Haven, 1972). In addition, at an age when pressures are high to conform to expected gender roles and behaviors, many girls do not want to be seen as "unfeminine" in a culture that equates math and science skills with "masculinity." The Benbow and Stanley study and its attendant sensationalized publicity will do little to dispel what Dean Jewell Cobb of Douglass College called the "notion that proficiency in mathematics is a sex-linked characteristic which is widespread among elementary school and high school teachers, college students and young mothers" (Quoted in *Science News*, Vol. 113, p. 200, 1978).

It is only recently that efforts have been launched to educate teachers and counselors away from sex-typing and channeling. In those schools where the environment is equally challenging to both sexes, studies produce quite different results from those of Benbow and Julian. Patricia Casserly of the Educational Testing Service in Princeton has studied 20 high schools where all the teachers have science, math, or engineering backgrounds, communicate enthusiasm for math, and *expect* women to advance as well as men. In these schools, girls and boys score equally well in Advanced Placement (college level) examinations (Kolata, 1980).

It is faintly ironic that not long after the Benbow and Julian study, living refutations of sex stereotyping and scientific sex delineations appeared within the same year, though they were not heralded, if noticed at all, by the popular press: 11-year-old Ruth Lawrence of England got the highest score in the mathematics entrance examinations at Oxford University's St. Hugh's College, which she was to enter in 1983 (*Ms*, June 1982); 17-year-old Laura Clark of Long Island was the only student out of 154,000 to score a perfect 800 on *both* sections (verbal and mathematical) of the Scholastic Aptitude Test (*Ms*, June 1982); for the third year in a row, a woman high school student (Reena Gordon of Brooklyn in 1982) was the winner of the National Westinghouse Science Talent Search Award (American Women in Science *Newsletter*, Vol. 11, # 4, Aug.-Sept. 1982); Nina Morishige, who received her BA and MA in mathematics at 18 years of age after attending Johns Hopkins University for two years, became one of the youngest recipients ever to receive a Rhodes Scholarship to Oxford in the 78-year history of the award (*Johns Hopkins Journal*, Spring, 1982).

There are other problems with the Benbow and Stanley study or with the authors' interpretation of the results. In suggesting inherent (they use the term "endogenous") superiority in mathematical reasoning in males, they overlook the substantial overlap in the distribution of scores of girls and boys; that is, among talented girls and boys, the scores are more alike than different, with a few exceptional cases. If some girls near the top are superior to most of the boys, then what does male "superiority" mean? Next, Benbow and Stanley state their belief that environmental factors affect mathematical *achievement*, whereas the SAT, which they used, measures aptitude, that is, "natural" ability. There is, however, a real question whether it is possible at all to make a distinction between achievement and aptitude; and, second, there is real doubt that the SAT is indeed capable of measuring aptitude, whatever that may be, as contrasted with achievement. A member of the Educational Testing Service of Princeton has written that "the developers of the SAT do not view it as a measure of fixed capacities," but instead, "The test is intended to measure aspects of developed ability" (Schafer and Gray, 1981). Susan Chipman of the National Institute of Education wrote that the math SAT samples "performance in a domain of learned knowledge and skill. . . . In a fundamental sense, we do not yet know what mathematical ability is . . ." (1981; see the same issue of *Science* for a number of excellent critiques of the Benbow and Stanley study in the *Letters* Section; see also Beckwith and Durkin, 1981).

Finally, Benbow and Stanley's study and conclusions stand in contradiction to a number of other studies that fail to confirm the assumption that boys are invariably superior in mathematics achievement before the grade levels when clear socialization factors appear (Fennema and Sherman, 1977, 1978; Sherman, 1980). Following two years of intensive study of students in grades 6 through 12, Fennema and Sherman (1978) found that "when relevant factors are controlled, sex-related differences in favor of males do not appear often, and when they do, they are not large" (p. 201). Furthermore, Fennema and Sherman have not found sex differences in spatial visualization at any age. But as one might anticipate, these negative results and the innumerable other studies that show *no* differences in performance or aptitude between the sexes do not excite attention or merit headlines and national news service coverage, and many are not accepted by journals for publication.

If the Benbow and Stanley study is flawed, why, one might ask, get so excited about it? It is because the message of the authors' conclusions has undoubtedly already had dire effects; it is an example of a self-perpetuating and reinforcing ideology. Teachers, counselors, and parents are told there is no particular point in encouraging seemingly talented girls because they are ultimately limited, and it tells girls directly that they should spare themselves grief and energy, even though they like math and are good at it. The study itself is likely to widen the sex-differential in performance or at least to offset the advances in confidence and achievement that have been hard-wrought by the women's movement and the more open atmosphere it has created. The predictable effects of the study and the unbridled enthusiasm of its media reception will be to confirm the comfortable stereotypes about women and men, and make it easier to keep women out of those fields that increasingly rely on sophisticated mathematical and computer knowledge—science, business, and the social sciences.

SUMMARY AND CONCLUSIONS

There is abundant evidence that estrogens, progestins, and androgens have a variety of effects on the structure and functioning of a number of cells, organs, and tissues, and that they contribute to some more biological and physiological sex differences, though the specific intracellular mechanisms of these effects are still largely conjectural and under investigation. It is also clear that these hormones interact with neurons. In laboratory animals, such specific interactions have been linked most clearly with cyclicity of ovarian function and some reproductive behaviors, and in some birds with singing. But even for behaviors in rodents, the influences of these hormones is not sex-specific and exclusive. While the administration of androgens will increase the frequency of mounting behaviors of female rats (but not of female hamsters), the fact is that normal female rats, like females of other species, mount other females without benefit of hormonal interventions. Similarly, while some female rats will fight other rats with less provocation after androgen injections, female hamsters and vervet monkeys normally fight more than their male counterparts, and females of most species will fight under some circumstances. As the editors of a collection of classical papers on the subject of the effects of hormones on the brain and behavior wrote, "Social factors that emerge over the lifetime of an organism, as it interacts with others, are important modifiers of hormonally mediated behaviors" (Silver and Feder, 1979).

This field of research is further complicated by the fact that much remains to be known and many contradictions still need to be resolved, despite great gains in information about hormonal interactions with the brain. Different metabolic forms of the same family of hormones, for example, estrogens or androgens, have different behavioral effects as do different dosages or the timing of the injections. Different species of laboratory animals or even particular strains within a species vary in their hormonal profiles and respond differently to hormonal manipulations. Because of these as well as other fundamental differences in biological and behavioral responses among different species of laboratory animals, it is unwarranted to extrapolate findings from the rat to the guinea pig or monkey and, certainly, to humans. But in addition, the results obtained in the controlled conditions of the laboratory, where animals are caged and have existed their entire lives under totally artificial circumstances, have no necessary relevance to their survival behaviors in the wild. As one investigator in the area of behavior writes in his review of a book on parental behaviors in rodents: ". . . the absence of modern fieldwork with three of the four species most commonly studied in laboratory situations combines [with other factors] to limit integration of the wealth of information available on reproduction in laboratory strains of rat, hamster, and gerbil with ecological and evolutionary concerns" (Galef, 1983, p. 743).

One object of laboratory rodent and primate studies is to discover and analyze the "fundamentals" of human behavior; that is, basic mechanisms "uncontaminated" by culture. At this behavioral level of investigation, that is an unrealizable goal because rodent or monkey behavior is not basic behavior minus culture; even in Primate Research Centers, rhesus monkeys learn and have a culture. Secondly, as discussed at length in Chapter 3, since learned or environmental factors affect the structure of the brain itself beginning prenatally and especially postnatally and also mold behaviors and attitudes from the time of birth, human behavior is always fundamentally social and cultural and cannot be pared down to reveal a core of untouched or essential basic biological mechanisms. Basic biological mechanisms or structures are there and important to understand, to be sure, in the form of neurons, synapses, pathways, and hormones, similar to those in other animals, but their influences are inextricable from learning and environmental effects, which interact at every level of the "basic biological mechanisms."

Am I claiming that investigations of basic mechanisms are useless or that such work on laboratory animals has no relevance to the human brain? No, but I am disputing interpretations that make these mechanisms explanatory of human behavior. Knowledge of these basic mechanisms has less and less predictive value about the behaviors of the animals in which they are studied the more complicated, flexible, and unpredictable the animals' behaviors are and the more complex and heterogeneous their environment and culture are. The comparative psychologist, Ethel Tobach, in her critique of hereditarian theories, which applies equally to any other theories of the biological determination of human behavior, views behavior

. . . as a derivative of many processes which may be analyzed on many levels of organization and integration. Behavior subsumes all levels in ascending order— biophysical and biochemical (including genetics), physiological, organismic, ecological. . . . The concept of levels of integration postulates that phenomena on one level are specific to that level and one cannot extrapolate from preceding, subsumed levels to the next higher level. For example, if one knows that thresholds at the membrane of a neuron are variably sensitive to circulating hormones, such as insulin, under different physiological conditions, one cannot predict whether a person will or will not break a diabetic diet when faced with a social situation in which everyone is drinking alcohol. Further, each level has its own appropriate forms of analysis, principles and laws. Therefore, to make people equivalent to lower levels of organization in the animal world, or to impute human characteristics to other animals results is the kind of pseudo-scientific thinking that is the basis of ethology, Skinnerian meritocracy and sociobiology. (1977, pp. 11-12)

To put this in the terms of this chapter: when an oil magnate is exhibiting leadership in the business world (one of the measures of "aggressivity"), he is operating at a level of behavioral integration (cognitive functioning in relation to all of the complexities of business, government, and politics) that simply cannot be compared with or extrapolated from the level of behavioral integration or organization represented by a laboratory rat that has been injected by testosterone and fights more with her cagemates.

It is for all of these reasons and more that the questions underlying the research discussed in this chapter are not valid questions. The underlying assumptions are that there are sex-differentiated behaviors, temperaments, and characteristics, and these differences are determined by biological factors. The question that is then explored is, What are the biological factors? A vast scientific enterprise is now devoted to measuring sex differences and to finding how the effects of hormones on the developing brain influence sex differences in adult behaviors and characteristics. As this chapter has shown, not only are the underlying premises and logic faulty, but the most influential of the studies involving humans are seriously flawed methodologically and do not support the claims made by their authors or justify their widespread and enthusiastic acceptance. Studies linking hormones with aggressivity, achievement, and intelligence or linking "innate" differences in brain structure with sex differences in verbal, mathematical, and visuospatial abilities have been methodologically, logically, and conceptually unsound and inconclusive.

Scientists are frequently unable to apply their usual critical standards to the findings and interpretations of studies that confirm their own beliefs and hypotheses, and at the same time they tend to ignore or disbelieve those that don't. But specifically in the areas of sex differences or hormones and behavior where the results of studies are often inconclusive, scientists attempting to establish the biological basis for sex differences in some human behavior will frequently pool the results of a number of inconclusive, ill-controlled, and often contradictory studies (of rodents, primates, and humans) and conclude that despite the incon-clusiveness and inadequacies of *each* of them, *together* they make a case simply because there are so many of them. This is like claiming that if you add three zeros together, you get zero, but if you add enough zeros together, say 25, then you'll get 25. But you don't. You still have nothing.

By their very methods of reporting trivial differences in the mean scores of large groups or populations of boys and girls as sex differences, these disciplines have helped, along with other cultural forces, to *create* the entity (gender differences) that they claim to explain and measure scientifically. By isolating, in the name of scientific rigor, the characteristics they measure from the social forces that mold their expression, they further create the illusion of the biological inevitability of the illusory differences.

A fundamental difficulty is that all the studies try ostensibly to establish clear-cut mutually exclusive biological differences between the sexes, such as in brain structure, lateralization, hormones, or genes, to explain behavioral sex differences that are in fact *not* mutually exclusive or sex specific. That is, tests of verbal or visuospatial or mathematical abilities or aggressivity or anything else may show small differences in the *mean scores* between some populations of boys and girls and no differences between other populations of boys and girls. The *range* of performance between women and men or boys and girls is the same, only the distribution of scores may vary. Where differences exist in mean scores, they are small and are between two groups in whom the differences in social expectations and in training in the relevant skills are, however, enormous. The majority of little boys, but the minority of little girls, are consistently primed from the time they walk to excel in those activities that sharpen the three-dimensional, eye-hand-body-coordinated abilities that constitute visuospatial skills. It is obvious that girls so trained are also superior. The enormous differences in socialization factors are more than adequate to explain the almost trivial differences that exist in mean scores without speculating about the differential evolution of female and male brains, of which nothing is known.

As many others have said, whatever characteristic is being measured, the range of variation is far greater *among* males or *among* females than *between* the two sexes. There is, in fact, far greater scientific and perhaps social justification for exploring and trying to understand the vast variance among individuals than the elusive, tiny variances between the sexes that elicit far greater attention and expenditure of research resources than they merit.

What the studies are in fact trying to explain are the more widespread differences that exist between the sexes in status, privilege, or power within known industrial, patriarchal systems, and they do this through attempting to scientifically establish biologically determined, sex-differentiated cognitive and personality characteristics that would make women's subordinate position inevitable.

REFERENCES

Barash, D. *The whisperings within*. New York: Harper & Row, 1979.
Beckwith, J., and Durkin, J. Girls, boys and math. *Science for the People*, 1981, *13*, 6-35.

Benbow, C., and Stanley, J. Sex differences in mathematical ability: fact or artifact? *Science*, 1980, *210*, 1262-1264.

Bleier, R. Myths of the biological inferiority of women: an exploration of the sociology of biological research. *University of Michigan Papers in Women's Studies*, 1976, *2*, 39-63.

Bleier, R. Social and political bias in science: an examination of animal studies and their generalizations to human behaviors and evolution. In R. Hubbard and M. Lowe (Eds.), *Genes and Gender II*. New York: Gordian Press, 1979.

Bleier, R., Byne, W., and Siggelkow, I. Cytoarchitectonic sexual dimorphisms of the medial preoptic and anterior hypothalamic areas in guinea pig, rat, hamster, and mouse. *Journal of Comparative Neurology*, 1982, *212*, 118-130.

Brophy, J. E., and Good, T. L. Teachers' communication of differential expectations for children's classroom performance: some behavioral data. *Journal of Educational Psychology*, 1970, *6*, 365-374.

Byne, T. E., Terasawa, E., Bleier, R., and Goy, R. W. Sequential estradiol benzoate (EB) and progesterone (P) administration induces a luteinizing hòrmone (LH) surge in gonadectomized male and androgen-sterilized female guinea pigs. *Abstract, Society for Neuroscience*, 1983, *9*, #319:10.

Chipman, S. Letter to the editor. *Science*, 1981, *212*, 114-116.

Conner, R. L., and Levine, S. Hormonal influences on aggressive behaviour. In S. Garattini and E. B. Sigg (Eds.), *Aggressive behaviour*. Amsterdam: Excerpta Medica, 1969.

Delefes, P., and Jackson, B. Teacher-pupil interaction as a function of location in the classroom. *Psychology in the Schools*, 1972, *9*, 119-123.

DeVoogd, T., and Nottebohm, F. Sex differences in dendritic morphology of a song control nucleus in the canary: a quantitative Golgi study. *Journal of Comparative Neurology*, 1981, *196*, 309-316.

Döhler, K. D., and Wuttke, W. Changes with age in levels of serum gonadotropins, prolactin and gonadal steroids in prepubertal male and female rats. *Endocrinology*, 1975, *97*, 898-907.

Edwards, D. A. Early androgen stimulation and aggressive behavior in male and female mice. *Physiology and Behavior*, 1969, *4*, 333-338.

Ehrhardt, A., and Baker, S. Fetal androgens, human central nervous system differentiation, and behavior sex differences. In R. C. Friedman, R. M. Richart, and R. L. Vande Wiele (Eds.), *Sex differences in behavior*. New York: Wiley, 1974.

Ehrhardt, A., and Meyer-Bahlburg, H. Psychosexual development: an examination of the role of prenatal hormones. *Sex, Hormones and Behaviour*, 1979, *62*, 41-57.

Ehrhardt, A., and Money, J. Progestin-induced hermaphroditism: IQ and psychosexual identity in a study of ten girls. *Journal of Sex Research*, 1967, *3*, 83-100.

Ehrhardt, A., Epstein, R., and Money, J. Fetal androgens and female gender identity in the early-treated adrenogenital syndrome. *Johns Hopkins Medical Journal*, 1968, *122*, 160-167.

Ernest, J. *Mathematics and sex*. Santa Barbara: Mathematics Department, University of California, 1976.

Etreby, M. F., Gräf, L. J., Günzel, P., and Neumann, F. Evaluation of effects of sexual steroids on the hypothalamic-pituitary system of animals and man. *Archives of Toxicology*, 1979, *2*, 11-39.

Fausto-Sterling, A. *Woman: a biological fantasy*. New York: Basic Books, in press.

Fennema, E., and Sherman, J. Sex-related differences in mathematics achievement, spatial visualization, and affective factors. *American Educational Research Journal*, 1977, *14*, 51-71.

Fennema, E., and Sherman, J. Sex-related differences in mathematics achievement and related factors: a further study. *Journal for Research in Mathematics Education*, 1978, *9*, 188-203.

Floody, O. R., and Pfaff, D. W. Steroid hormones and aggressive behavior: approaches to the study of hormone-sensitive brain mechanisms for behavior. *Aggression*, 1974, *52*, 149-185.

Fried, B. Boys will be boys will be boys: the language of sex and gender. In R. Hubbard, M. S. Henifin, and B. Fried (Eds.), *Women look at biology looking at women*. Cambridge: Schenkman, 1979.

Galef, B. Reproductive behavior. *Science*, 1983, *221*, 742-743.

Goldberg, S. *The inevitability of patriarchy*. New York: Morrow, 1973.

Goldfoot, D., Wallen, K., Neff, D. A., McBrair, M. C., and Goy, R. W. Social influences upon the display of sexually dimorphic behavior in rhesus monkeys: isosexual rearing. *Archives of Sexual Behavior*, in press.

Gorski, R. The neuroendocrinology of reproduction: An overview. *Biology of Reproduction*, 1979, *20*, 111-127.

Gorski, R., Gordon, J. H., Shryne, J. E., and Southam, A. M. Evidence for a morphological sex difference within the medial preoptic area of the rat brain. *Brain Research*, 1978, *148*, 333-346.

Gorski, R., Harlan, R. E., Jacobson, C. D., Shryne, J. E., and Southam, A. M. Evidence for the existence of a sexually dimorphic nucleus in the preoptic area of the rat. *Journal of Comparative Neurology*, 1980, *193*, 529-539.

Goy, R., and Phoenix, C. H. The effects of testosterone propionate administered before birth on the development of behavior in genetic female rhesus monkeys. In C. H. Sawyer and R. A. Gorski (Eds.), *Steroid hormones and brain function*. Berkeley: University of California Press, 1971.

Goy, R., and Resko, J. A. Gonadal hormones and behavior of normal and pseudohermaphroditic nonhuman female primates. In E. B. Astwood (Ed.), *Recent progress in hormone research*, 1972, *28*. New York: Academic Press, 1972.

Greenough, W., Carter, C. S., Steerman, C., and DeVoogd, T. J. Sex differences in dendritic patterns in hamster preoptic area. *Brain Research*, 1977, *126*, 63-72.

Gurney, M. Hormonal control of cell form and number in the zebra finch song system. *Journal of Neuroscience*, 1981, *1*, 658-673.

Gurney, M., and Konishi, M. Hormone-induced sexual differentiation of brain and behavior in zebra finches. *Science*, 1980, *208*, 1380-1383.

Hardyck, C., Tzeng, O., and Wang, W. Cerebral lateralization of function and bilingual decision processes: is thinking lateralized? *Brain and Language*, 1978, *5*, 56-71.

Harris, G. Sex hormones, brain development and brain function. *Endocrinology*, 1964, *75*, 627-648.

Harris, G., and Levine, S. Sexual differentiation of the brain and its experimental control. *Journal of Physiology*, 1965, *181*, 379-400.

Haven, E. W. Factors associated with the selection of advanced academic mathematical courses by girls in high school. *Research Bulletin* 72-12. Princeton: Educational Testing Service, 1972.

Hilliard, J., Scaramuzzi, R. J., Penardi, R., and Sawyer, C. H. Progesterone, estradiol and testosterone levels in ovarian venous blood of pregnant rabbits. *Endocrinology*, 1975, *93*, 1235- 1238.

Jacklin, D. Methodological issues in the study of sex-related differences. *Developmental Review*, 1981, *1*, 266-273.

Karsch, F. J., Dierschke, D. J., and Knobil, E. Sexual Differentiation of pituatary function: Apparent difference between primates and rodents. *Science*, 1973, *179*, 484-486.

Kessler, S., and McKenna, W. *Gender. An ethnomethodological approach*. New York: Wiley, 1978.

Kihlstrom, J. E. A male sexual cycle. In A. Ingelman-Sundberg and N. O. Lunell (Eds.), *Current problems in fertility*. New York: Plenum Press, 1971.

Knobil, E., Plant, T. M., Wildt, L., Belchetz, P. E., and Marshall, G. Control of the rhesus monkey menstruel cycle: permissive role of hypothalamic gonadotropin-releasing hormone. *Science*, 1980, *207*, 1371-1373.

Kolata, G. Math and sex: are girls born with less ability? *Science*, 1980, *210*, 1234-1235.

Kulin, H., and Reiter, E. O. Gonadotropin and testosterone measurements after estrogen administration to adult men, prepubertal and pubertal boys, and men with hypogonadotropism: evidence for maturation of positive feedback in the male. *Pediatric Research*, 1976, *10*, 46-51.

Leinhardt, G., Seewald, A. M., and Engel, M. Learning what's taught: sex differences in instruction. *Journal of Educational Psychology*, 1979, *714*, 432-439.

Maccoby, E., and Jacklin, C. *The psychology of sex differences*. San Francisco: Stanford University Press, 1974.

MacLusky, N., and Naftolin, F. Sexual differentiation of the central nervous system. *Science*, 1981, *211*, 1294-1303.

McGlone, J. Sex differences in human brain asymmetry: a critical survey. *The Behavioral and Brain Sciences*, 1980, *3*, 215-263.

Mitchell, G., and Brandt, E. Behavioral differences relate to experience of mother and sex of infant in the Rhesus monkey. *Developmental Psychology*, 1970, *3*, 149.

Money, J. Pre-natal hormones and intelligence: a possible relationship. *Impact of Science on Society*, 1971, *21*, 285-290.

Money, J., and Ehrhardt, A. *Man & woman, boy and girl*. Baltimore: Johns Hopkins University Press, 1972.

Money, J., and Lewis, V. IQ, genetics and accelerated growth: adrenogenital syndrome. *Bulletin of Johns Hopkins Hospital*, 1966, *118*, 365-373.

Moore, C., and Morelli, G. Mother rats interact differently with male and female offspring. *Journal of Comparative and Physiological Psychology*, 1979, *93*, 677-684.

Morris, J. *Conundrum*. New York: Harcourt Brace Jovanovich, 1974.

Nottebohm, F., and Arnold, A. Sexual dimorphism in vocal control areas of the songbird brain. *Science*, 1976, *194*, 211-213.

Overpeck, J., Colson, S., Hohmann, J., Applestine, M., and Reilly, J. Concentrations of circulating steroids in normal pre-pubertal and adult male and female humans, chimpanzees, rhesus monkeys, rats, mice, and hamsters: a literature survey. *Journal of Toxicology and Environmental Health*, 1978, *4*, 785-803.

Parke, R., and Suomi, S. Adult male-infant relationships: human and nonhuman primate evidence. In K. Immelmann, G. Barlow, L. Petrinovich, and M. Main (Eds.), *Early development in animals and man: proceedings of the Bielefeld interdisciplinary conference*. Cambridge: Cambridge University Press, 1981.

Parsons, J. *The psychology of sex differences and sex roles*. New York: McGraw-Hill, 1980.

Phoenix, C. H., Goy, R. W., Gerall, A. A., and Young, W. C. Organizing action of prenatally administered testosterone propionate on the tissues mediating mating behavior in the female guinea pig. *Endocrinology*, 1959, *65*, 369-382.

Quadagno, D., Briscoe, R., and Quadagno, J. Effect of perinatal gonadal hormones on selected nonsexual behavior patterns: a critical assessment of the nonhuman and human literature. *Psychological Bulletin*, 1977, *84*, 62-80.

Raisman, G., and Field, P. Sexual dimorphism in the preoptic area of the rat. *Science*, 1971, *173*, 731-733.

Raisman, G., and Field, P. Sexual dimorphism in the neuropil of the preoptic area of the rat and its dependence on neonatal androgen. *Brain Research*, 1973, *54*, 1-29.

Ramey, E. Men's cycles. *Ms*, 1972, *preview issue*, 8-14.

Resko, J., Ploem, J., and Stadelman, H. Estrogens in fetal and maternal plasma of the rhesus monkey. *Endocrinology*, 1975, *97*, 425-430.

Rubin, J., Provenzano, F., and Luria, Z. The eye of the beholder. Parents' views on sex of newborns. *American Journal of Orthopsychiatry*, 1974, *44*, 512-519.

Salzman, F. Aggression and gender: A critique of the nature-nurture question for humans. In R. Hubbard and M. Lowe (Eds.), *Genes and Gender*. New York: Gordian, 1979.

Schafer, A., and Gray, M. Sex and mathematics. *Science*, 1981, *211*, 229.

Shapiro, B. H., Goldman, A. S., Bongiovanni, A. M., and Marino, J. M. Neonatal progesterone and feminine sexual development. *Nature*, 1976, *264*, 795-796.

Sherman, J. *Sex-related cognitive differences: an essay on theory and evidence*. Springfield: Charles Thomas, 1978.

Sherman, J. Mathematics, spatial visualization, and related factors: changes in girls and boys, grades 8-11. *Journal of Educational Psychology*, 1980, *72*, 476-482.

Sherman, J., and Fennema, E. Distribution of spatial visualization and mathematical problem solving scores: a test of Stafford's x-linked hypotheses. *Psychology of Women Quarterly*, 1978, *6*, 157-167.

Silver, R., and Feder, H. Environmental regulation of sex hormones. In R. Silver and H. Feder (Eds.), *Hormones and reproductive behavior*. San Francisco: W. H. Freeman, 1979.

Silverstein, A. *Human anatomy and physiology*. New York: John Wiley & Sons, 1980.

Star, S. L. Sex differences and the dichotomization of the brain: Methods, limits and problems in research on consciousness. In R. Hubbard and M. Lowe (Eds.), *Genes & Gender II*. New York: Gordian Press, 1979.

Tobach, E. Interview. *AWIS newsletter*, 1977, *6*, 1-12.

Toran-Allerand, C. D. Gonadal hormones and brain development: cellular aspects of sexual differentiation. *American Zoologist*, 1978 *18*, 553-565.

Valdés, E., del Castillo, C., Gutiérrez, R., Larrea, F., Medina, M., and Pérez-Palacios, G. Endocrine studies and successful treatment in a patient with true hermaphroditism. *Acta Endocrinologica*, 1979, *91*, 184-192.

Walker, P. A., and Money, J. Prenatal androgenization of females. In M. Marois (Ed.), *Hormones*. Basel: Karger, 1972.

Wittig, M. The category of sex. *Feminist Issues*, 1982, *2*, 63-68.

Wittig, M. A., and Petersen, A. *Sex related differences in cognitive functioning*. New York: Academic Press, 1979.

Chapter 5
Theories of Human Origins and Cultural Evolution: Man the Hunter

To reappropriate the biosocial sciences for new practices and theories, a critical history of the physiological politics based on domination that have been central in animal sociology is important. The biosocial sciences have not simply been sexist mirrors of our own social world. They have also been tools in the reproduction of that world, both in supplying legitimating ideologies and in enhancing material power.

Donna Haraway, 1978, p. 25

Thus far I have described and criticized biological theories and experimental work aimed at establishing the genetic or hormonal or otherwise biological basis for temperamental and behavioral sex differences and the kinds of social relationships that characterize our gender-stratified cultures. Implicit in such biological explanations is the assumption that the human behaviors and forms of social organization, such as hierarchies and relationships of dominance and subordinance that we see in our Western industrialized cultures, have always characterized human existence. Thus, until recently, efforts by the traditional disciplines to reconstruct the course of human evolution, as another approach to understanding how we came to be the way we are (or seem to be) and why we behave as we do, have assumed, as though eternally present, the very hierarchical and gender-differentiated characteristics and behaviors that they were seeking to explain. The results, predictably enough, have been theories that appear perfectly and logically to explain the development of the human cultures with which we are most familiar.

The predominant theory relevant to human cultural evolution for at least two decades has been the Man-the-Hunter theory. The theory that humanity originated in the club-wielding man-ape, aggressive and masterful, is so widely accepted as scientific fact and vividly secure in our popular culture as to seem self-evident. This is the view of the male as provider of food for his dependents; bonding with other males to hunt and to defend; inventing, creating, speaking, and evolving.

In a very real sense our intellect, interests, emotions, and basic social life—all are evolutionary products of the success of the hunting adaptation. (Washburn and Lancaster, 1968, p. 293)

115

To assert the biological unity of mankind is to affirm the importance of the hunting way of life. . . . The biology, psychology, and customs that separate us from the apes—all these we owe to the hunters of time past. (Ibid; p. 303)

And, of course, " . . . it was the men who hunted the game, fought the enemies and made the decisions" (Fox, 1967). Where, we may wonder, were the women? Was their only role and destiny in our evolutionary history to be incubators, as is clearly implicit in Man-the-Hunter theories of human origins?

It may help in appreciating how pervasive and at the same time almost unconsciously implicit these theories about our human origins are in our minds if we stop here for a moment and allow whatever representation of prehistoric life we have to rise to consciousness. For most of us a cultural stereotype will appear. It will be a small band of fierce-looking, purposeful males carrying weapons and stalking game. If women appear at all, they are at the edge of the picture, placid-looking, holding babies, squatting by the fire, and stirring the contents of a pot. Scientific theory, in yet another form, has become a part of popular culture and of an ideology that finds modern social arrangements and gender relationships to be part of the natural order of things now and for millions of years past.

The Man-the-Hunter theory, in essence, describes the process whereby our increasingly upright bipedal (male) ancestors, from about 15 to 4 million years ago, used their freed hands to fashion tools and weapons for hunting (Washburn and Lancaster, 1968). Men banded together to hunt large animals and to share in the kill that they carried back to their female and young dependents. This primary sexual division led to an intensification of the sexual division of labor and of sexual differentiation in psychological and temperamental characteristics. The Man-the-Hunter theory thus explains female dependence upon males for survival and the evolution (among males) of cooperation and sharing, communication, and the invention of tools, weapons, equipment, *and* art. The origin of men as hunters is also linked with the origins and evolution of a presumed "killer" instinct in males that accounts for war, torture, homicide, and modern day hunting; and with the origins of male competitiveness, aggressivity, daring, and creativity that account for male dominance over women in all aspects of personal, social, political and economic life.

One is next led to wonder whether such a theory emerged from a mass of incontrovertible "facts" and just happens so felicitously to explain modern day social arrangements and inequalities, or instead represents a creation or construction argued back from the uncomfortable awareness that men's contributions to civilization have never been separate from their acts of violence, destruction, and domination. A theory that can show the positive contributions and the violences alike to be inevitable consequences of the same characteristics that ensured the survival and evolution of the species—the courage, strength, and aggressivity of man, the hunter—is a welcome addition indeed to social scientific theory and popular lore.

In this chapter I shall indicate some of the scientific roots of Man-the-Hunter theories of human cultural evolution and then show how available evidence from archeology, primatology, and anthropology suggests that the social hunting of large animals is a relatively recent development and could not explain either human origins or the uniquely human aspects of our cultures. At the same time I shall present alternative interpretations of the same bodies of data and suggest that the nature of the evidence and of processes of change cannot support any Single Cause theory of human cultural evolution.

SOME SCIENTIFIC ROOTS OF CONTEMPORARY THEORIES OF HUMAN CULTURAL EVOLUTION

Studies and theories from a multitude of disciplines have converged in the efforts to explain the origins and evolution of the social and political organization of human "society" (in reality, of Western patriarchal, industrialized societies): primate anatomy and physiology, animal sociology (animal behaviors and social groups), physical anthropology and paleontology (the study of variations in structure and function and the correlations between them among humans, other primates, and fossil remains), comparative (across species) psychology or psychobiology, sexual and reproductive physiology and neuroendocrinology, population genetics, evolutionary and ecological field biology, and social or cultural anthropology. The major contributors to evolutionary speculations have usually synthesized theories and observations from a number of these disciplines.

In two recent essays, Donna Haraway (1978) has provided an analysis of the historical and philosophical development since the early 1900s of the ideas linking the human organism and animal sociology with a natural economy of the body politic and leading to contemporary theories and beliefs about human origins and human "nature." She describes the powerful ideological, linguistic, and metaphorical connections that have been made for many centuries between the political and the physiological. The perception of human society, of the social order or body politic, as an organism has permeated political theory since the time of the ancient Greeks. During the period of the Industrial Revolution, that link was especially evident in the concepts and terminologies ("survival of the fittest") shared by political theories of the marketplace and by biological theories as influential as those of Darwin. The significant element in that union of the political and physiological that Haraway considers to be critical for our understanding of the full social impact of science is that it

'. . . has been a major source of ancient and modern justifications of domination, especially of domination based on differences seen as natural, given, inescapable, and therefore moral. (p. 22)

Haraway shows that the principle of domination is deeply embedded in the theory and practice of contemporary natural sciences, especially those that seek to explain human behaviors and social organization. The particular field that has been important in this regard has been animal sociology, particularly primatology, where, Haraway documents, implicit political ideas of domination became an analytical principle; human social relations became embodied in the content and procedures of these presumably descriptive natural sciences. Those sciences then served to reinforce a "vision of the natural and cultural necessity of domination" (p. 37). In particular, "animal sociology has been central in the development of the most thorough naturalization of patriarchal division of authority in the body politic and in reduction of the body politic to sexual physiology" (p. 26).

Haraway begins her historical analysis, which will be only briefly described here, with the work of Clarence R. Carpenter, who trained in the laboratories of Robert M. Yerkes, a pioneer in psychobiological studies of captive apes in the 1920s, 1930s, and 1940s, and was also a central figure linking science, government, foundations, intelligence testing, and "human engineering." Yerkes, whose work was commented upon in Chapter 2 by Josie, Ruth Herschberger's chimpanzee spokesperson, was influential in promoting sexuality as a subject for scientific investigation. Through his observations and interpretations linking female chimpanzee sexuality to male power and privilege (females trading sex for food and status), thus making an economic link between physiology and politics, he sought to establish sex, reproduction, and male dominance among primates as the bases for the emergence of human social relationships. These were assumptions that Carpenter automatically incorporated into his own pioneering observations of free-ranging Asian monkeys which he collected and transported to an island off Puerto Rico. Placing his findings within the framework of influential functionalist, evolutionary, biological, and social scientific theories between the two world wars, he based his work "on principles of hierarchical order of the body and body politic" (p. 31). Carpenter was convinced of the importance of male dominance and male hierarchies in intragroup organization. He perceived male dominance to be strongly correlated with successful sexual access to estrous females, and hence clearly evolutionarily significant and advantageous, since genes for "aggressivity" would be selectively transmitted. During this era covering approximately the first three decades of the twentieth century, Haraway concludes that the political principle of domination became transformed into the "legitimating scientific principle of dominance as a natural property with a physical-chemical base. Manipulations, concepts, organizing principles—the entire range of tools of the science—must be seen to be penetrated by the principle of domination" (p. 35).

An English physician and scientist, Solly Zuckerman, combined interests in paleontology, physical anthropology, reproductive physiology, and zoology to make significant theoretical contributions in the 1930s and later decades, when he also became a most influential figure in British science and administration. He held the conviction that "sexual physiology is the foundation of primate social order" and that hunting had crucial consequences for the sexual division of labor and the universality of the institution of the human family. Beginning in the early 1950s, Sherwood Washburn, a physical anthropologist and primatologist, made important contributions to evolutionary theory by formulating the possible relationships among bipedalism, upright posture, increased hand use, tool using, and the development of the brain and language, as described in Chapter 3. He is also the person primarily associated with the Man-The-Hunter theory of human cultural and psychological evolution as outlined briefly earlier in this chapter, further developing with collaborators the concept of the evolutionary importance of aggression and hierarchical ordering among monkeys, apes, and humans. Haraway presents the interesting parallel analysis of the primatologist Thelma Rowell, who, operating within the same theoretical framework as Zuckerman, rejected his theories of female passivity and male dominance and the association between male aggressivity and reproductive success; and of the anthropologists Nancy Tanner and Adrienne Zihlman, who, operating within Washburn's theoretical framework of social and evolutionary functionalism, rejected his Man-The-Hunter theory and provided a sociobiological account of human evolutionary descent from woman, the gatherer. Washburn himself, while providing an important theoretical context for use by Sociobiologists, has been a critic of the new Sociobiology and of uncritical extrapolations from apes to human behavior (see Chapter 2) and, as Haraway points out, has also been an important influence and advisor for feminist and traditional investigators alike.

There are other important contributors within the Man-The-Hunter tradition who present interesting paradoxes that can be added to Haraway's account. Frank Beach, a comparative psychologist, has been a pioneering investigator over the past three decades in studies of the sexual and reproductive behavior of animals and the influences of hormones on that behavior. He had been careful to affirm the importance, however, of social context in understanding animal (or human) behaviors, as well as the principle that hormones cannot "cause" the occurrence of particular behavior patterns (Beach, 1974a). These convictions did not, however, interfere with Beach's writing a lengthy philosophical article on evolution, within the Yerkes-Zuckerman-Washburn tradition that Haraway outlines, that would pass today as the production of a committed Wilsonian Sociobiologist. Among other things, he wrote:

> Male genotypes that were above average in promoting those characteristics specifically related to effective performance of the hunter role were especially adaptive from the point of view of group survival. (1974b, p. 351)

Beach states in another paragraph that these genetic characteristics are "certain emotional tendencies such as less fearfulness and greater willingness to venture from the safety of the home base." He continues:

> Within the female population, natural selection favored perpetuation and dissemination of those gene patterns which contributed most to behavior consonant with nonhunting, with gathering, with remaining near the home base. (Ibid; p. 351)

The circumspection Beach advocates with respect to interpretations about the role of hormones on behavior, his own area of expertise, he casts aside in his speculations about the evolutionary origins of presumed gender differences and the function of genes in determining such dubiously biological characteristics as fearfulness, adventuresomeness, nonhunting, and remaining near home base.

But then within the context of a symposium (and subsequent book), Beach was clearly stung by the casual dismissal of comparative psychology, which is Beach's discipline, in E. O. Wilson's book, *Sociobiology* (1975). He reacted logically enough, as perhaps a feminist scholar might to the trivialization of her life's work by one of the eminent fathers in her field. Wilson had proclaimed that comparative psychology is "destined to be cannibalized by neurophysiology and sensory physiology from one end and sociobiology from the other" (p. 6). This is necessary because "the future, it seems clear, cannot be with the ad hoc terminology, crude models, and curve fitting that characterize most of contemporary ethology and comparative psychology." In response, Beach refers to Wilson as "the high priest of sociobiology" (1978, p. 116) and proceeds to dismember Sociobiological methodology with sarcasm:

> I recognize that in . . . sociobiology the postulates are sacrosanct by definition and need never be proved. . . . However, a distressing myopia impedes my labored search for reassuringly tangible connections between . . . the sociobiologist's formidable postulates and impeccable mathematical theoretical models and . . . the grubby raw material of empirical evidence with which a pedestrian comparative psychologist perforce must deal. (1978, p. 117)

This interchange perhaps suggests more poignantly than any theoretical formulation that I may offer the fragil and subjective nature of theory making and the influence that scientists' personalities, experiences, and beliefs have on the perspectives they incorporate into and express by their scientific writings.

With the advent of Sociobiology in the late 1970s, evolutionary reconstructions passed beyond speculation and hypotheses to become stated as fact:

> What we can conclude with some degree of confidence is that primitive men lived in small territorial groups, within which males were dominant over females. (E. O. Wilson, 1975, p. 567)

. . .sexual selection would tend to be linked with hunting prowess, leadership, skill at tool making, and other visible attributes that contribute to the success of the family and the male band. (Ibid., p. 569)

But also during the 1970s, countercurrents were beginning to stir. In a landmark paper first appearing in 1971, Sally Slocum (1975) discussed the problem of male bias in anthropology, pointing out that the choice of asking certain questions *and not others* grows out of the cultural context in which anthropologists exist. While by 1971 Western anthropologists had begun to recognize their ethnic, racial, class, and academic biases, Slocum first demonstrated the *male* bias in the Man-The-Hunter theory of evolution. She described her alternate version of evolution, which takes into account the participation of women as gatherers and mothers, and suggested the critical role such activities may have played in the evolution of food-sharing, cooperation, and the invention of containers and tools, all essential features for the evolution of the cooperative activity of large-scale social hunting. This line of investigation and writing has been carried forward by Nancy Tanner and Adrienne Zihlman (1976) and others as will be described in succeeding pages.

During the past decade, it has become clear that there is a paucity of data either to support any theory of the signal importance of large-scale hunting as a driving force in evolution millions of years ago or to suggest that it even existed earlier than about 100,000 years ago. Furthermore, studies from a number of disciplines suggest a variety of interpretations of data bearing on our evolutionary history. In evaluting these studies, which I shall describe, some general considerations need to be taken into account.

GENERAL PROBLEMS IN THE RECONSTRUCTION OF HUMAN CULTURAL ORIGINS

First, it is important to remember that we are discussing a time frame of millions of years over which these evolutionary developments occurred from the time of *Ramapithecus* to *Homo sapiens*. The developments all represent interacting evolutionary and cultural *processes* that occurred unevenly among different populations over different time spans and in particular places and environments; there was no smooth and uniform progression of evolution everywhere from one form or phenomenon to another. As a corollary to the above, it is not profitable or reasonable to seek Single Event hypotheses of the causality of any evolutionary phenomenon, whether it is human inventiveness or female subordination.

A second problem involved in the reconstruction of early human life and cultural evolutionary processes concerns the nature of the fossil and archeological records. The fossil record available for study in no way represents an adequate sample of the human populations once inhabiting the planet. For example, there is a fossil gap of about 4 million years between about 8 or 9 and 4 or 5 million years ago. For the other millenia, many parts of the puzzle are also still missing. Another facet of the sampling problem concerns the differential perishability of fossil and archeological remains. Many behaviors, social relationships, and activities either leave no material by-products or are associated with material remains that, under most conditions, would not survive processes of decay. Thus, materials such as stone, bone, tooth, or horn are likely to be preserved in the archeological record, while plant materials, wood, bark, or other perishables will not be represented at most sites. It is for this reason that Leakey and Lewin (1977) suggest that the importance of tool making and using as driving forces in evolution may well have been exaggerated, since for a very long time bone, tooth, and stone tools have been the only fossil evidence we have had to indicate what our prehistoric ancestors *did*. This need not, however, lead to the conclusion that such tools or weapons represent the *only* or even the most important thing that they did. For similar reasons Isaac (1978) believes there has been an overemphasis on the importance of meat-eating, since bones become fossilized while plants generally do not. Isaac states,

> It is clear that as long as we do not correct for the imbalance created by the durability of bone as compared with that of plant residues, studies of human evolution will tend to have a male bias! (p. 121)

Theories concerning human evolution must take into account these difficulties in sampling. Reconstructions must account for and be consistent with all of the fossil evidence that does exist, and, on the other hand, must consider those aspects of material culture that did not leave fossilized residues. Important omissions are a pervasive problem in Man-The-Hunter theories. In order to complete the research process, we must draw on other sources of information, such as observations of the living nonhuman primates and modern gatherer-hunting societies. Studies of great apes can suggest what behaviors may have been within the physical and intellectual capabilities of early hominid bipeds under similar ecological conditions. The study of modern gatherer-hunter groups can show the range of foods, patterns of resource procurement and tool use, and the material by-products of various social arrangements characteristic of groups generally adapted to their environments. Such studies provide information suggesting the types of problems and solutions that may have characterized the life of our prehistoric ancestors in various areas until agriculture began to replace foraging as a means of subsistence about 10 to 15 thousand years ago. These two sources of information, if used cautiously, can be utilized to supplement and enhance our interpretations of the archeological remains.

Even armed with the maximum amount of information currently available for study—the fossil and archeological records and studies of living human and nonhuman primates—the amount of knowledge we do *not* possess is so vast that no one can claim a definitive theory of human origin and evolution, either morphological or cultural. That is, as previously noted, the fossil record is fragmentary and subject to varying interpretations concerning dating, classification, and inference. Second, relatively few contemporary foraging societies have been studied, and those findings are variously interpreted by different anthropologists; in fact, anthropologists are still defining appropriate methods of studying relict gatherer-hunter groups as a means of better interpreting the archeological record. Third, the field of primatology is still in its early stages of development. While a number of superbly detailed studies have been conducted of particular populations of primates in specific ecological settings, much remains to be learned about other species or other groups of the same species in different habitats. Accordingly, the information available does permit the generation of testable hypotheses, but not the neat and tidy packages that are promoted quite regularly as final answers to the questions of how we have come to be the way we are. While our ignorance is immense, there is sufficient information to make it conspicuous when popularizers of theories ignore contradictory evidence, fail to indicate the unknowns, or distinguish between their speculations and what appears to be known.

Even though I shall present what are generally accepted as "facts," for example, that modified stone tools date back to about 2 to 2.5 million years ago, it must be understood that someday new archeological findings or interpretations may change current notions and could, for example, date stone tool-making to 3 million or more years ago. Finally, I should like to make it clear before examining the relevant archeological, primatological, and anthropological record, that I do not like the Man-The-Hunter theory of human evolution because it does not take women into account in *human* evolution, and because it starts with a set of assumptions concerning the eternal nature of the characteristics, temperaments, roles, responsibilities, and capacities of women and men and the relationships between, and forms of social organization of, the two sexes. I consider these to be serious philosophical, conceptual, and methodological problems that make the theory scientifically weak. It is, furthermore, not supported by available evidence from archeology, anthropology, or primatology and for this reason has been seriously criticized also by anthropologists and archeologists working in this field (Lovejoy, 1981; Slocum, 1971; Tanaka, 1976; Tanner and Zihlman, 1976; Teleki, 1975;). We can, then, proceed to an examination of the evidence from those three disciplines.

ARCHEOLOGICAL EVIDENCE BEARING ON HUNTING; HUNTING AS SYMBOL AND RITUAL

The archeological record indicates that the oldest known definite stone artifacts date back to about 2 to 2.5 million years ago. These are small hand-sized stones from which flakes were chipped leaving edges that may have been used for cutting or scraping (Isaac and Leakey, 1979; Leakey and Lewin, 1977). There is no reason to infer that these tools were weapons used to kill animals. The earliest association of cutting or scraping tools with the bones of large animals dates to the period between 1.5 and 0.5 million years ago. It is assumed by most anthropologists and archeologists that they were used to remove the flesh from animals found dead, sick, or mired and unable to flee (Isaac, 1978; Leakey, 1971; Tanner and Zihlman, 1976; Zihlman, 1978). The earliest evidence of actual systematic hunting dates to a site 500,000 years old in Spain, where elephants were regularly mired and butchered in a narrow pass (Crompton, 1980; Tanner and Zihlman, 1976). It was not until the Neanderthal period, 100,000 to 35,000 years ago, that the first composite tools appeared; that is, attached flaked stone heads or points to wooden shafts to make hafted axes or spears that could be used as projectile weapons to kill large animals for the kind and scale of hunting that is postulated to be the signal force in human cultural evolution (Fagan, 1980). The earliest undisputed evidence for hunting large animals with weapons, an elephant with a spear between its ribs, was found in a site dating back about 100,000 years (Tanner and Zihlman, 1976), and bows and arrows appeared only about 15,000 years ago. In contrast to the sites in Africa, Europe, and northern Asia, no archeological collections of animal bones and stone tools have been found in southeast Asia, even though the fossil evidence for hominids is abundant. Zihlman (1978) concludes that *Homo erectus* in southeast Asia relied on plant foods, insects, and small animals rather than large game animals.

In short, the fossil evidence suggests that upright, bipedal humans evolved without benefit of the social hunting of large animals from the time of *Ramapithecus* about 15 million years ago or *Australopithecus* of 3 to 4 million years ago to the period between *Homo erectus* of 500,000 years ago and *Homo sapiens neanderthalensis* of about 100,000 years ago, a period constituting over 99 percent of hominid evolutionary time. During that same period of time, the brain increased dramatically from the estimated 300 cc. size of *Ramapithecus* or the 400 to 600 cc. of various australopithecine and *Homo habilis* brains to the neanderthal *Homo sapiens* brain of 100,000 to 35,000 years ago, which is approximately the size of the average modern *Homo sapiens'* brain (1450 cc.). Thus, as described in Chapter 3, the hominid brain experienced a growth spurt beginning around 3 million years ago and was already levelling off when large-game social hunting evidently developed. The dramatic enlargement of the brain tapered off around the period (100,000 to 35,000 years ago) during which a dramatic foward leap occurred in cultural complexity: not only large-scale co-operative hunting with hafted weapons, but also rituals, symbolization, language, representational art, and increased sophistication of toolmaking. Rather than being a cause of the uniquely human aspects of hominid evolution and the human mind, cooperative hunting appears to have been one of the cultural developments made possible by an advanced technology and a brain close to the capacity of modern *Homo sapiens*.

There is no denying, however, that once established among various peoples, cooperative social hunting itself became a significant cultural force in evolving hominid societies. But this is not necessarily because of the features obviously intrinsic to hunting itself, such as the obtaining of meat for the diet. Meat as a dietary supplement had probably always been available and eaten in the form of small game (where it existed), gathered as a part of regular foraging activities, as in contemporary foraging societies. Nor would its significance necessarily lie, as has been claimed in the Man-The-Hunter theory, in its being the prime force generating uniquely human characteristics, such as language, planning, advanced toolmaking, and cooperation. These capacities had probably largely developed by the time large-scale hunting appeared. Rather, during the period between 100,000 and 35,000 years ago (the period during which ritual and symbolic systems appear in the archeological record), large animal cooperative hunting, mainly by men, may have begun to attain greater significance in some cultures for ritual and symbolic reasons. These ritual and symbolic meanings could be quite separate from the meat-obtaining rewards of hunting and, in any particular society, would have particular significance within the context of that society's history, ecology, technology, and symbolic system. The symbolic meanings could be related, for example, to the significance of male networks of cooperation and exchange or to the establishment of a male sphere of authority separate from the women's spheres of production and reproduction.

More specifically, it is possible that the development of large-scale hunting with hafted weapons as a male activity symbolized, embodied, and perhaps even advanced an important aspect of gender differentiation in the division of labor. Emerging, as it appears to have done, during the period when a quantitative leap forward occurred in tool and weapon technology, hunting may have represented (in some places or times) differential access by women and men to tools and weapons and to tool and weapon technology. While the specifics vary from one culture to another, Tabet (1982) argues that it is a common feature of contemporary preindustrial cultures—hunting-gathering, fishing, horticulture, and agriculture—that women are underequipped and a technological gap exists between women and men. This general characteristic manifests itself in a number of ways. In foraging societies, even when the major contribution to the group's subsistence is produced through women's work in gathering, hunting or fishing, as is usually the case, women's tools are rudimentary—sticks and nets or baskets—while the more advanced tools—harpoons, spears, spearthrowers, axes, knives, bows and arrows, and boats—are made, used by, and reserved for men. While both women and men can and do use rudimentary tools, women, in general, are prohibited the use of weapons or weapon-tools and the use of the more complex instruments of production. Usually woman's main tool is the primitive digging stick or her bare hands for the gathering of plants, animals, or fish. Tabet emphasizes the importance of the male monopoly of weapons in hunting-gathering societies (or their prohibition to women) to the relations between the sexes, both because of the significance of weapons in themselves and because weapons, such as the spearthrower, often are also privileged and more advanced tools of production.

In horticulture and agriculture, the work of soil preparation, seeding, weeding, and harvesting is done by digging sticks and hoes, usually by women, but it may be done by women or men; where the plow is introduced, it becomes a male tool. The work of clearing the fields and building fences requires stone or metal axes, knives, or machetes, and these are used almost exclusively by men. Further, when tools can be activated by wind, water, or animals, they are used by men, while women continue such operations by hand with tools like grinding and pounding stones and sticks and mortar and pestle. Tabet describes another area of gender differentiation with respect to tools and labor that results in male control over women's production. Hard materials, such as metals, stone, bone, wood, and shell are worked exclusively by men in 94 percent (horn and shell) to 99.8 percent (metal) of contemporary foraging and other nonindustrial societies. Soft or pliable materials can be worked by women or men, using bare hands or crude tools, whereas hard materials require more advanced tools. This means that all tools and weapons are also made almost exclusively by men, including the tools of women, such as the primitive digging stick and mortar and pestle. Tabet's argument is that the sexual division of labor is always a relationship of control and is the result not the cause of differential use of and access to tools.

While we do not yet know when or how gender differentiations developed, archeologists interested in the origins of language have dated the development of symbolization, abstraction, and ritualization to the same period in which evidence appears, from other archeological findings I have cited, for large-game social hunting and advanced tool-and weaponmaking. It seems likely that these are related evolutionary phenomena. I am suggesting that large-scale social hunting was one of the many ritualized forms in which gender differentiations began to develop in the period between 100,000 and 35,000 years ago, when the human capacities for symbolization, language, and ritualization fully appeared and when tool and weapon technology was sufficiently advanced to make differential access a social possibility.

PRIMATOLOGICAL EVIDENCE BEARING ON HUNTING

In theorizing about early hominid evolution of hand use with bipedal posture, it is reasonable to assume that early hominids continued, with increasing skill, to do those same activities that were part of the selection forces that favored upright posture and bipedal locomotion. We assume these activities primarily comprised food gathering–foraging for seeds, nuts, fruits, plants, and insects; digging for roots; and catching small animals first in forests, then in savanna-woodland-fringe forest areas over the hundreds of thousands or millions of years when forests were receding. Among present-day chimps, it has been estimated that about 95 percent of the diet consists of fruits and plants; 5 percent consists of insects, eggs, and small animals (Zihlman, 1976). Gorillas appear to be strict vegetarians. Individual chimpanzees forage, find, and eat their own food on the spot. Occasionally they carry animal prey to a tree to eat or carry nuts a short distance in order to break them open. Chimpanzees have been observed to use tools: stripped twigs, bark, or grasses to fish for termites and ants; rocks to crack open nuts and fruits; sticks to knock down bananas; crumpled leaves to mop up water from hollows or brains from the skulls of dead animals (Goodall, 1968).

In addition to the fact that chimpanzees prepare and use tools, occasionally walk upright, share food, and communicate social and environmental information, they also are similar to humans anatomically and genetically. Comparative studies of proteins, DNA, and chromosomes have shown a virtual identity of many of these molecules, suggesting to some molecular biologists an evolutionary divergence between the two species about 5 to 6 million years ago (Sarich and Wilson, 1967). For these reasons chimpanzees may be viewed, though cautiously, as indicating some features and behaviors that may have characterized some hominid populations ancestral to Australopithecines and other hominids millions of years ago (Tanner and Zihlman, 1976). (I am not suggesting that this is because such behaviors have been genetically transmitted but rather may have been within the biological and social capacity of our ancestors.)

In his detailed critique of Man-The-Hunter theories of hominization (i.e., of the divergence of humans from apes) and of human behavioral evolution, Geza Teleki (1975) refutes what he considers to be myths of human uniqueness in subsistence patterns and the false dichotomizations made of the diets and subsistence behaviors of apes and humans. He sees the basic erroneous assumption to be that hunting behavior originated within the primate evolutionary sequence as a uniquely human pattern, which in turn generated other unique human behaviors. The myths and false dichotomizations that follow the assumption include the following: that humans are carnivores and great apes are frugivors (fruit-eaters) and vegetarians; that men hunt and apes do not; that men hunt cooperatively but apes do not; that the pursuit and capture of game requires an advanced technological base; that language is necessary for cooperative hunting; that men share or exchange meat and apes do not; that men transport meat and apes do not. Teleki focuses his attention in this analysis on Sub-Saharan Africa, a region extending from South Africa to Ethiopia and including a range of ecological conditions from desert to savanna to forests, where he and others have extensively studied chimpanzee and baboon behaviors. Since this is also the region presently inhabited by three well-studied gatherer-hunter populations—the Mbuti Pygmies, the Hadsa, and the Kalahari Desert !Kung—and formerly inhabited by our hominid ancestors whose fossil remains provide the most complete archeological record presently available for one area, Teleki was able to impose some historical and geographic continuity upon his analysis.

The first important observation Teleki makes is that with the exception of the specialized leaf-eating colobine monkey, primates—monkeys, apes and humans—

are omnivorous, with the generalized primate diet including leaves, buds, fruits, berries, bark, nuts, seeds and grains, roots and bulbs, honey, eggs, insects, fish and molluscs, reptiles, birds, and mammals. As I shall discuss in more detail later, meat constitutes only about 20 to 30 percent of the diet of most gatherer-hunter peoples, most of it in the form of small game that is collected or trapped. And just as humans are not carnivores but omnivores, so are monkeys and apes not vegetarians but also omnivores, since they eat meat too. Chimpanzees and baboons not only opportunistically seize and eat immobilized prey they happen to come across, but actively engage in the seeking out, pursuit, and capture of prey.

The next dichotomy Teleki refutes concerns cooperative hunting. He points out that most, but not all, hunting by humans is a solitary or paired activity, so that while group cooperative hunting occurs, it is by no means diagnostic of humans or essential for success. On the other hand, Teleki and others have observed many cases of adult chimpanzees in groups of two to five stalking prey together, coordinating their movements over long periods with great precision (although without vocalizations or gestures) until they had isolated and cornered their prey or decided, in some fashion not discernible to the human observers, to give up the chase. Once the predators catch, kill, and divide up the prey, each attracts a cluster of chimpanzees who request a share by a variety of gestures and characteristic vocalizations. These efforts to procure a share are successful more often than not. Teleki notes that food-sharing is the only aspect of the hunting process that is characterized by communications through vocalization and gesture. After the sharing process and the initial eating, individual chimpanzees have been seen carrying some of the prey around with them during the day or to the nest to eat at night. The sharing of meat among human hunters is variable, ranging from nonexistent to persistent. In short, chimpanzees cooperate in hunting, communicate requests, share and transport food.

Bringing together the recent evidence on the subsistence activities of contemporary baboons, chimpanzees, and humans in Africa, Teleki shows both the similarities as well as the differences existing among primate species that coexist in the same habitat. He suggests that prior to the time that hominids and possibly the great apes evolved, there was an evolutionary development beginning with omnivorous forest-dwelling primates among whom predation on mammals arose in some species. He argues that predation would have emerged at many spatial and temporal loci, appearing and disappearing within various populations before becoming fixed as a species trait. He furthermore believes that while environmental factors are, and probably always were, important in molding dietary habits at particular habitats, the occurrence, extent of, and social relationships around predation or hunting have also been influenced by social factors among all primates. It is these social factors that account in part for the observed differences in subsistence behaviors among primate species that live in the same habitat.

Thus, Teleki sees few qualitative or exclusive differences in subsistence behaviors between humans and apes but rather suggests:

The nutritional as well as behavioral components of primate subsistence can be scaled along a single spectrum whereupon some species may occupy shorter or longer segments than do others, but most occupy overlapping and interlocking segments rather than discrete intervals. No species, in other words, exhibits exactly the same subsistence parameters as does another species on the spectrum, yet each species holds some features in common with all other species. For instance, the Gombe chimpanzees differ from the Kalahari bushmen in some specific patterns (e.g., weapon technology), but their collector-predator and gatherer-hunter lifestyles overlap on many broad patterns (e.g., cooperation in pursuit, distribution of meat). Our assumptions about man as the hunter of game and about ape as the collector of plants seem, as a result, to be no longer tenable, and since it was these assumptions which formed our current concepts of human origins and evolution, the concepts themselves may no longer be tenable. (p. 155)

His analysis and conclusion leave open the possibility, as I suggested previously, that the unique contribution that humans made to hunting, in some cultures at least, was not the technological advancement of a basic subsistence activity, but rather its elevation to an activity endowed with symbolic and ritual significance and meanings.

ANTHROPOLOGICAL EVIDENCE BEARING ON HUNTING

The oldest hominid teeth thus far found indicate that early upright hominids were also basically plant-eaters or omnivores rather than carnivores. *Australopithecus* and her contemporary *Homo habilis* cousins had the large, worn, grinding molars of plant-eating animals and not the long, tearing canines of carnivores. Studies of modern gatherer-hunter nomadic groups have shown that the gathering of plant foods and small animals, mainly by women, is the most dependable food source in most environments and contributes 60 to 90 percent of the total diet by weight and calories (Gould, 1980; Lee, 1968, 1979). On the basis of his study of the Kalahari San cultures, Richard Lee concluded that the hunting of mammals is the least reliable source of food and, therefore, should be generally less important than either gathering or fishing. To test this hypothesis, he examined data from 58 societies in Africa, Asia, Australia, and South and North America and found that half of them emphasize gathering, one-third, fishing, and the remaining one-sixth, hunting of mammals (1968). Kay Martin and Barbara Voorhies (1975) examined 90 societies, using the same ethnographic sources as Lee, and found gathering to be the primary food-obtaining activity in 58 percent and hunting in 25 percent. Hunting of land and sea mammals is of most importance only in the coldest of climates where there is "no viable alternative subsistence strategy" (Lee, 1968, p. 42). Lee concludes that "the people we have classified as 'hunters' apparently depend for most of their subsistence on sources *other* than meat . . . " (p. 42). And further, "Since a 30 to 40 percent input of meat is such a consistent target for modern hunters in a variety of habitats, is it not reasonable to postulate a similar percentage for prehistoric hunters?" (p. 43). He ends by suggesting a shift of focus away from the dramatic and exceptional, away from ancient hunters and toward gatherer-hunters.

The book in which this article of Lee's appeared provides another example of the dissonance that may develop between cherished beliefs and more or less objective evidence. The book, edited by Lee and DeVore, was an outgrowth of a conference on nomadic foragers, where it had repeatedly been shown that gathering by women was the primary subsistence activity, but it was nonetheless entitled *Man the Hunter*. Similarly, a subsequent book also edited by Lee and DeVore (1976) was devoted to the !Kung San and provided evidence once again that gathering is the primary subsistence activity among the various nomadic bands. Yet in its Foreword, Sherwood Washburn wrote " . . . it may well be that it was the complex of weapons-hunting-bipedalism which accounts for the evolutionary origin of man" (p. xv).

Jiro Tanaka, an anthropologist in Lee's group, notes that in all the African sites where hominization is thought to have taken place, gathering is the basis of subsistence of extant foraging groups even in areas such as the East African savanna where game is abundant. He concludes

> . . . we can hardly imagine that the ancient inhabitants of Africa once derived their diet primarily from hunting even if we take into account the difference in environment between the Pleistocene and the present. (1976, p. 116)

Despite the importance of gathered food in the diet, meat is nonetheless generally more prized than plant food, and hunting may be viewed as more prestigious. In some places this may be because game is more scarce and unpredictable or because hunting has been invested with symbolic and ritualistic significance, as I have discussed previously.

The record, then, shows that today the gathering of plant foods and small animals is the primary subsistence activity of the majority of nomadic gatherer-hunters and that women participate prominently. Unless ecological circumstances were vastly different millions of years ago, and the paleoecological record does not suggest this, it appears likely that early hominids were also principally gatherers, even after the development of the hunting of large mammals with weapons about 100,000 years ago.

ALTERNATIVES TO THE MAN-THE-HUNTER THEORY OF HUMAN CULTURAL EVOLUTION

If, then, data from archeology, primatology, and anthropology do not confirm the importance of hunting and weaponmaking as prime causal factors in the evolution of human intellect, inventiveness, language, and art, what alternative scenarios do they suggest? Starting with the assumption that prehistoric women were foragers who, unlike men, carried their nursing babies with them for three to four years (like the contemporary !Kung), Slocum (1975), Tanner (1981) and Tanner and Zihlman (1976) have suggested alternative reconstructions of the course of cultural evolution.

Since one of the evolutionary consequences of upright bipedal posture and locomotion was the loss of the grasping ability of the feet and since hominids were also losing their body fur, there came a time when babies could not cling to their mothers' backs or abdomens in the fashion of the hairy apes. At the same time, hominid babies were born even more immature and remained helpless and dependent for a much longer time than other primates. For these reasons, Slocum suggested that it would have been very important for mothers to invent baby slings to carry nursing babies on their backs, leaving their hands free for gathering. These could have been made from vines, leaves, ostrich eggshells, hides, bark, or human hair. The idea and techniques for carrying babies could then have been extended to the idea of carrying food when it became possible or necessary to collect and carry more food than could be eaten on the spot. Excess food may have been collected for the purposes of sharing, processing, or storing. On the basis of this reasoning, Slocum, as well as Tanner and Zihlman, suggest that it was probably the requirements of gathering and collecting plants, fruits, and small animals, rather than hunting large and dangerous animals, that provided the impetus for this first type of material technology—carrying devices. Furthermore, they suggest, the same requirements also provided the impetus for the use of tools: sticks, bones, and handstones to extend the reach for fruits and nuts in trees, to pry up roots and tubers, dig out burrowing animals, pulverize and chop tough plants, and crack open nuts and seeds.

Tanner and Zihlman consider an important implication and consequence of their interpretation of early human evolution to be that the amiable atmosphere of gathering plants and catching of small animals by women and men poses no natural selection pressures for aggressivity and competitiveness (at least under adequate ecological circumstances). Such pressures are an integral part of Man-The-Hunter theories, which pose a gender-dichotomous biocultural evolution. Tanner and Zihlman's assumptions are supported by the observations that most contemporary gatherer-hunters lead well-paced lives with leisure time, sociability, adequate food, and the absence, with rare exception, of aggressivity and competitiveness. They suggest that those cognitive, inventive, and social skills that are associated with the gathering-hunting mode are most responsible for early human survival and consequent evolutionary success. These include the mapping and recognition of food sources, ability to communicate this information to others, the development of complex social relationships, planning, and the teaching and learning of subsistence techniques. Furthermore, extrapolating from recent primate studies that emphasize the role of females in *selecting* sexual partners (rather than being passively *receptive to* the most successfully competitive and aggressive males, as the classical stereotypes assume), Tanner and Zihlman propose that prehistoric women selected more sociable males as those likely to participate in the care, feeding, and protection of their children. (There is no reason, however, to assume that women did not also select sociable females as sexual partners, as well as partners in the care and protection of infants and children. In fact, it is likely that proscriptions concerning sexual activity and sexual partners were a fairly recent social invention.) They argue that selection pressures were for cooperation and sociability rather than competition and aggressivity. As Haraway points out, Tanner and Zihlman provide us with an outlook that avoids "telling a tale of obsolescence of the human body caught in a hunting past" (1976, p. 59). Thus, they turn the tables on other sociobiologists by suggesting that sexual selection and human evolution were guided by sociable women rather than competitive and aggressive men.

Slocum's and Tanner and Zihlman's arguments need not imply simply a counter-theory to Man-The-Hunter; namely, that it was only Women-as-Gatherers who did the inventing and who thus account for human cultural evolution. Rather, one could say that for many millions of years, hominids (women and men) evolved as gatherers of plant and small animal foods, as available evidence suggests. It is reasonable to start with an assumption that early hominids, like contemporary chimpanzees, each foraged for his/her own needs, eating as they roamed, since little else was possible before carriers and campsites became possible. It would have been during that long period from about 15 to 5 million to about 100,000 years ago that inventiveness and technology were evolving along with those characteristics and capabilities of mind and brain, such as communication, symbolization, language, and cooperativeness, that eventually made possible the development of the social organization of all subsistence and other activities that served to minimize the risks and enhance the chances of survival. There is nothing intrinsic to hunting that distinguishes it from other social and cooperative forms of relationships around subsistence activities in its significance either for survival (except in very cold climates) or as a motive force in human cultural evolution. Because the hunting of large mammals is usually a male social venture in its contemporary forms, it has been invested with singular evolutionary importance by Western male meat-eating anthropologists.

One important value of Tanner and Zihlman's viewpoint is that it does not begin with the assumption of woman's passivity and dependence as a basis for scenario-building of human evolution. It recognizes, unlike other evolutionary scenarios, that such a premise finds no supporting evidence from any species of animals nor, with only rare and historically recent exceptions, from human cultures. Their view attaches great importance to women's childbearing and lactation, as do other biosocial theories. Unlike other biosocial theories, however, they do not see reproduction as a force leading inevitably to helplessness and dependence. Rather, they view it as a social force leading to selection for innovativeness, sociability, and cooperativeness, since they consider early foraging mothers with dependent children as being highly motivated to increase their food-gathering capabilities, to invent tools and carriers for that purpose, and to be the protectors of their young against predators. It is unlikely that we shall ever know all of the forces contributing to inventiveness, the invention of tools, and human sociability, but the value of the controversy as posed by Slocum and Tanner and Zihlman is immense, since it opens the mind to the possibility of alternative arguments that are at least as plausible and logical as traditional androcentric versions.

The models of Slocum and Tanner and Zihlman do carry the risk, however, of perpetuating single-cause or primary-event explanations of evolution and consequent assumptions about the universal and uniform course of the evolution of forms of social organization and behaviors. More specifically, they could serve to perpetuate assumptions that biological phenomena, like reproduction and, by implication, motherhood, determine the course and forms of social relations and cultural evolution, a controversial issue to be discussed in the next chapter.

Other anthropologists have proposed other factors as keys to understanding human cultural evolution. For example, Richard Lee, in a paper delivered in 1968 and recently printed for the first time in his book *The !Kung San* (1979), posed the carrying device as "the essential prerequisite, the sine qua non, of human economy." He argued that the development of food exchange and campsites were basic features of the hominid way of life. These two features made it possible, he suggests, for persons on a given day to forage in different areas, concentrate on different foods, engage in hunting with the attendant risks of catching nothing, or simply sit and develop new tools, secure in the expectation of being fed by others if their own efforts to procure food produced no edibles that day. But, Lee emphasized, neither food exchange nor homebases would be possible without the carrying devices to transport collected foods, raw materials for the manufacture of tools, and tools themselves.

Leakey and Lewin (1977), like Gordon Hewes (1964), also emphasize the singular importance that the ability to carry things would have had in allowing early hominids a certain degree of freedom with respect to their environment. Being able to transport food or water provided greater flexibility in foraging patterns as well as migration routes. It would have become possible, for example, to develop the notion of establishing campsites near a scarce resource like water in a relatively arid area and then to forage widely for plant and animal foods. Both Mary Leakey (1971) and Glynn Isaac (1978) have uncovered evidence that hominids around two million years ago carried stone tools to the site of probably mired or dead large mammals, like hippopotami, to cut away the meat. Both have also analyzed other sites dating to the same period where stone tools were associated with large collections of animal bones from a variety of species: hippopotamus, giraffe, pig, porcupine, gazelle, waterbuck, etc. These constitute the oldest known campsites. Isaac suggests that not only stones and stone tools, but also meat was transported to particular sites, an activity not observed among living nonhuman primates except for chimpanzees, who carry parts of carcasses to their nests for the night. Isaac suggests that these concentrations of stones and animal remains signify some division of subsistence tasks and organized food sharing, which would probably have included plant foods, though no fossil evidence for them exists. He believes that food-sharing is central to an understanding of human evolution over the past two million years, incorporating as it does a number of significant human developments: the ability to carry things, to fashion and use tools, to communicate, and cooperate.

SUMMARY AND CONCLUSIONS

No single factor or event, such as hunting or gathering, carrying devices or campsites, tool-use, food-exchange, or language can in itself provide *the* key to human evolution. They all represent interdependent stages of hominid development, appearing variably in different populations of prehistoric hominids, and each is a product of many interrelated processes. The degree to which any behavioral complex became developed or significant for any society was (or is in today's gatherer-hunter societies) highly variable depending on that society's particular ecological, demographic, historic, social circumstances, and symbolic systems.

One has but to read accounts of our prehistory (see for example, Fagan, 1980) to begin to appreciate the diversity of subsistence patterns and social subsistence organization developing within the varied conditions of extreme ecological variations. Thus, within Africa, for example, economic specialization arose from environmental necessity. Foraging bands on the shores of lakes and rivers lived by fishing; those in the open savanna captured game and gathered seasonally in woodlands; and those in rain forests relied on plant foods. Peoples in frigid zones live by the hunting of sea and land mammals. In addition, ecological diversity was drastically modified over many parts of the earth's surface, over time spans of tens or hundreds of thousands of years, with periods of glaciation and shifts in rainfall patterns that had significant effects on game populations and grasses (Fagan, 1980). Clearly in some areas and time periods, obtaining meat was and is essential to survival, just as vegetable foods or fish have been critical in others.

Subsistence activities within any particular habitat, whether hunting, gathering, or fishing, could have generated both the social communication and cooperativeness and the technological innovativeness that survival in particular circumstances might have required: digging sticks, stone pounders, choppers and grinders, and carrying receptacles for gathering; hooks, nets and eventually harpoons for fishing; clubs, rocks, stone flaked tools, and eventually spears and bows and arrows for hunting. Many of these innovations appeared only in the past 100,000 years, such as composite or hafted weapons, or as late as 15,000 years ago, such as bows and arrows. Nomadic foragers, with diverse subsistence techniques, constituted all the peoples of the earth until the period between 15,000 and 10,000 years ago when sedentarism and domestication of plants and animals began to develop in some parts of the world. By 2000 years ago, nomadic foragers had become a minority (Fagan, 1980) but still exist today in Africa, Australia, and elsewhere.

It is important to avoid single-cause theories of human evolution (or any other human phenomena), since they interfere with our ability to see and seek relevant data that could lead to some unforeseen and unpredetermined conclusions. They also impede our efforts to understand the complex processes and interrelationships and the non-uniform course that characterize human cultural evolution. The Man-The-Hunter theory has been such a conceptual framework, which straightjackets observations, interpretations, and understanding. One reason for its attractiveness and uncritical acceptance may be that it neatly ties together a number of puzzling and disparate phenomena of modern social existence: women's economic dependence on men, the sexual division of labor, war, and male aggressivity. Yet therein lies its central flaw. In the effort to explain the *origins* of present-day gender-associated behaviors and social arrangements, popular theories of human evolution, such as Man-The-Hunter, start with implicit assumptions about the biological basis of such behaviors and characteristics and the existence of a woman's "nature" and a man's "nature." They then reconstruct earliest evolutionary history according to an idealized image of modern industrial societies. Their central actor is the fearless, aggressive, creative, and dominant male, who generated civilization and, through his bonding and hunting with other men, fed and protected the passive, dependent, subordinate female, who generated babies. They postulate for their prehistoric model the very conditions that they are presumably attempting to understand and explain—the sexual division of labor with women as economic dependents and men as providers and doers. However, the record, inadequate as it is, strongly suggests that someone besides man was also evolving, and that she, too, was very busy.

One also suspects that the origins and consequent popularity of the Man-The-Hunter theory of evolution reflect other common ethnocentric views. Since meat-eating is a central preoccupation and seems always to have been important in our recorded Western civilizations, it is assumed to have always been central to human diets everywhere if not to survival itself. Since hunting for sport or for sustenance has been primarily a male pursuit in written history and in today's world, it has been invested with much significance and is assumed to have always been a male accomplishment of central importance to the evolution of human civilization.

While foragers may always have gathered and eaten small animals, if they were available, along with plant food, the archeological record suggests that large-scale cooperative hunting with hafted weapons developed only about 100,000 years ago. This was at the beginning of the Neanderthal period and the Mousterian culture, during which rituals, complex symbolization, representational art, perhaps language, and complex tools also appeared. I have suggested that big game social hunting may have begun at that time to assume particular cultural significance for symbolic or ritual reasons, and that these may have been related to the emergence of differential access to tools and weapons and tool-weapon technology, sexual divisions of labor, and other gender asymmetries.

REFERENCES

Beach, F. Behavioral endocrinology and the study of reproduction. The fifth annual Carl G. Hartman Lecture. The society for the study of reproduction. 1974. (a)

Beach, F. Human sexuality and evolution. In W. Montagna and W. Sadler (Eds.), *Reproductive behavior*. New York: Plenum, 1974. (b)

Beach, F. Sociobiology and interspecific comparisons of behavior. In M. S. Gregory, A. Silvers, & D. Sutch (Eds.), *Sociobiology and human nature*. San Francisco: Jossey-Bass, 1978

Crompton, R. Old bones shatter hunter myths. *Science for the people*, 1980, *12*, 5-34.

Fagan, B. M. *People of the earth. An introduction to world prehistory*. New York: Little, Brown, 1980.

Fox, R. *Kinship and marriage*. Baltimore: Penguin, 1967.

Goodall, J. The behavior of free-living chimpanzees in the Gombe Stream Reserve. *Animal Behaviour Monographs*, 1968, *1*, 165-311.

Gould, R. *Living archaeology*. Cambridge: Cambridge University Press, 1980.

Haraway, D. Animal sociology and a natural economy of the body politic, part I: a political physiology of dominance. *Signs*, 1978, *4*, 21-36.

Haraway, D. Animal sociology and a natural economy of the body politic, part II: the past is the contested zone: human nature and theories of production and reproduction in primate behavior studies. *Signs*, 1978, *4*, 37-60.

Hewes, G. Hominid bipedalism: independent evidence for the food-carrying theory. *Science*, 1964, *146*, 416-418.

Isaac, G. The food-sharing behavior of protohuman hominids. *Scientific American*, 1978, *238*, 90-108.

Isaac, G., and Leakey, R. *Human ancestors*. San Francisco: Freeman, 1979.

Leakey, M. *Olduvai gorge excavations in bed I and I, 1960-1963*. Cambridge: Cambridge University Press, 1971.

Leakey, R., and Lewin, R. *Origins*. New York: Dutton, 1977.

Lee, R. What hunters do for a living, or, how to make out on scarce resources. In R. B. Lee and I. DeVore (Eds.), *Man the hunter*. New York: Aldine, 1968.

Lee, R. *The !Kung San. Men, women, and work in a foraging society*. New York: Cambridge University Press, 1979.

Lee, R., and DeVore, I. *Kalahari hunter-gatherers*. Cambridge: Harvard University Press, 1976.

Lovejoy, C. O. The origin of man. *Science*, 1981, *211*, 341-350.

Martin, M. K., and Voorhies, B. *Female of the species*. New York: Columbia University Press, 1975.

Sarich, V., and Wilson, A. Immunological time scale for hominid evolution. *Science*, 1967, *158*, 1200-1203.

Slocum, S. Woman the gatherer: male bias in anthropology. In R. R. Reiter (Ed.), *Toward an anthropology of women*. New York: Monthly Review Press, 1975.

Tabet, P. Hands, tools, weapons. *Feminist Issues*, 1982, *2*, 3-62.

Tanaka, J. Subsistence ecology of central Kalahari San. In R. Lee and I. DeVore (Eds.), *Kalahari hunter-gatherers*. Cambridge: Harvard University Press, 1976.

Tanner, N. *On becoming human*. Cambridge: Cambridge University Press, 1981.

Tanner, N., and Zihlman, A. Women in evolution. Part I: Innovation and selection in human origins. *Signs*, 1976, *1*, 585-608.

Teleki, G. Primate subsistence patterns: Collector-predators and gatherer-hunters. *Journal of Human Evolution*, 1975, *4*, 125-184.

Washburn, S., and Lancaster, C. S. The evolution of hunting. In R. B. Lee and I. DeVore (Eds.), *Kalahari hunter-gatherers*. Cambridge: Harvard University Press, 1976.

Wilson, E. O. *Sociobiology: the new synthesis*. Cambridge, MA: Harvard University Press, 1975.

Zihlman, A. Sexual dimorphism and its behavioral implications in early hominids. In P. V. Tobias and Y. Coppens (Eds.), *Les plus anciens hominides*. Paris: C.N.R.S., 1976.

Zihlman, A. Women in evolution, part II: subsistence and social organization among early hominids. *Signs*, 1978, *4*, 4-20.

Chapter 6
The Subordinance of Women:
A Problematic Universal

> Empirically, women's social relations are neither universally dependent nor universally subordinate; women have been making culture, political decisions, and babies simultaneously and without structural conflicts in all parts of the world.
>
> Karen Sacks, 1979, p. 6

A central premise in biological explanations of the asymmetrical positions of women and men in present-day cultures is that the subordinate position of women is a universal—across all time and all cultures. It is, as well, a central premise in evolutionary theories, such as Man the Hunter, that seek to describe and explain the origins of such asymmetries.

This universal served as an unexamined assumption in traditional anthropology until work over the past decade or two by feminist and other nontraditional anthropologists brought into question not only that particular universal but the validity of the universalistic lens and framework by which Western male anthropologists have viewed and interpreted non-Western, nonindustrial cultures.

This field, one of the most dynamic and influential areas of feminist scholarship, has revealed the ethnocentric biases in Western anthropological concepts of dominance and subordinance, hierarchy, power and authority; in anthropological views concerning production and reproduction, nature and culture, domestic and political spheres, private and public life; and, finally, in anthropological assumptions concerning the cross-cultural meaning of gender. Even the gender categories of *man* and *woman*, generally assumed as universal biological givens, require analysis as cultural constructs, concepts to be understood only in relation to the cultural context that shapes their meaning and significance.

Universalistic assumptions and conclusions have always invited biological explanations: woman is eternally and everywhere subordinate because childbearing and motherhood limit her productive contributions, her mobility, and her participation in the public (the important) sphere of human activity; man is aggressive and universally dominant because of his genes, selected by the evolutionary requirement for hunting prowess and successful sexual competition and his male sex hormones. And there are others. Because the ultimate argument for the inevitability (that is, the biological determination) of female subordinance and of male dominance is the claim that women have had an inferior status in all places and all times, it seems necessary to discuss briefly some of the important recent conceptual and empirical work of feminist and other anthropologists that calls into question an entire canon of traditional anthropological beliefs, viewpoints, and assumptions.

Since it is at present an unresolvable question, I am not arguing here so much against the universality of women's subordinance today as I am against the traditional *assumptions* of such and against the assumption of women's subordinance across all time. Whatever tentative conclusions arise from continuing scholarship, the importance of the work is to show the complexities and contradictions, the historicity of development, and the extraordinary variations in the processes, in different places and different times, leading to the subordinate positions of women as we observe them today. It is necessary to examine the assumptions, interpretations, and predetermined conclusions underlying claims for the biological bases and, hence, the immutability and inevitability of women's subordinance.

Because of the richness of the growing anthropological literature on women and because feminist scholars by no means present a unified viewpoint or approach or even philosophical framework for their investigations of questions relevant to "women's position" in various societies, I am not presenting a comprehensive review of this work. Rather, I highlight some of the major issues and questions raised by feminist anthropologists. I attempt to show first that gender inequality is a complex issue that cannot be analyzed successfully in terms of universals, and secondly that women's subordinance developed unevenly and historically and does not require biological explanations.

PROBLEMS IN EXAMINING THE POSITION OF WOMEN CROSS-CULTURALLY

It has been customary in anthropology, with notable exceptions in the past two decades or so, to assume (rather than demonstrate) certain universals and to record observations of other cultures and make interpretations that appear to confirm the (assumed) universals. The assumptions simply represent the generalized ideas we have about how all people and societies are, based upon the experiences we have had within our own culture. It has been taken as a logical assumption, for example, in our Western, industrial, hierarchically organized class societies where men hold power and authority that all human (and other primate) societies are organized into male dominance hierarchies. Experiences in such a society create a mind set that organizes thoughts, values, and beliefs into categories that act as prisms through which other cultures are viewed. The mind set includes the conceptual framework that is used to organize and interpret such perceptions. In short, the experiences derived from our own society are inappropriately projected onto the institutions and behaviors of other societies: dominance hierarchies and sexual stratifications are constructed where they do not exist: women are seen (or, more accurately, not seen) as subordinate and peripheral regardless of what they are doing, since what women do, by definition, is unimportant. Such pre-conceptions are then reinforced by observing only what men do, since, again by definition, it is men who do the important things.

Thus, observations and conclusions of Western male anthropologists have reflected not only their own ethnocentric assumptions, beliefs, values, and experiences, but also the biased sources of their knowledge concerning the values and beliefs of the cultures they have studied. Most ethnographic reports have focused on data gathered from male informants, such information being considered to represent the realities of the culture as a whole. Yet, as Rogers (1978) has emphasized, two quite different and contradictory views or ideologies may, and indeed often do, exist side by side within cultures. Male perceptions that male activities are predominantly important are not necessarily shared by the women, whose "cultural systems might give superior value to the roles and activities" (p. 143) of women. Thus, anthropological reporting that men are dominant because their activities are more highly valued may seriously distort the social reality if the information is based on male perceptions alone. Since, in the past, ethnographic investigations have relied primarily on reports of male informants, it is easy to understand how notions of universal male dominance gained currency. One is led also to wonder about the biasing effects operating in the responses female informants make to anthropologists who are male, as the overwhelming majority have been in the past. Rogers cites a number of societies where gender-differentiated and contradictory value systems exist side by side and other instances that suggest separate female and male ideologies. For example, in different societies, women and men may perceive of themselves as "separate entities" or "different breeds"; collective antagonistic actions may be taken by one sex against the other; separate and independent prestige systems may be constructed by each sex; or marked social and economic segregation by sex exists, with *each* sex being excluded from the domain of the other.

Another problem has to do with the concept of "women's position." Careful cross-cultural comparisons have begun to document not only that there can be no simple statement of a *universal* "position" of women in society, but that even *within* most societies there is no such simple entity as "women's status." As Naomi Quinn (1977) has emphasized, it is more useful to view women's position in any culture as a "composite of many different variables, often casually independent one from another" (p. 183). In any given society women may have what appears to an observer to be an inferior position with respect to some areas of life and an equal or superior one in others. It is important, however, as Atkinson (1982) warns, not to ignore the significance of sexual stereotypes or to presume "that women's influence in one context cancels out their degradation in another" (p. 248). Thus, to understand women's position within any given society, it is necessary to examine the particularities of their experiences in the entire social context of their culture and not selectively use excerpts from it. Furthermore, within any area of a society's life, the "position" of women will often be variously affected by class or age or kin relationships, as well as by the history of that culture.

The method of using selective examples from different societies in order to "prove" the existence of universals is one we validly view with suspicion when it is used in other contexts. For example, we do not accept the Sociobiological argument that all females are coy because "coy" behaviors may be cited in a variety of species. Argument from analogy may be used to support any universalist statement, however outrageous. Not only does it remove particular behaviors from their social and historic contexts, as noted above, but it also uses different measures or definitions of the particular feature being examined, such as participation in religious rituals or office holding or deference gestures or gang rape, as equivalent measures of position or authority. But while the method uses different measures, it imputes the same meaning or significance to the behaviors, whether or not they bear some resemblance to each other.

And finally, the method of citing specific behaviors from each of several societies as analogous indicators, for example, of women's subordinance, ignores the possibility that the meaning and significance of the behaviors for the people involved may be (and probably is) quite different from the interpretations placed on them by outside viewers who have their own values, beliefs, and preconceptions. This is, then, an approach that fails to consider how the women themselves interpret their own behaviors (Collier & Rosaldo, 1981). The "reality" of sexual stratification, for example, may exist only within the framework and terminology of outsiders, who from the perspective of their own value systems, impute hierarchies of worth, status, and power where they do not exist for the people observed. We must recognize that measures we may choose for discussing women's position, such as autonomy, independence, or decision-making power are culture-bound. They have relevance for women in our Western industrial cultures but not necessarily for women in other kinds of societies.

The problem seems to me to be similar to the one of trying to understand or perceive how language itself shapes and constrains our perceptions of reality and therefore our reality itself. That is, how do we step outside of language, our perceptual prison and springboard, both to examine its intrinsic limitations and to catch a glimpse of the realities that it both signifies and creates? Infused as it is with human subjectivity, desire, and intent, our own language may distort and hide other interpreted realities from view. We must extend our own conception of culture to the point where it can articulate underlying concepts that are significantly different from those generated by our own particular culture and that can give us more illuminating explanations of our observations of other cultures (Wagner, 1975). The problem is to understand each culture "in terms of its own unique sets of underlying concepts" (Millar, 1983, p. 2). It is within that vacuum of our incomprehension (i.e., that there are symbolic frameworks or conceptual systems of which we are totally unaware) that our own frameworks have served as the context for interpreting others' behaviors.

Whether or not one comes up with generalizations, universals, or laws probably does not depend so much on whether there are such to be discovered, but on whether one finds it necessary or desirable to do so, which in turn reflects one's philosophical approach to anthropological observations. In this regard Geertz has written

> Believing, with Max Weber, that man is an animal suspended in webs of significance he himself has spun, I take culture to be those webs, and the analysis of it to be therefore not an experimental science in search of law but an interpretive one in search of meaning. (1973, p. 5)

The final problem to be discussed here concerning efforts to establish universals through ethnographic comparisons is the ahistorical aspect of some anthropological analysis. As Mona Etienne and Eleanor Leacock emphasize, there remains an implicit assumption that societies "without written history have no history," and that contemporary cultures not yet modernized represent "an intact remnant of an unchanged past" (1980, p. 5). It is an approach that fails to recognize or acknowledge that there is hardly a place in this world that has not been touched by European, and more recently American, colonization over the past five to six centuries even when this is not directly evident. It was the English, French, Spanish, Portuguese, and Dutch ancestors of present-day anthropologists who drastically changed or wiped out the cultures or the very existence of the peoples inhabiting the lands they colonized. The effect has been the imposition of a cultural uniformity that their anthropological heirs now declare to represent human *nature* and the natural order of things.

At the same time, however, it is not useful to idealize or romanticize precolonial, prestate, and preindustrial societies. While colonialism debased North and South American and African women and men and introduced slavery and exploitation in places where they did not exist before, many precolonial and present-day traditional societies themselves have been class-stratified and have also condemned "women to a prescribed fate of subsistence, subservience and silence in the political world" (Christian, 1983, p. 27). In Nigeria and many other societies, slavery existed prior to colonization, and most slaves in Nigeria and elsewhere were women. In today's world, genital mutilation of women is defended as traditional culture, a realm assigned to women to preserve. And gang rape, as well as other techniques for male control of women in various traditional cultures, makes the analysis of the position of women in so-called simple cultures a difficult problem indeed.

Like Etienne and Leacock (1980) in their discussion of North and South American Indian women, Christian stresses the strength and adaptability of African women as actors, not merely victims, in the precolonial and postcolonial worlds. But there has also been "waste, tragedy, and loss" (Christian, p. 27). Within a meshwork of colonialism, technological development, capitalism, and socialism, enslavement, oppression and exploitation—waste, tragedy and loss— have been the conditions of existence for women and men of every race and color throughout the world; and women, within their own racial, class, tribal or national group usually have known, for millenia past, a doubled burden of oppression.

While pristine foraging cultures may have been egalitarian, stratifications by class and gender developed in different places and times and under differing circumstances. As Deere and León de Leal (1981), Safa and Leacock (1981), Scheper-Hughes (1983), Tabet (1982) variously argue, the sexism of colonialism of the past, as well as that of today's capitalist "modernization" schemes for the nonindustrial world, was more easily established in some cultures because of the availability of traditional ideologies and practices that were part of the "continuous and collective history of women's oppression under ancient forms of patriarchy . . ." (Scheper-Hughes, 1983, p. 36).

UNIVERSALIST ASSUMPTIONS ABOUT WOMEN

Traditional assumptions begin with the tenet that there has always been a particular sexual division of labor based on biological categories, namely, women's childbearing capacity and men's strength. From this basic division, it is assumed, all the other sexual divisions of tasks and responsibilities are derived, the sexual dichotomies in temperament and behaviors, and the gender asymmetries in power, authority, worth, and status with which we are familiar. From this point of view, it appears natural and inevitable that women have been eternally and universally subordinate to men. These assumptions construct an evolutionary scenario that sees women as physically constrained by pregnancy, lactation, and infant care to virtual immobility and evolutionary stagnation, and sees men as fundamentally unconstrained and creative, capable of bonding with each other, inventing weapons, and bringing home the meat, each to his dependent domestic unit (Barash, 1977, 1979; Lovejoy, 1981; Washburn and Lancaster, 1968). This point of view—a world view—interprets society as being characterized by a particular set of dichotomies based on *natural* oppositions: woman-man, nature-culture, private- public, domestic-political, and subordinate-dominant, with woman residing, of course, in the sphere of the natural, the private, the domestic, and the subordinate.

The Question of a Universal Sexual Division of Labor Based on Female Reproduction and Male Production

One problem in attempting to trace the origins of sexual divisions of labor is the virtual absence of fossil data that are relevant to the question. While all social scientists recognize that gender is an important organizational element in the social/economic/political life of perhaps all societies, the study of gender has not been a focus in archeological research, nor has much attention been paid to a consideration of possible methodologies that could be useful for relating archeological findings to possible gender-related activities of the prehistoric actors.

All of the archeological evidence suggests that for many millions of years, until about 15,000 years ago, humans were associated in nomadic foraging bands. It is reasonable to assume that all persons did what they were physically capable of in the gathering of plants and small animals, depending on their size, strength, endurance, speed, skill, experience, and age. There is no reason to assume *a priori* that sex was a differentiating attribute or that women, unlike all other species, sat around waiting to be fed because they were mothers. It is extremely doubtful that such a species could survive to evolve. The fossil evidence available suggests only minimal sexual dimorphism in australopithecine body size (Zihlman, 1976), and everything that we know about modern-day women in gathering-hunting or industrial societies indicates that their physical endurance for work or long-distance walking is no less than that of men. By the end of an average day of foraging, a !Kung woman (who weighs about 90 pounds) may be carrying on the six-to-ten mile return walk to the campsite up to 33 pounds of vegetable foods on her back, as well as a child or even two, adding between 7 and 40 pounds. If she is also carrying some of her possessions plus water, as she does on long trips, her load increases another several pounds (Lee, 1979). Strength among foragers would not appear to be an important differentiating factor. It seems possible, however, that the fairly constant association across cultures of women with the processing of foods to increase their digestibility had its origins in mothers' efforts to provide food supplements for infants and wean children from breast milk. Siskind (1978) suggests similar origins (that is, the social responsibility of women for their children's subsistence) for the association of women with the more dependable forms of obtaining food, such as gathering rather than hunting. Since the particular divisions of tasks by sex have, with this exception, differed so widely among cultures, it would appear that nonbiological considerations, such as ecology, demography, technology, and ideology have influenced the distribution of responsibilities between the sexes in particular societies.

VERSATILITY OF WOMEN'S PRODUCTIVE AND REPRODUCTIVE ROLES

In all societies we know about in recorded history, there has been some form of sexual division of labor, though the particular tasks done and rituals performed by women and men have differed radically among cultures; in some societies, for example, only the women build the houses; in others, only the men do; in yet others, women or men. With few exceptions among gatherer-hunter societies today, men are associated with the hunting of large mammals and women with most of the collecting and processing of plant and small animal foods. Beyond that sexual division, however, societies vary in the tasks they perceive to be the responsibilities of women and men, including child care, or perceive to be neutral with respect to sex.

In analyzing the ethnographic data describing the division of labor by sex in 224 societies, Karen Sacks (1979) shows the enormous range of economic activities that women perform. In fact, rather than finding women to be economically peripheral, she suggests that "men's tasks are largely determined by what women do not do" (p. 93). In different societies women may be primarily responsible for "mining and quarrying, stone work, lumbering, herding, clearing the land for agriculture, burden carrying, and grain grinding" (p. 68). (However, as noted elsewhere in this chapter and Chapter 5, women are virtually universally excluded from metalworking in the contemporary nonindustrial societies that have been studied.) The work record of all societies studied over time shows that

> Almost every productive task undertaken by humanity is assigned to women in one or another place. Yet "men's work" and "women's work" have been defined very differently by different societies. (p. 67)

Sacks concludes that this variation in what different societies consider to be women's or men's work is an obvious indication that tasks are not assigned to one sex or the other on the basis of any particular biological or temperamental characteristics of women and men.

Furthermore, Sacks found that in all societies women combine these physical activities of producing food and material objects with the physical activities of childrearing and motherhood.

> While carrying, bearing, and nursing babies is certainly productive labor, no human society has defined this as the totality of women's labor. (p. 67)

A most significant conclusion of Sacks', directly contrary to most analyses, is that it has been women's subsistence or *productive* activities that have shaped her relationships to *reproduction* and the conditions of her motherhood rather than the converse. Some further support for Sacks' conclusion comes from the observation that the women of the !Kung, nomadic gatherers of the Kalahari Desert, nurse their babies for three years. Since nursing inhibits ovulation, the typical spacing between births is about four years. It is reasonable to assume that !Kung women know that nursing stops menstruation and therefore pregnancy, and they are thus scheduling their childbearing to fit the requirements and capacities of their essential foraging and other productive activities, which provide the majority of the group's food and water.

The converse view, that woman's childbearing has determined her productive activities and social relationships is commonly assumed in most disciplines and accepted by many feminist and Marxist scholars. This reflects the fact that sooner or later in looking for ultimate explanations of woman's condition, the one irreducible and incontrovertible difference between women and men is women's capacity to bear children, and this must, therefore, account for all the other dichotomies and inequalities, whether or not they follow logically. This view unfortunately employs a fundamental assumption of biological determinist theories and reflects our own ethnocentric blindness to alternate modes of interpretation. It is important to see that, unlike breathing, for example, the biological capacity to reproduce does not necessarily mean that one *has* to reproduce or even be heterosexually active, nor does it dictate the social arrangements for child nurturance and rearing or determine how child rearing affects one's participation in other cultural activities. Whether or not we bear, nurse, or mother children is just as much a function of cultural, social, political, economical, and, no more importantly, biological factors as whether we are poets or soccer players.

Thus, the ethnographic and ethnohistorical evidence demonstrates that there has not been a universal basic division of labor into the categories of women's reproduction and men's production, and that women have not been universally excluded from any sphere of productive activities by their childbearing capacity or by child care.

THE SEXUAL DIVISION OF LABOR AND GENDER RELATIONSHIPS

An important concept that the work of some feminist anthropologists as well as data from recent field studies of gatherer-hunter societies have established is that sex roles, or the division of tasks by sex, do not necessarily imply inequality of economic, social, or political status; relationships of subordinance and dominance; or hierarchies of value, worth, autonomy, or decision-making power. Whether or not relationships of inequality exist in any society depends in part upon its social-economic structure as a whole and the existence within it of cultural conceptions requiring hierarchical ordering (Leacock, 1977).

Karen Sacks (1976) attributes a particular set of "ethnographic blinders" to what she calls "state bias," since in state societies hierarchical social relations are reflected and reinforced in hierarchical ways of thinking. She points out that it is erroneous to assume that one sex must be dominant if women and men play different roles, since in some nonstate societies, the sexes or their roles and responsibilities may be sharply separated yet may be viewed as equal in worth and status.

Among contemporary nomadic gatherer-hunter societies, women are the primary gatherers of vegetable and small animal food and provide from 50 to 90 percent of the group's food and water, the proportion depending upon ecological circumstances. Women of the !Kung San engage in gathering expeditions about every other day. They are gone up to ten hours a day and often travel eight to ten miles from camp (Draper, 1975, 1976). If they have nursing children, they carry them along. The other children remain in the camp in the care of adults who are not away working that day, and these are as likely to be men as women. Women control the distribution of the products of their foraging and share equally in group decision making. In nomadic foraging societies, ties of economic dependency link each individual to the group as a whole, decision making is dispersed, and decisions are made by and large by those who will have to carry them out. Neither girls nor boys are socialized to be child caretakers, and neither have such responsibilities. Aggresivity and dominance are not exhibited by women or men and are devalued by the group as a whole. Since authoritarianism does not exist with !Kung society, fathers have no "authoritarian" role within the family or outside it. Authority, as it is understood in our industrial societies, is the ability to have control over resources and to withhold them from others. This concept, for whatever reason, does not exist or is actively discouraged within many foraging tribes, though there is an idea of personal influence. This does not appear to be sex-linked and is validated in daily life in terms of an individual's general contribution to the well-being of the group. These patterns have changed dramatically as some !Kung have settled near the westernized Bantu.

While this description outlines the basis for women's and men's economic equality within at least some !Kung societies, it leaves unexplored many other aspects of gender meanings and relationships in such nomadic gathering-hunting societies. For example, in examining the relationships between politics and gender in "simple" (that is, hunter-gatherer, hunter-horticulturist, brideservice) societies, Collier and Rosaldo (1981) describe the varying patterns of "male-female co-operation, dominance and independence" (p. 316). They show that marriage and motherhood, sex and reproduction, despite their prevalence and their functional logic, have different meanings and social uses in different societies and embody relationships between women and men that are conditioned by the social order. It is Collier and Rosaldo's view that marriage in brideservice societies (where husbands provide services or goods to in-laws) organizes obligations, and these obligations shape political life. Marriage creates an asymmetry between women and men because men need marriage and women do not. Men need a wife to acquire a committed network of in-laws, which gives them adult status, prestige, and autonomy. Thus, while the wife provides her husband with adult prestige and equality with other men through her kin network, she loses the sexual autonomy and freedom she had before marriage.

An example of a form of complementary egalitarianism has been provided by studies of the Iroquois societies of the seventeenth and eighteenth centuries.

in social relationships and organization that characterize patriarchal cultures developed historically and did not evolve from biological necessity. The problem is, how did women as a class come to lose autonomy and control over almost every aspect of their own lives in the course of the evolution of those particular cultures or societies that became patriarchal cultures and came to dominate world civilization? To explore this question it is necessary first to trace what is known or believed about human prehistory, as it is described in traditional texts.

THE EVOLUTION OF HUMAN SOCIETIES
FROM NOMADIC FORAGING TRIBES TO STATES

The Archeological Record

The archeological record suggests that 10 to 15 thousand years ago virtually everyone still lived by gathering, hunting, and fishing, that is, nomadic foraging. By A.D. 1500 about 15 percent of the world's population were still foraging (Fagan, 1980). Even today, more than a third of the 563 societies in Murdock's 1981 *Atlas of World Cultures* are nomadic or seminomadic. Cultivation and domestication of animals and sedentarism began to appear around 12,000 years ago in the Near East and in various parts of the world over the following 7,000 to 8,000 years. The first villages were temporary and seasonal as the seminomadic peoples combined cultivation with seasonal scheduling of their gathering, hunting, or fishing activities. The earliest permanent agricultural villages that have been excavated date to about 6000 B.C. and by 5500 B.C. included irrigation (which implies some organization of authority) and painted pottery. It was over the following 3000 years that sedentarism became widespread in the Near East. Chiefdoms, which were multicommunity or supra-village political units, first emerged in Mesopotamia about 5500 B.C. and were followed in subsequent millenia by city-states, states, and then empires. Developments similar to these occurred over the same time period from 6000 to 3000 B.C. in Anatolia, Greece, and Italy and from 2000 B.C. to 1200 A.D. in the New World.

The Anthropological Record

Along with the archeological record there is a contemporary anthropological record, and together these suggest the evolutionary course of social organization at the various stages just described. First they suggest that the earliest forms of social organization among nomadic foraging bands were egalitarian (lacking political or economic stratifications) and communal (Fagan, 1980; Flannery, 1972). Such bands probably constituted all of societies until between 15,000 and 10,000 years ago. By 7000 B.C. in the Near East, 3000 B.C. in Peru, and 1300 B.C. in Mesoamerica (Flannery, 1972), tribes appeared. These were economically and politically egalitarian societies whose segments were kinship-based groups (clans, lineages). They communally produced their subsistence and communally shared the means of production. This form of organization characterized nomadic foraging tribes, seminomadic and semisedentary tribes, and early settled villages as well as some later agricultural societies, as in Mesoamerica. Modern examples are the New Guinea Highlanders and Pueblo Indians of the southwestern United States.

Among those societies that did not remain egalitarian and communal, the next stage was the development of ranked societies in autonomous villages. Archeological excavations have made it possible to infer the development of social or class stratifications as early as 5300 B.C. in Mesopotamian farming villages. As is true for all complex prehistoric phenomena, there are different theories concerning the origins of social and economic stratification and the relative importance of a variety of factors. It is not central to the argument here, however, to do more than list some of the more obvious relevant factors, such as technological advances making the production of surplus food and goods possible; differentiation of tasks and specialization of labor; trading and warring leading to differential access to products and strategic resources; and the ideology, power, and motivation to produce and appropriate surpluses of food and goods from producers and redistribute them to those who did not produce, such as the priestly and chiefly clan and village elites. In any case, there developed classes of craftsworkers, farmers, merchants, traders, and clan or village elites with a chief who was both the secular and religious leader. What this development meant was that kinship groups such as clans became hierarchically organized rather than being the egalitarian base for the communal ownership of land and other resources. The next stage was the horizontal associations of clan and village chiefs or elites into interclan and intervillage structures of authority. As suggested later, since these structures were probably the outgrowth of male interclan and intervillage networks, the egalitarian position of women within their kin corporations was undermined.

This next stage and level of political development appears to have been the chiefdom, considered by some to be the precursor of the state (Carneiro, 1981). The chiefdom is a type of political organization that transcends village autonomy—an intertribal, intervillage, autonomous political unit or system under the control of a paramount chief with a secondary hierarchical level made up of the village chiefs. Chiefdoms were made up of Neolithic villages and towns with well-developed social and economic stratifications that either voluntarily associated under a single authority in defense against nomadic raiders and neighboring chiefdoms or were amalgamated into the victor's chiefdom following defeat in war. One of the most important goals of warring was to acquire control of trade routes that would provide luxury items for the ruling elite and noble classes. Because of the increasing power of chiefdoms to appropriate goods and labor and acquire resources, commodities, and slaves, they became extremely stratified socially and economically as well as politically. At some stage, chiefs became noble and divine and elite rank became hereditary.

After chiefdoms, kingdoms and states developed. These represented a third hierarchical level of political authority produced through the aggregation of two or more chiefdoms into a larger political unit (Carneiro, 1981). Carneiro considers the functional criteria of a state to be that it "is an autonomous political unit, encompassing many communities within its territory and having a centralized government with the power to draft men for war or work, levy and collect taxes, and decree and enforce laws" (p. 69). The next development was the formation of empires, around 2500 B.C. in Mesopotamia and around 1790 B.C. in Babylon. Empires thus represent the fourth level of hierarchical political authority and power, the amalgamation of states by conquest.

THE POSITION OF WOMEN IN SOCIAL FORMATIONS AND THE ORIGINS OF PATRIARCHAL CULTURES: A THEORETICAL FORMULATION

But now we must return to the central issue: how do women fit into these "sociopolitical" developments; how does one account for the development of patrilineality, patriclans, and women's loss of status and control over production and products in those cultures? How, in short, can one visualize the origins and evolution of patriarchal cultures that have reached a contemporary peak expression in industrial nations?

There are few sources to use in trying to answer these questions and to trace the roles and positions of women from egalitarian nomadic bands to modern patriarchal civilizations. Traditional texts describing prehistory and the rise of civilizations or the origin of states, as I have just recounted it (Fagan, 1980; Jones and Kautz, 1981), do not mention or discuss women, gender, or the patriarchal organization of power and authority, or recognize that the "civilization" they describe is a patriarchal civilization. That there may be important connections between the development of male hegemonic authority and the particular directions in which dominant human cultures, that is, civilization, evolved has not been considered by traditional scholarship of prehistory. That is because civilization, as recorded, was a male creation; it is *the* truth to be described by male scholarship, which "does not comprehend its own perspectivity" (MacKinnon, 1982, p. 538).

In speculating about the possible origins and evolution of gender stratifications, I would first of all assume that the egalitarianism of nomadic foraging and horticultural societies, recognized by prehistorians with respect to the lack of class stratifications, held also for the relationships between women and men. This is, however, not known and may have been the case in some cultures but not others. It is known, however, that in the earliest settled villages where such questions have been asked of the archeological data, gender differences in possessions and status appeared to be absent during the time when there was general economic and social equality. For example, excavations of Chinese coastal neolithic burial sites in three provinces and spanning three millenia from 5000 B.C. to 2000 B.C. suggest that in the early period there was some sexual division of labor, since certain tools were found more frequently (but not exclusively) in female or male graves, but that there was equal distribution of possessions and rank among women, men, and children. The period of 2750–1750 B.C. shows "increasing wealth and social differentiation and a decline in the status of women and children" (Pearson, 1981, p. 1086). Lineages became more important, possibly with a shift from matriliny to patriliny, and males appeared to have increasing importance, power, and wealth. Similar patterns have been found in Mesopotamia and Mesoamerica.

Excavations of Catal Hüyük, an advanced Neolithic society in Anatolia, have been interpreted to indicate the high status of women in that town during the period studied, from around 6250 B.C. to 5400 B.C. (Rohrlich, 1980). The people of Catal Hüyük practiced intensive irrigation agriculture and had highly developed arts, crafts, and religion, complete with symbolism and mythology. Even though there was occupational specialization, examination of the burial sites suggested communal ownership of primary resources and also a matrilineal and matrilocal clan structure. Figurines and other artifacts indicate that women were of central importance in agriculture, engaged in hunting, and were long-distance traders, ritual leaders, and deities. In fact, it appears that the principle deity was a goddess.

Catal Hüyük is considered to be the earliest known prototype of an advanced Neolithic society, from which the Sumerian state developed beginning about 4000 B.C. Rohrlich (1980) analyzes the extensive excavations of Sumer, which have provided one of the most complete records of the transformation of women's position from one of preeminence in the early city-state to one of subordination in the established state around 2400 B.C. Similar developments have been documented for societies in Mesoamerica beginning about 800 A.D. (Rohrlich and Nash, 1981).

With the establishment of chiefdoms and then the city-state of Sumer, there arose a managerial class of people who were also the ritual leaders. (Rohrlich does not use the term *chiefdom*, but I think it is implied in her description of different levels of political organization.) This class of chiefly priests retained a large amount of the surplus wealth produced in the city and increasingly appropriated the labor and land of farmers, who lost autonomy as the priesthood became detached from the interests of the community. The kin corporate egalitarian clan structures of land ownership were thus eroded and clan chiefs became incorporated into the ruling elite. In early Sumer, women ruled as queens; they were priests and managers, scribes, musicians, craftsworkers, healers, warriors, and deities. They owned land and they ran businesses.

Evidently, as the need for more land, natural resources, commodities, and luxury items increased, warring became a paramount activity, and generals became the rulers separate from the priesthood. The priesthood, however, retained elite status and important ritual and ideological roles. With increasing militarism in the third millennium B.C., class stratifications became more extreme, especially with the institution of slavery. The earliest slaves were women who had been captured in war and also wives who were sold to pay off debts. Women slaves were used for breeding, labor, and prostitution.

It is Rohrlich's thesis that in the context of chronic warfare, which became a male occupation, rigid economic stratification, and political consolidation in the hands of a male ruling class, kinship relationships were subverted and women became subordinate. She considers the subjugation of women to have been an integral part of these interacting processes that resulted in state formation in Sumer.

Rapp (1977) and Sacks (1979) also point out that the kinship networks that organize prestate societies resisted and became eroded by the ruling class formations that eventually led to the state. It is within kin corporations that women shared authority with men, often as sisters rather than wives, and also within them that women's subordination appears to have developed. Through warfare, women were acquired by force as slaves and concubines for labor power and the reproduction of labor power. They were also exchanged through marriage and other alliances in order to extend kinship networks and, through such networks, to gain increased access to natural resources, commodities, and trade routes. However, it is at the same time important to take into account that appropriation and trade have not been exclusively male functions (Rapp, 1977). Women were traders in Mesopotamia and the Incaic empire, and they have been active as traders in Africa, the Caribbean, and the Andes to this day. It is also an oversimplification, Rapp points out, to consider there to be a necessary "association of warfare and an elevation of male status at the expense of female autonomy" (p. 312), since in some early societies (Spartan, Roman, Athenian) women gained in civil power and authority during warfare. It was a significant step in the development of patriarchal social orders that, with the increasing importance of land and private property appropriated through wars and women, its generational transmission became secured through the male line by law. The earliest legal code found (2415 B.C.) imposed monogamy on women only, making polyandry equivalent to adultery and punishable by death. It also legalized the beating of women for subordinance. Enforcement of monogamy for women only is interpreted to signify a shift from matriliny to patriliny, since men can be assured, at least officially, of their paternity and their own descent line for purposes of passing on property and rank. The patriarchal family became legally established in Sumer and was a prime force in the socialization of children for gender and class hierarchies. By the time of Hammurabi's empire around 1792 B.C., all the scribes were men, and women were excluded from education and therefore the knowledge that became inseparable from independence or power.

IDEOLOGICAL CONSIDERATIONS IN PATRIARCHAL STATE FORMATION

While the description of patriarchal origins and evolution I have sketched pays much attention to forms of social organization around subsistence and commodity production and acquisition, such evolution was without doubt influenced by a variety of other factors. Even with similar subsistence activities and techniques, groups living in the same ecological setting differ in the structure of their daily lives and relationships, and individuals within groups differ among themselves. And so it doubtless always was. An important intangible in attempting to reconstruct the various forces and forms of cultural evolution is the role of individuals and their ideas. One has to look to more than environmental-ecological and subsistence activities to explain, for example, the development from early farming villages to the spectacular Olmec and Mayan civilizations during the first millenia B.C. and A.D., with their highly complex and integrated sociopolitical systems and remarkable achievements in technology, arts, monumental architecture, and complex rituals and ideology, much of it recorded in their hieroglyphic writings (Flannery, 1972; Willey, 1982). While ideas, fantasies, ceremonial rituals, religions, and their deities may have been a response to material, subsistence requirements, to problems, uncertainties, and needs generated by interactions with environments, they cannot be dismissed as "mere" epiphenomena. They served as forces in the evolution of civilizations as necessary to be considered as the material forces that leave fossil records. It is known, for example, that elaborate rituals and ceremonial deities have important functions in preclass and prestate societies as regulatory or levelling mechanisms that prevent the accumulation of wealth or power in egalitarian cultures (Flannery, 1972).

Flannery sees such epiphenomena as lying at the heart of any society's environmental and interpersonal regulation and therefore integral to any comprehensive ecological analysis of cultural evolution. Flannery's framework could provide a useful approach for the systematic analysis of the role of ritual and ideology in the evolutionary development and maintenance of patriarchal orders. This would be a study of the ways in which ideology and ritual changed from levelling mechanisms in egalitarian societies, benefitting the majority, to forces that enabled the privileged few to appropriate the fruits of a civilization from the hands of those who produced them—a role they play, of course, in class stratified and patriarchal societies such as our own. Studies of state formation in South America have suggested the important roles played by religious iconography and art in spreading ideology and effecting the ideological transformations necessary for the legitimation of hierarchies, conquest, and expansion within Aztec and Incan empires (Jones and Kautz, 1981). While these studies on the origins of states do not concern themselves with the issues raised here, the argument that systems of belief actually structure social action and play a critical role in processes of stability and change is highly relevant to any exploration of the origins and maintenance of patriarchal power. There can be no doubt that patriarchal ideologies and the awesome power of the state and other cultural institutions to disseminate them have been central to the acceptance by women and men of women's subordination. Thousands of years ago knowledge became a limiting resource for women from which their exclusion became enforced with the establishment of institutions of formal education and training. This exclusion of women from education was important enough that it has been tenaciously defended for at least the last 4000 years. The exclusion of women from education makes it more easily possible to create a scholarship that "demonstrates" women's intellectual inferiority, as well as to show that the absence of women from the ranks of scholars itself "proves" their inferiority.

Mary O'Brien (1981) gives a central position to a sex-differentiated reproductive consciousness in the evolution of patriarchal ideology and institutions. While women experience childbirth itself in an immediate way, men are biologically alienated from the birth process as soon as ejaculation of sperm occurs. A woman knows her own child through direct experience as the product of her labor, while a man can never be certain of his paternity of any child. Women directly *experience* themselves as part of genetic continuity, while men only have *knowledge* about paternity. That knowledge of the relationship between sexual intercourse and conception came as a historical discovery. O'Brien suggests that men's solution to the uncertainty of paternity and to their estrangement from verifiable genetic continuity was through the development of institutions to provide such continuity: female monogamy to increase the certainty of paternity; marriage, which O'Brien sees as a treaty among men to permit each other sole access to one woman in order to restore "integrity to male reproductive consciousness" (p. 154); and the appropriation and ownership by men of a particular woman's sexuality and her offspring. As social substitutes for a genetic continuity they could not be certain of, men created institutions and ideologies that transcend life-spans, such as legal codes, constitutions, monarchies, hereditary property, and the idea of the State.

SUMMARY AND CONCLUSIONS

I have had several purposes in this chapter. One has been to examine the validity of certain universals that have been important assumptions in anthropological research until the past few years. Once rid of traditional universalist and essentialist assumptions about the position of women today and throughout human history as subordinate to men by virtue of their biological role in reproduction and motherhood, it is possible to look afresh at the variety of relationships and responsibilities that have characterized the position of women throughout prehistory and history and to begin to analyze the unique complex of factors that may account for the particular patterns in any culture.

The other major purpose of this chapter has been to examine evidence and propose some hypotheses relating to the question of how in the course of the cultural evolution of human civilizations women came to lose control over most aspects of their lives in those societies that became patriarchal. Recognizing that the subordinance of women to men is a historical development characterizing patriarchal cultures that have come in the most recent millenia to dominate world civilization, it becomes possible to reject the ideology of its "naturalness" and inevitability and to work for its elimination.

There are serious problems and weaknesses in the traditional use and concept of *universals* in human social behaviors, characteristics, and organization. The most obvious is that the anthropological evidence simply does not support traditional assumptions of such key universals as the subordinance of women or their historical biological segregation to reproductive and otherwise nonproductive labors. Secondly, the assumption of universals, such as the subordination of women, has mystified the phenomenon universalized, placed it outside of the realm of any historical analysis of the dynamics of change and interaction, and made explanation both impossible and unnecessary. Instead of historical and social analyses, such mystification invites further mystification by automatically assuming an equally universalistic explanation. Since the only phenomenon as universal as women's presumed subordination is women's reproductive capacity, biology becomes the obvious explanation for the inferior position of women. But the historical and ethnographic reality is that the significance of woman's biology, of her reproductive capacity, is itself culturally constructed. In some cultures, motherhood is irrelevant for the cultural definition of *woman* and for the significance of women's position and roles. While the *biology* of reproduction and sociology of motherhood have not limited the range of roles and responsibilities women have assumed historically and across cultures, the *consciousness* of reproduction (O'Brien, 1981), necessarily different for women and men, may, however, have had profound effects on the course of cultural evolution and the development of patriarchal ideologies and institutions.

Not only are universals often not reflective of generalized "truth," but it may also be that the very concept or idea of universals plays an integral role in culture-bound ideological frameworks. Such a framework constructs a particular reality that is coherent with the world view of those who are making the theories and, accordingly, obscures relationships and processes that are not coherent with that view. In the main this is a world view derived from experiences of the hierarchical and asymmetrical relationships that characterize our recent history.

Recent studies suggest, however, that in the past, and still today, there have been egalitarian, classless societies in which there were no hierarchical relationships between individuals or relations of dominance and subordination between the sexes. This probably characterized all or most societies until important changes occurred in the organization of subsistence activities and productive relationships in particular societies, perhaps in response to population and ecological pressures and technological change. Each society's response to survival threats and technological advances would have been shaped by a variety of factors, not the least of which would have been its beliefs, ideas, and values—its interpretive framework and cultural history to that point. For some cultures the framework does not include concepts of gender stratification or hierarchies of power, however natural such categories appear to us to be.

It seems likely that with the establishment of horticulture, herding, the sedentary way of life, and agriculture, more widespread and far-reaching changes began to develop in some societies in relationships both among people and between women and men with respect to economic and political position. While the archeological record has established that economic and status stratifications appeared in the early villages of 5000 B.C. and later, it has been relatively silent (perhaps because the questions have rarely been posed) about the origins of gender stratifications that led to patriarchal societies.

I have suggested that in those cultures that evolved toward patriarchies, patterns of the sexual division of labor following sedentarization facilitated the formation of interclan and intervillage male networks of control, authority, and information. With the increasing importance of these networks in the acquisition and control of natural resources and commodities through raiding, warfare, trading, and the enslavement and exchange of women, the roles and authority of women became more circumscribed as women were separated both from control of the products of their labor and from positions of authority in kinship networks. Following the development of more complex horizontal systems of interclan and intervillage hierarchical authority, more rigid social, economic, and political stratifications, more centralized control and warring, chiefdoms became established as amalgamations of villages under a paramount chief and his retinue of village and clan chiefs, forming a male ruling class engaged primarily in warfare. These developments further dichotomized and stratified public and private domains and the positions of men and women. Chiefdoms and their equivalents were thus the sociopolitical patriarchal forerunners of the state. Neither the state nor patriarchy *appeared* at some point in prehistory; rather structures, relationships, and ideologies that characterize them both evolved gradually in parallel fashion and in many mutually reinforcing and interdependent ways.

The state represents, thus far, the most complete codification and institutionalization of patriarchal authority and the separation of women and men into private and public spheres. With the establishment of the state (as in Sumer), monogamy for women only was enforced by law, patriliny succeeded matriliny, and the patriarchal family became legally established to bring women's sexual autonomy under male control, ensure paternal descent lines, establish patriarchal authority at home, and ensure the ideological development and socialization of children for their proper gendered and class position in the sociopolitical hierarchy. Thus, states were able to codify into law the economic, social, and political subordination of women.

The state has continued to be, among other things, the means through which men have controlled women's sexuality. Laws control access to women's sexuality through their regulation of the degree to which rape, battering, incest and child abuse, abortion, pornography, contraception, and divorce are permitted. Since it is the business of the state to regulate the most intimate aspects of life within the family, it is obvious that the dichotomy drawn between private and public spheres, as corresponding to female and male spheres, is false, not only for nonstate and preindustrial cultures, but also for the modern state. Women have indeed been excluded from participation in the political and public spheres, but the private sphere, the family, has been the intimate and unofficial arena for women's official—public, political—subordination.

Another essential function and capability of state centralized authority is the control of the content and the flow of information and ideology, an ability vastly amplified with the expansion of empires. An essential part of this state and patriarchal function was the institution of education and the restriction of access to it to the ruling and managerial classes. Women were effectively excluded from formal education for the last 4000 years. Integral to changes from tribes and clans to patriarchal chiefdoms and states would have been the development of ideologies (including the myths, rituals, religions, and traditions that both embody and transmit gender ideologies) that motivated, supported, "explained," and gave transcendent and naturalistic meanings to the subordinance and inferiority of women as a class. While women's sexuality and its control may have become an important subject in the ideology of the period during which chiefdoms became consolidated, it was perhaps the special contribution of state ideologies, particularly of Western state ideologies, to elaborate, ritualize, mystify, and institutionalize motherhood as the core element in the enforcement of patriarchal relationships of power. Motherhood became the means and metaphor for women's subordination.

With the establishment of vast civilizations, empires, and colonialism, the power of ideologies surpassed territorial and societal borders. It was an integral part of the radical transformation of some societies that they were able to impinge upon, influence, and change to a greater or lesser degree almost all other societies in the world. That is, from an evolutionary point of view, cultures became established that were uniquely characterized by their advanced technological capacity, by their ideas and control of the means of communication, and by economic and ideological necessity to expand into and dominate (change, accelerate) the course and direction of the evolution of most other cultures in the world. It became both possible and necessary to export and impose cultural values along with technology upon other cultures, a process continuing into the present moment. The near universals in relationships that thus became established in the industrial world and its colonies, such as asymmetries in position, possessions, prestige, or power based on sex, class, or color, came to be justified and viewed as natural and essential.

However, by taking the broadest historical and anthropological view of the question of stratifications in control and authority, it is easier to see that the pervasive sexual asymmetries in position and value in industrial and other societies of the recent historical period are neither biologically determined nor eternal nor inevitable.

REFERENCES

Atkinson, J. Anthropology. *Signs*, 1982, *8*, 236-258.

Barash, D. *Sociobiology and behavior*. New York: Elsevier, 1977.

Barash, D. *The whisperings within*. New York: Harper & Row, 1979.

Brown, J. K. Iroquois women: an ethnohistoric note. In R. R. Reiter (Ed.) *Toward an anthropology of women*. New York: Monthly Review Press, 1975.

Carneiro, R. L. The chiefdom: precursor of the state. In G. D. Jones and R. R. Kautz (Eds.) *The transition to statehood in the new world*. Cambridge: Cambridge University Press, 1981.

Christian, B. Alternate versions of the gendered past: African women writers vs. Illich. *Feminist Issues*, 1983, *3*, 23-28.

Collier, J. F., and Rosaldo, M. Z. Politics and gender in simple societies. In S. B. Ortner and H. Whitehead (Eds.), *Sexual Meanings. The cultural construction of gender and sexuality*. Cambridge: Cambridge University Press, 1981.

Deere, C. D., and León de Leal, M. Peasant production, proletarianization, and the sexual division of labor in the Andes. *Signs*, 1981, *7*, 338-360.

Draper, P. !Kung women: contrasts in sexual egalitarianism in foraging and sedentary contexts. In R. R. Reiter (Ed.), *Toward an anthropology of women*. New York: Monthly Review Press, 1975.

Engels, F. *The origin of the family, private property and the state*. New York: International Publishers, 1942.

Etienne, M., and Leacock, E. *Women and colonization. Anthropological perspectives*. New York: Praeger, 1980.

Fagan, B. M. *People of the earth. An introduction to world prehistory*. Boston: Little, Brown, 1980.

Flannery, K. The cultural evolution of civilizations. *Annual review of ecology and systematics*, 1972, 399-426.

Geertz, C. *The interpretation of cultures*. New York: Basic Books, 1973.

Jones, G. D., and Kautz, R. R. *The transition to statehood in the new world*. Cambridge: Cambridge University Press, 1981.

Leacock, E. Ideologies of sex: archetypes and stereotypes. *Annals of the New York Academy of Sciences*, 1977, *285*, 618-645.

Leacock, E. Women's status in egalitarian society: implications for social evolution. *Current Anthropology*, 1978, *19*, 247-275.

Lee, R. *The !Kung San. Men, women, and work in a foraging society*. New York: Cambridge University Press, 1979.

Lee, R. Politics, sexual and non-sexual, in an egalitarian society. In E. Leacock and R. Lee (Eds.), *Politics and history in band societies*. Cambridge: Cambridge University Press, 1982.

Lovejoy, C. O. The origin of man. *Science*, 1981, *211*, 341-350.

MacKinnon, C. Feminism, Marxism, method, and the state: An agenda for theory. *Signs*, 1982, *7*, 515-544.

Millar, S. On interpreting gender in Bugis Society. *American Ethnologist*, 1983, *3*, 477-493.

Murdock, G. *Atlas of world cultures*. Pittsburgh: University of Pittsburgh Press, 1981.

O'Brien, M. Feminist theory and dialectical logic. *Signs*, 1981, *7*, 144-157.

Ortner, S., and Whitehead, H. *Sexual meanings. The cultural construction of gender and sexuality*. Cambridge: Cambridge University Press, 1981.

Pearson, R. Social complexity in Chinese coastal Neolithic sites. *Science*, 1981, *212*, 1078-1086.

Quinn, N. Anthropological studies on women's status. *Annals of Anthropology*, 1977, *6*, 181-225.

Rapp, R. Gender and class: An archaeology of knowledge concerning the origin of the state. *Dialectical Anthropology*, 1977, *2*, 309-316.

Rogers, S. Woman's place: A critical review of anthropological theory. *Comparative Studies in Society and History*, 1978, *20*, 123-162.

Rohrlich, R. State formation in Sumer and the subjugation of women. *Feminist Studies*, 1980, *6*, 76-102.

Rohrlich, R., and Nash, J. Patriarchal puzzle: State formation in Mesopotamia and Mesoamerica. *Heresies*, 1981, *4*, 60-65.

Sacks, K. State bias and women's status. *American Anthropologist*, 1976, *78*, 565-569.

Sacks, K. *Sisters and wives. The past and future of sexual equality*. Westport, CT: Greenwood Press, 1979.

Safa, H., and Leacock, E. Preface. *Signs*, 1981, *7*, 265-267.

Sanday, P. R. *Female power and male dominance*. Cambridge: Cambridge University Press, 1981.

Scheper-Hughes, N. Vernacular sexism: An anthropological response to Ivan Illich. *Feminist Issues*, 1983, *3*, 28-37.

Siskind, J. Kinship and mode of production. *American Anthropologist*, 1978, *80*, 860-872.

Tabet, P. Hands, tools, weapons. *Feminist Issues*, 1982, *2*, 3-62.

Wagner, R. *The invention of culture*. Chicago: University of Chicago Press, 1975.

Washburn, S. and Lancaster, C. S. The evolution of hunting. In R. B. Lee and I. DeVore (Eds.), *Kalahari hunter-gatherers*. Cambridge: Harvard University Press, 1968.

Willey, G. Maya archeology. *Science*, 1982, *215*, 260-267.

Zihlman, A. Sexual dimorphism and its behavioral implications in early hominids. In P. V. Tobias and Y. Coppens (Eds.), *Les plus anciens hominides*. Paris: C. N. R. S., 1976.

Chapter 7
Sexuality, Ideology, and Patriarchy

That the true business of civilization has been in the hands of men is the lesson absorbed by every student of the traditional sources. How this came to be, and the process that kept it so, may well be the most important question for the self-understanding and survival of the human species; but the extent to which civilization has been built on the bodies and services of women—unacknowledged, unpaid, and unprotested in the main—is a subject apparently unfit for scholarly decency.

Adrienne Rich, 1979, p. 135.

In her discussion of patriarchy[1] as a fatal disease in *Three Guineas*, Virginia Woolf connected the father's fear that forbids freedom in the private house with the public fear of the patriarchy that prevents freedom in the political sphere; she connected the tyrannies and servilities of the private house with the massed tyrannies and servilities of the public world. She saw no essential difference between the tyrannies of her republican country and those of the dictatorships of the 1930s, since they both required war as well as the domination and humiliation of women.

The relationships between the patriarchal family and the patriarchal public world have been complex, contradictory, and everchanging. The patriarchal family was a brilliant social invention that secured the individual and collective consciousness, sexuality, loyalty, and subordination of women to individual men and to the (undefined and invisible) male collectivity, the patriarchy, and its ideologies. It has been idealized as a haven from a harsh and ruthless world, as the private sphere ruled by angels. At the same time, it has been the battleground for the violent resolution of the most intense human emotions—fear, anger, hatred, frustration, denial, deception—through the domination and battering of women and the physical, emotional, and sexual abuse of children. It has held for women a promise of freedom and security at the same time as it has been a trap with no escape and no safety. While the home and family are viewed as

---

[1] By patriarchy I mean the historic system of male dominance, a system committed to the maintenance and reinforcement of male hegemony in all aspects of life—personal and private privilege and power as well as public privilege and power. Its institutions direct and protect the distribution of power and privilege to those who are male, apportioned, however, according to social and economic class and race. Patriarchy takes different forms and develops specific supporting institutions and ideologies during different historical periods and political economies.

the private (and sexual) sphere of human activity, it is the primary site for the most intimate public intrusions by the state through its regulation of birth control, abortion, marriage, divorce, welfare, employment and education. At the same time, the state has also remained aloof from intrusions that would threaten the integrity of the traditional, idealized nuclear family no matter what the costs to the life and safety of wives and children. And as the New Right of the 1980s has shown again, the family becomes the primary target of manipulation by the state as the nodal point for solutions to crises in the capitalist economy and challenges brought by the women's movement to patriarchal authority.

The body of ideas, assumptions, values, rituals, and forms of thought and language that constitute an ideology stands in a complicated relationship to the real circumstances and experiences in people's lives. It reflects what is apparent, while it also mystifies reality and molds what could be. It serves mainly to obscure the realities and sources of oppression and to give the experienced realities of living the appearance of naturalness and inevitability. The power of patriarchal ideology lies in the fact that it "remains within the consciousness of individual women as it does within the social and political structuring of political society" (Eisenstein, 1981, p. 10). One source of the power of patriarchal ideology is its obvious pervasiveness, since it affects every family intimately regardless of class or race. Another source lies in the nature of the liberal political philosophy that is part of the heritage of feminism. Most of us were reared in an atmosphere of liberal philosophic rhetoric, which speaks of freedom for all *men*, of individualism, and equality of opportunity. But like all other of the great liberalizing and progressive advances of "mankind" (for example, the Renaissance), women were not included either by intent or by language, except in the works of Harriet Taylor and John Stuart Mill. While Locke and Rousseau wrote, in the seventeenth and eighteenth centuries respectively, of the need to end patriarchal (that is, aristocratic, feudal) control in the public economy, it was an integral part of their liberal philosophy and program to maintain and strengthen patriarchal control in the private and separate realm of the family (Eisenstein, 1981). It was assumed that the public realm was male. Thus women were rendered nonpersons in what became the dominant liberal ideology in capitalist societies, except insofar as they nurtured men and children within the family. Even granted the mystification and obfuscation of state or ruling class power and control with respect to class and race, liberal ideology speaks the language of individualism and equality of opportunity, but for (white) men only. The Bill of Rights, after all, specifically excluded slaves and women. Women, whatever their class or race, were specified as "noncitizens and nonrational beings" (Eisenstein, 1981, p. 16). Their innate (biological) inferiority has been implicit.

In our Western industrial and capitalist states, a central ideology (and its institutionalization) is motherhood. The day-to-day mechanism of enforcement is through the control not only of women's sexuality but of women *by* sexuality within a culture of institutionalized heterosexuality that appropriates women's sexuality for the benefit of men at the same time that it also organizes it for the purposes of reproduction and specifies how women must be, look, act, and view themselves. In Catharine MacKinnon's words, "the organized expropriation of the sexuality of some for the use of others defines the sex, woman." And she adds, concerning sexuality,

> Heterosexuality is its structure, gender and family its congealed forms, sex roles its qualities generalized to social persona, reproduction a consequence, and control its issue. (1982, p. 516)

The kingpin in the patriarchal formations that serve to oppress women is sexuality and the heterosexual structuring of consciousness and institutions. That is, underlying all forms of the oppression of women in patriarchal cultures— physical, economic, political, legal, emotional, ideological—are the assumptions of the institution of heterosexuality or heterosexism: specifically, the assumptions that men own and have the right to control the bodies, labor, and minds of women.

This chapter will suggest how this is so and demonstrate the special contributions medicine and biology have made to the effort.

SCIENCE, SEXUALITY, AND IDEOLOGY

The interdependence between patriarchal social orders, sexuality, and science is profound, based in the ideology, structure, and practice of all three cultural institutions. As other feminist writers have documented (Jordanova, 1980; Merchant, 1980; Smith-Rosenberg and Rosenberg, 1973), the biological and medical sciences have been "suffused" (Jordanova) with sexual metaphor and imagery from the seventeenth century and, conversely, science and medicine have constructed women's sexuality and temperament and provided naturalistic explanations for the sexual division of labor that maintains women's subordinate position in society. In part, through the scientific and medical constructions of women's sexuality, stereotypic notions of the nature of women as passive, all-enduring creatures became universal assumptions.

There is a more abstract level at which the interconnections among science, sexuality, and patriarchal order may be analyzed. A patriarchal mode of thought dichotomizes the world into systems of control and domination. From the patriarchal division of the "civilized" world into public and private spheres that institutionalized the division into the political world of men and the domestic world of women, there has developed a coherent scheme of dualities: men are to women as culture is to nature, as mind is to body, as subject is to object, as domination is to subordination. (See Ortner, 1972, for the early exposition of this theme of nature-culture duality.) Science has been viewed as the objective investigation of nature for the purpose of both knowledge and its control and domination by "man." Since objectivity has been seen as the differentiating characteristic of the male mind and control as the male mode of being, science, by definition, is a male activity. That control and domination of nature by scientific man has historically been expressed in sexual imagery, viewing as natural (as an extension of nature) the control of women and women's sexuality by men. Jordanova (1980) described the science and medicine of eighteenth and nineteenth century Britain and France as activities "associated with sexual metaphors which were clearly expressed in designating nature as a woman to be unveiled, unclothed and penetrated by masculine science" (p. 45).

Then, at the level of palpable reality, the connection between patriarchal order, science, and sexuality is that sexuality, in its theory and its practice, is the method par excellence of the day-to-day control of the minds and bodies of women in patriarchal cultures.

DEFINITIONS OF SEXUALITY

Sexuality, in the writings of the modern Western world, has generally been treated as a *thing*, a universal given, an essence—implicitly understood, assumed by all, not requiring definition (Padgug, 1979). Yet across cultures or individuals, sexual reality includes an enormous range of social and individual acts and attitudes that engage mind and body in manifold and diverse ways. "The forms, content and context of sexuality always differ" (Padgug, 1979, p. 11) from culture to culture; and within any culture, sexuality takes different forms and meanings depending on one's gender, class, or position in a kinship or other kind of hierarchy. Its forms, meanings, and symbols are socially learned and transmitted, whether one considers intercourse itself or kinship relationships or art or fantasy. As Padgug (1979) points out, "The members of each society create all of the sexual categories and roles within which they act and define themselves" or at least *ought* to act, since these categories are indeed normative and ideological. Thus, the meanings even of the categories *women* and *men* vary among cultures as well as among classes. The concept of *homosexuals* and *heterosexuals* as categories of people or of *homosexuality* as a set of qualities or acts defining people is not "natural" and self-evident and did not develop until the seventeenth century (Padgug, 1979).

Our individual beliefs and ideas about what sexuality is may be as varied as sexual practices themselves. At one extreme is the conviction that our sexuality is truly who we are; that all of our life activities, energies, and relationships represent how, from birth on, we have deployed our infantile (innate) desires and sexuality; that is, that "libido shapes our consciousness and our world" (O'Brien, 1981, p. 20). This assumes some innate, unchanging essence that is covered over with layers of social and personal proscriptions and could, or should, under some circumstances be uncovered or released. Another quite contrary view is that our consciousness, our world, shapes our libido. It sees sexuality, including obvious biological components that may be a part of one's sexual responses, as socially molded from early childhood, like any other facet of our personalities, and it does not allow for notions of innateness.

For the individual, I believe there is no fixed sexual "essence" or "nature" that lies buried beneath layers of social ordering, any more than there is a core female or male "nature." Our individual sexualities, like our natures, are socially constructed from our individual histories of interactions with people and society, and they continually change. Our sexuality comes to symbolize and mean different things, and different things come to have symbolic meaning and significance for our sexuality. Our sexuality is one interface we as individuals have with the external world and other people: a dense zone of interactions with the world, with constantly changing and unique physical, emotional, and symbolic meanings. As the concept of God can symbolize, in vastly different ways, a relationship to the world for both the devout and the atheist, so sexual reality can include, for one person or for one moment, an experiencing of a piece of music just as, for another person or moment, it can be an arena of political struggle.

While it may be a common view of sexuality that it is what lies at the very core of one's being and represents the real person, I suggest it may be instead a rather inchoate and charged representation of our entire history of our closest and earliest relationships in the context of our particular culture. I suspect our expressions of our sexuality represent how we are or want to be in relationship to the world and to other people. For example, a person's sexuality may express a desire or need to be vulnerable to another person or, alternatively, a determination never to be vulnerable to another person. It can express a general need to experience commitment to, dependence on, submission to, transcendence with, or physical-psychic unity with another person. It can express a need to always be in control of oneself, of another person, of all situations, or of all people one develops any relationship with. On the other hand, it can express the need to be, for once, *not* in control, but to surrender control to another. Sexuality can be seen also as a survival mechanism; a trading of needs and desires, a desire to be liked, needed, wanted, indispensable, the highest priority in someone else's life. Sexuality can be perceived as a measure of one's attractiveness to other people, as a route to intimacy, as the way to be entrusted with another's vulnerability. Perhaps too obvious to mention is the possibility that sexuality may also have something to do with love (though I do not dare to discuss its meaning) and with (uncomplicated?) physical pleasure. And, of course, our sexuality can express many of these needs at different times and even simultaneously.

In a sense, sexuality, like intelligence, is a learned relationship to the world, with an important and necessary, but not in itself determinate, biological component. For intelligence, it is not enough to have a brain and billions of neurons and synapses. Intelligence develops out of experience and learning, and, as we have seen, even the shape and size of neurons and their synaptic arborizations are influenced by environmental input. So in sexuality, there is a real biological substrate for a range of sexual responses that involve the brain, hormones, muscles, and blood vessels—tinglings, flutterings and flushes; engorgements, secretions, and muscular contractions—and are elicited for any individual only by certain stimuli: a particular person or type of person, a scent, a scene, a sound; a physical experience, a psychological situation; violence or pornography. But whatever or whoever arouses us, as well as our biological responses to arousal, are, I believe, individual characteristics that develop from childhood as part of one's history of experiences and interactions with the external world. As palpable, visible, perceptible, and even measurable as are the physiological stages of sexual responses, there is nothing about desire, arousal, orgasms, or feelings of transcendent oneness that "comes naturally." Too familiar to require discussion here is our knowledge of the elusiveness, the contingency of physical sexual feelings. For most women, orgasms, the most unequivocal of biological responses, are a complicated mental and psychological production.

It is possible that sex and sexuality are viewed as centrally important for individuals because they are the acceptable territory for the playing out of issues of truly central importance to one's character and desires—issues of control, self-control, dependence, expressivity, vulnerability. For women in particular sexuality may be viewed as the *one* way to be seen as a person, providing circumstances under which we can reveal who we truly are and at the same time show love and trust by the willingness to risk the vulnerability that always accompanies the making of oneself visible and accessible. It is precisely because sexuality is so charged for women with psychic and emotional significance and so inextricable from issues of vulnerability and expressivity that it is so powerful a weapon for the social control of women.

One of the specific contributions of the contemporary women's movement, of feminist and lesbian-feminist writings, has been to loosen women's physical sexual pleasure from the weight of traditional constraints. Regardless of the significance or obligations (concerning commitment, desire to please, etc.) that women may invest in a sexual relationship, many have learned over the past two decades what some women have always known: a sense of excitement and the nearly limitless possibilities for physical pleasure to be experienced by, in, with our bodies, whether alone, with women, or men. Beginning with the landmark paper of Koedt (1970) that unhooded the clitoris from generations of oblivion and mystery and used it as a rallying cry for women's sexuality, more women have begun to understand not only the possibilities for, but their rights to, sexual enjoyment, active participation, or the exercise of control, rather than resigned acceptance. At the same time, the serious and questioning attitude that the women's movement has directed at issues of sexuality has made it possible for some women to *choose* celibacy as their preferred and positive mode of being and interacting, rather than only experiencing it as imposed or unwelcome or socially humiliating.

SCIENCE, MEDICINE, AND SEXUALITY

Not only is our sexuality, or our understanding of it, constructed from our entire personal and social history of relationships with others, but our perceptions of our own and of women's sexuality in general have been seriously influenced by the theories, practices, and writings of men for many centuries. An understanding of the intimately learned, complex, and obscure construction of our individual sexuality is immensely complicated by the *cultural* constructions of sexuality. In the following paragraphs I do not in any sense attempt a history of writings about women's sexuality but will discuss some important periods and theories by way of illustrating the impact of science and medicine on the subject.

One of the things that the witch-hunts from the fourteenth through the seventeenth centuries in Europe accomplished was the removal of large numbers of women who had knowledge of women's sexuality from the healing arts and, consequently, from positions of authority. This killing off of women healers as witches accompanied centuries-long efforts by university-trained male physicians to eliminate women healers. Even though barred from universities, they had developed an understanding of bones, muscles, herbs, and drugs to guide their practice of medicine, in contrast to the superstition, astrology, and theology that then characterized much of the formal training for medical practice (Ehrenreich and English, n.d.) With the advent of drugs and obstetrical forceps in the late eighteenth century, their increasing use in the nineteenth century along with the introduction of anesthesia, and hospitalization for childbirth in the early twentieth century, the last wisewomen or midwives were finally excluded from medical practice. Along with the midwives, the rest of a birthing woman's female support system— her friends and relatives—was gradually excluded from the birthing room and the entire birthing process (Leavitt, 1983).

It was, however, not only for their healing but for their sexuality that estimated millions of women were burned at the stake in Germany, France, and England over four centuries (and in the 1600s in New England). It was the Church's teaching that "All witchcraft comes from carnal lust, which in women is insatiable" (Ehrenreich and English, p. 10). As we all know, this view of women has existed for centuries side by side with the view of woman as angel, pure, and pallid. Whatever the particular views physicians held, it is clear that women were equated with sexuality, and the medical profession accepted the responsibility for containing that sexuality by whatever heroic measures were required.

Barker-Benfield (1978) has described the widespread use and acceptance by the medical profession in the United States of clitoridectomies and castrations (ovariectomies) as modes of control of women's sexualities, minds, and bodies throughout the last half of the nineteenth and early twentieth centuries. These were treatments for what male physicians diagnosed as hysteria, insanity, masturbation, nymphomania, other sexual "transgressions" (contraception, abortion, orgasm), and dissatisfactions with women's standard (that is, "normal") roles within the family. In Barker-Benfield's view, there was a variety of beliefs and motives underlying the diagnoses and treatments: that women by their very biological nature (that is, because of their ovaries, menstruation and pregnancies) always are but a step from hysteria, insanity, and criminality; that these biological tendencies led them to sexual transgressions and deviations from the social norms for middle- and upper-class women; that just being female was a disease. Upper- and middle-class husbands and fathers handed over their fatigued, ailing, deviant, or disorderly women to physicians, who became involved with their patients in a cycle of drug prescribing and operations, often removing one ovary and tube at a time—an approach that only served to make women more dependent, demanding, and sickly. Many women, believing that ovaries and the uterus were the source of their troubles, sickness, or unhappiness, requested their removal themselves, according to gynecologists of the time.

Theories and practices of physicians often reflected the fears and hostilities of other upper- and middle-class men in the face of challenges by women of their class (and their own home) to the sexual status quo as women began to demand education and the vote, birth control, and abortion (Bullough and Voght, 1973; Smith-Rosenberg and Rosenberg, 1973). Education would, and did, some believed, not only ruin women's health but threaten the purity, robustness and even continuance of their "race," also a matter of concern to middle- and upper-class men because of the end of slavery and the increase in European immigration. However ludicrous and scientifically unsupported these medical arguments appear to us, physicians contributed significantly to traditional patriarchal ideology and constraints on women of all classes.

> When the belief structure of the physician is threatened, even in fields outside of medicine, he often uses his medical expertise to justify his prejudices and in the process strikes back with value laden responses which have nothing to do with scientific medicine. Unfortunately, since he is assumed to speak with authority, his response, perhaps as he intended, has influence far beyond that of the ordinary men. (Bullough and Voght, 1973, p. 66)

While diagnoses and treatments of women doubtless reflected prevalent social attitudes and male expectations of women, it is also the case that women were victims of profound medical ignorance about disease processes and effective treatments. In addition, middle- and upper-class women were also the victims of standards and mores that had their bodies pathologically constricted and distorted by corsets, weighed down by layers of heavy materials, and prohibited from physical exercise. Like their working-class sisters, who were also caught up by dress standards, confined in corsets, and weighed down by 15 to 18 hours of arduous labor under abominable circumstances, they probably were, by and large, a sickly and exhausted lot.

Prevailing medical theories viewed individuals as having a given, limited supply of energy and vitality. Middle- and upper-class women were not to dissipate theirs by too much mental stimulation, thereby jeopardizing their reproductive capacities (clearly not an issue of concern regarding working-class women). Conversely, since women were primarily reproductive beings, the medical profession tended to view any symptoms as reflections of disordered functioning of one or another of their reproductive organs, requiring its removal. That the theorizing was not consistently or logically applied to men—they were, after all, not castrated for being sexually promiscuous and wasting their creative energies through excessive ejaculations—suggests that the application of even the best of ignorance is socially and differentially determined.

Perhaps the most powerful and pervasive shaping of consciousness and belief concerning women's sexuality and its proper expression, at least in the United States in the twentieth century, was Freud's accomplishment. Recognizing the clitoris as a sensitive and erotogenic site from the time of infancy, a condition which Freud considered to be one of "childish masculinity" (1962), Freud decreed that a transference of excitability must take place from clitoris to vagina for sexuality to be mature. During the transference, the vagina may be anesthetic and this anesthesia of the vaginal orifice, so common to women, he acknowledged, "may become permanent if the clitoridal zone refuses to abandon its excitability . . . " (p. 87). Just to be female is to be flawed. To have a sensitive clitoris is to be incorrect by male and scientific standards. Obscured by this scientific mysticism about pleasure and women's eroticism was scientific information that only the modern women's movement made widely available to women—that the clitoris is richly supplied with nerve endings, while the vagina, including the "anesthetic" orifice of the "immature" woman, is not so supplied (the anesthesia is biological, not emotional), as women can very well perceive (or think they perceive). Instead of sexual surgery, the far more subtle and pervasive medical "treatment" of women for their sexuality or their restlessness became their assignment to neurotic immaturity and psychoanalysis.

Freud's theory of the vaginal orgasm required women to deny their own senses and knowledge about their own eroticism in order to be mature and female, a truly debilitating and depressing enterprise. The effects were profound and far ranging. For many women it was a fruitless effort that only deepened a sense of inferiority, inadequacy, and guilt. As a theory to explain and cure "frigidity," it ensures lack of orgasm by requiring women to have sex in precisely the way it is most difficult for them to experience an orgasm. It laid the scientific basis for the social proscription of masturbation, though for many women, masturbation is the only way they learn about their own sexual pleasure and orgasms. It reinforced the phallocentricity of sexuality by defining women's sexuality in terms only of the penis and her sexual "normality" in terms of her orgasmic ability in the conventional missionary position of heterosexual intercourse. The solution for many women was to fake orgasm with vaginal intercourse, a recommendation also made in gynecological textbooks at least into the 1960s (Scully and Bart, 1973). It seems hardly necessary to point out the self-serving aspects of the theory of the vaginal orgasm, since the vagina is central to most men's sexual satisfaction. If the clitoris is recognized as central to many women's sexuality, it is a challenge to both phallic and male supremacy since it means fingers, or tongue, *or* another woman can do better. Given the economic and political equality women were seeking, women might dispense with men altogether if left to their clitorality.

While the writings and practices of physicians of the late nineteenth and early twentieth centuries may be seen as part of the general male response to the increasing efforts of women to emancipate themselves from domestic servitude, I wonder what additional role may be attributed to increasing male apprehension about the intensity of emotional relationships within the homosocial world of middle- and upper-class women in nineteenth-century America. This may have been the context for Freud's preoccupation with the clitoris. From her examination of the letters and diaries of hundreds of women, Carroll Smith-Rosenberg (1975) began the reconstruction of this world where daughters grew up within a close-knit female network of love, loyalty, support, and friendship that included their mothers, sisters, aunts, cousins, and friends and existed alongside, though apart from, their heterosocial world. In their everyday lives as well as at times of crises—childbirth, death, illness—it was within their homosocial world that women received and gave love and support. Intense and emotional friendships developed between women that were unaffected by marriage or geographical separation and often lasted a lifetime. The letters, full of tenderness and emotional intensity, spoke of their contentment when they were last together, their despair at separation, their loneliness and longings for each other, often in physical terms. If they were able, women who were separated geographically often spent long vacations together, and it seemed quite natural and expected that when they visited each other's homes, the husband would relinquish the marriage bed and bedroom so the two women could spend every moment together.

From Smith-Rosenberg's study, this homosocial world, with its woman-centered primacy and devotion, appears to have been acceptable and possibly desirable and necessary within the Victorian society of the late nineteenth century when inhibitions and constraints were directed against physical and emotional intimacy and contact in heterosexual relationships. While these intimate homosocial relationships seem frequently to have been also physical, it is not clear whether they were sometimes or ever perceived as lesbian relationships, in today's terms. But this may not have been a male fear in the nineteenth century, if men were convinced of their own representations of (their) women's basic purity and asexuality and if, in any case, most women were still economically and politically dependent and unable to disturb patriarchal relationships in the public realm or within the private sphere of the family. Perhaps by the twentieth century, women had made sufficient (however limited) gains in breaking out of the Victorian and patriarchal stereotypes and in progressing toward at least the possibility of some economic autonomy that their primary emotional commitments to other women as well as their (clitoral) sexuality became of intense concern at least to middle- and upper-class male society and its physicians. Freud's theories of penis envy and the vaginal orgasm together explained and dispensed with (that is, relegated to the immature and neurotic) women's aspirations for emancipation (penis-substitutes), clitoral sensuality, homosociality, and lesbianism.

In Freud's twentieth century, we have seen first a disintegration or destruction of the nineteenth-century homosocial world of women, at least in the white middle and upper classes where that world has been documented, and an increasing emphasis on, if not obsession with, the heterosexual nuclear family—tight, together, and exclusive—by the dominant culture. This has meant the breaking up of a tradition of female networks and the isolation into individual homes of the large numbers of white middle-class and working-class women who were not employed in large numbers until or after the second world war. We can see in these processes the interlocked needs and mechanisms of control of a capitalist economy and a patriarchal social order. A patriarchal resistance to the increased possibilities for women's autonomy because of new educational and job opportunities was coupled with capitalism's economic needs to regulate the size of its labor force, with women constituting the auxiliary resource that could be manipulated.

Freud's theories on women's sexuality seeped into popular consciousness with remarkable pervasiveness and were also incorporated into everyday medical opinion and practice. Mainstream gynecological textbooks taught generations of medical students and physicians into the 1970s about the maturity of the vaginal orgasm, the primacy of the male sex drive, and women's passivity and "frigidity" as the usual female state, and they largely ignored the findings of Kinsey and of Masters and Johnson on the importance of the clitoris to women's sexual responses (Scully and Bart, 1973). Textbook statements are important factors in shaping or validating physicians' attitudes about women, attitudes that then serve to reinforce beliefs and social perceptions held by women themselves.

An important feature of sex desire in the man is the urge to dominate the woman and subjugate her to his will; in the woman acquiescence to the masterful takes a high place. (Jeffcoate, 1967, p. 726)

The traits that compose the core of the female personality are feminine narcissism, masochism and passivity. (Willson, 1971, p. 43)

In the 1970s at least one physician, Dr. James Burt, had resumed the more aggressive approach to women's sexual problems and by 1978 had helped 4000 women have orgasms by "reconstructing the vagina to make the clitoris more accessible to direct penile stimulation . . . " (Kunnes, 1978). He fashions and moves his "Mark II Vagina" and clitoris by lengthening the pubococcygeal muscle; by Dr. Burt's report, this operation has been 100 percent successful.

Knowledge about the clitoris, made widely accessible by the women's movement, along with increasing acceptability and openness of discussion around masturbation, lesbianism, and other critical issues have greatly advanced the liberation of women's sexual pleasure from mere service to men's sexuality, from male standards and values in sexual practices, and from phallocentrism. As might be expected, women respond in a variety of ways to this new consciousness, including the making of previously unheard of demands on male partners. The Mark II vagina is a medical response both to the "new" knowledge of the importance of the clitoris for women and the continued commitment to the pursuit of orgasms in the standard fashion most pleasing and convenient for men. This solution is reminiscent of the efforts of liberal reform movements in other areas to reconcile antagonistic interests but always in favor of the ruling class and without basic disturbance to the status quo.

MEDICINE, SCIENCE, AND HOMOSEXUALITY

With this history, one would, of course, expect that medicine and biology have paid attention to the "problem" of homosexuality. It has been considered by physicians in the twentieth century to be either a symptom of mental illness — a neurosis, obsession, or perversion—that should be treated and cured or a biological, constitutional aberration that can only be pitied and ignored. While psychiatrists have recently officially deleted homosexuality from their list of mental diseases, it is far from accepted in psychiatric, medical, or popular cultures as just one more ho-hum way to be sexual. Starting with the assumption that heterosexuality is *the* biological norm, some biologists and physicians have looked for an aberrant hormonal basis for homosexual behaviors in humans and animals. The most careful studies done of humans fail to demonstrate differences that some may have expected; that is, lesbians do not have higher testosterone levels than heterosexual women nor do male homosexuals have lower levels than heterosexual men. In the laboratory, modern speculations began with studies of the effects of castration and administration of opposite-sex hormones on stereotypical mating postures in rats: lordosis (raised rump posture) in females and mounting in males. It must be noted at the outset, however, that these are not exclusive behaviors; that is, untreated females of most species will mount other females or males, and males will mount other males. Early experiments showed that female rats, given androgens at birth, more frequently mount other females or males than untreated females do (Barraclough and Gorski, 1962; Harris and Levine, 1965). Conversely, male rats that are castrated at birth and given estrogens as adults exhibit lordosis in the presence of other male rats (Feder and Whalen, 1965; Grady, Phoenix, and Young, 1965). But all studies did not produce such straightforward and expected results. Androgens given to prepuberal females may *enhance* rather than abolish lordosis (Beach, 1942), whereas estrogens may *abolish* rather than enhance lordosis (Levine and Mullins, 1964) and may *increase* mounting activity with estrous females (Sodersten, 1972). Furthermore, estrogens can inhibit rather than increase lordosis if given to a neonatally castrated male (Feder and Whalen, 1965), and large doses of androgens can *abolish* male mounting and other sexual behaviors (Pollak and Sachs, 1975). In short, estrogens do not necessarily determine typical female mating behaviors and may, in fact, abolish them and enhance male mating behaviors; conversely, androgens do not necessarily determine male mating behaviors or inhibit female behaviors, but may instead abolish male and enhance female mating behaviors.

These contradictions do not, however, inhibit speculations that male homosexuals, like castrated neonatal male rats, suffered as fetuses from an inadequate level of androgens, resulting in "feminized" brains and therefore adult feminine sexual behaviors (making male homosexuality equivalent to lordosis in rats) (Dörner *et al.*, 1975). Conversely, the fetal brains of some girls are seen as somehow masculinized by androgen overdose and consequently molded for adult lesbian sexual behaviors (equivalent to mounting in rats). Nor did the ambiguities and serious flaws in the research prevent the application of these findings to the "treatment" of homosexuality with brain surgery to destroy parts of the hypothalamus or to its "prevention" in males by treating pregnant women with androgens (Meyer-Bahlburg, 1977).

The theory itself suffers from many flaws. First, it makes the simplistic assumption that stereotypical mating behaviors in animals, mounting and lordosis, are equivalent to and a measure of human homosexuality, a behavioral, psychological, and social complex that can not be characterized or measured by stereotypical sexual postures. The second major flaw is the assumption that heterosexuality is *the* biological norm of sexual behavior, and homosexuality is "caused" by a hormonal aberration. If we are to look to biology for normality, then we see that most species of animals frequently engage in physical and sexual (play?) behaviors with same-sex partners, actually mating heterosexually only when the female is in estrus. For them, heterosexual mating is a response to hormonal cues. For humans, the cues—the imperatives—are social. Indeed, if heterosexuality is so normal and natural, one wonders at the overwhelmingly powerful pressures that society brings to bear to maintain it—an "institutionalized compulsion" far beyond the present biological needs of the species (Rich, 1976, p. 210). For humans, cultural cues operate from the time of our earliest perceptions to construct a consciousness of unquestioned heterosexuality. While directed at both girls and boys, women and men, this falls with greatest force on girls and women, since their *heterosexual* identity—as objects of desire, as wives and mothers— constitutes the *totality* of their identity in our culture. To be sure, men are expected to be virile and are punished if they are not, but they *are* something else also; they are depicted as having a social identity and value apart from their sexuality and certainly regardless of their fatherhood.

It is within the field of the "scientific" investigation of homosexuality that the inextricable and highly charged connection between sexuality and gender is revealed. While gender is socially constructed (with culturally specific meanings and significance), it is also sexually constructed. An integral part of society's or an individual's own definition of gender is who one has sex with and how. To be masculine is *to screw*, to take, penetrate, invade, dominate, assert—if necessary, by force. Macho displays before one's peers of sexual interest in passing women is, after all, part of a boy's or man's self-confirmation and peer-confirmation that he is a real man. It is part of the gender definition of female to *be screwed*, to be passive, compliant, accepting, submissive; to be seductive, inviting, attractive. This reflects a sexual culture that expresses contempt for and the objectification of what is female (piece of ass) and glorification of what is male (virility and dominance). It sees sexual "normality" and identity only in the context of male domination of a woman. Within the psychiatric and medical professions, homosexuality is seen, if not as sheer mental illness, then as a disorder of gender identity, since it does not conform to that cultural conception of sexual normality. Scientific studies of sex hormonal disturbances (e.g., Dörner, Ehrhardt, Money) usually concern themselves with the subjects' *gender identity*, the underlying assumption being that it is likely to be disturbed and that it is an indicator or determinant of homosexuality. Lesbians are assumed not to identify themselves as women or gay men as men. Because the sex of the person one has sex with and how one is believed to perform sexually are part of the definition of gender, and because gender and heterosexuality are made to appear biological and natural, homosexuality is both viewed and investigated as a biological disorder of gender identity.

Yet, within this heterosexist cultural context, little girls, like little boys, are part of a homosocial female world that includes female relatives and friends and, later, teachers who are usually women.

The first knowledge any woman has of warmth, nourishment, tenderness, security, sensuality, mutuality, comes from her mother. That earliest enwrapment of one female body with another can sooner or later be denied or rejected, felt as choking possessiveness, as rejection, trap, or taboo; but it is, at the beginning, the whole world. Of course, the male infant also first knows tenderness, nourishment, mutuality from a female body. But institutionalized heterosexuality and institutionalized motherhood demand that the girl-child transfer those first feelings of dependency, eroticism, mutuality, from her first woman to a man, if she is to become what is defined as a "normal" woman—that is, a woman whose most intense psychic and physical energies are directed towards men. (Rich, 1976, pp. 218-219)

In view of these conflicting forces, that is, one's earliest and strongest emotional ties to a woman or women, our cultural tradition of women's networks of love and friendship, and the subsequent cultural pressures toward heterosexuality, the question becomes not so much why anyone is a lesbian or, for that matter, a heterosexual woman, but at what costs one comes to identify as either. If we could imagine a culture free of values and constraints concerning sexuality, human beings would probably express their sexuality, physicality, friendship, and loving emotions in a variety of ways that would not be necessarily influenced by others' biological sex. But that *if* is central to the problems of concern here in our patriarchal cultures.

DISCOURSE AND THE CONSTRUCTION OF SEXUALITY

Michel Foucault (1980) has written that the history of sexuality since the seventeenth century, rather than being one of the repression of sexuality in its various forms and expressions, has been a history of discourses on sex that express and generate relationships of power and feelings of pleasure and, in general, serve as mechanisms of dissemination and incitement of sexualities. The important things to discover about the discourses are, he believes, not what they "uncover" about sex, but why the discourses take place, who does the speaking, the institutions prompting people to speak, the forms power takes, and the channels through which it affects behaviors associated with desire and pleasure. Rather than there being truths and falsehoods about sex to be revealed, the effect of discourses has been to constitute, to construct sexualities and to organize sexuality, its expression, and the social forms and prescribed norms around it. The discourses on sexuality that have purported to liberate sexuality *from* repression and *for* its open discussion and expression are, rather, traps "set by the relations of power themselves to mask their mechanism and functioning" (Hussain, 1981, p. 169).

Foucault finds the technique of the nineteenth- and twentieth-century science of sexuality rooted in the Christian penance and its ritual of the confession, which began around the thirteenth century. "The confession became one of the West's most highly valued techniques for producing truth. . . . Western man has become a confessing animal" (p. 59). The confession in the Christian West was the first technique for producing the truth of sex. Foucault suggests that rather than the requirement being to root out a sex that was hidden within oneself, with the confession being simply the final step in the process, the real requirement was that people had to make confessions. Thus, there had to be something to confess, and the more elaborately and intricately it was concealed, the more elaborate and intricate the rituals around the confession had to be. From a philosophic point of view, it has been maintained that to confess, that is, to bring forth the truth, is a liberation, since power enforces silence; confession thus overcomes constraints on truth and freedom. It is, however, a deception or an inversion to believe that what is fundamental is a repressive force or power on speaking and thinking from which confession liberates us, and that the forces exhorting us to speak and confess are seeking to liberate us. To the contrary, Foucault argues, the *production* of truth, the confession, is primary and is imbued with relations of power, and the effects are control rather than liberation.

It was but a short step from the confessional to the nineteenth-century medical office and the psychoanalytic couch. The medicalization of sex introduced some refinements, however, to the confessional. First were the techniques of the physician: the history, the examination, questionnaires, hypnosis, etc. Then, since sex was considered to be established as a causal and explanatory factor in every aspect of one's present and future physical and mental health, the confession had to be meticulous, thorough, and constant. There was hardly a sickness or complaint that was free of some degree of sexual causation. Next, since sex is elusive, evasive and devious, the examination/confession had to elicit not only what the patient wished to hide from others but what was also hidden from the patient. Thus, bringing the truth to light required the efforts of confessor and examiner alike. But then the truth is not revealed by its confession alone; it must be validated through the interpretative and transforming knowledge of the examiner, the expert in truth. And finally, the process itself of the confession and its effects came to be therapeutic procedures, important because a generalized and unstable sexual morbidity was being defined for the first time. Sex, its instincts, expressions, and images could now be classified, no longer simply as error and transgression, but as either normal or pathological.

One could then describe (probably elaborating somewhat on Foucault's ideas) several of the most important aspects of the confessional process (both as Christian penance and in psychotherapy, recognizing that there are or may be differences between priest and psychotherapist in methods, motives, and goals). This process establishes, expresses, embodies, or enforces a set of power relationships between the participants: one, the authority who compels, questions, prescribes, judges, punishes, forgives, deciphers, and interprets; and the subject who sins, speaks, and receives interpreted truth. Also the confession itself provides the discourse on sex, the dissemination and reinforcement of heterogeneous sexualities, the knowledge of sex. It is self-affirmatory in that the rituals or sciences and discourses around the confessional have themselves constructed the sexuality that is required of people to find hidden within their natures and to bring forth for interpretation by the organizers of these rituals. The truth is further validated (an intrinsic psychotherapeutic postulate) by the very difficulty of bringing it forth; the greater the obstacles and resistance, the more true the product. Furthermore, the confession itself affirms the process, redeems, and purifies; one feels so much better for wrenching out the truths that it seems obviously harmful to have kept them hidden. But another, more elaborate scheme also remains hidden: the subject has played out a series of requirements: she has interiorized particular aspects of a *socially* constructed sexuality that she has been taught to consider personal, solitary, "innate" aspects of a secret nature that will harm her unless she extricates and shares them with someone who can examine, judge, forgive, understand, interpret, and help her to know herself. In this way our society, through its science of sexuality, has ordered knowledge about sex and, as I shall suggest, about *woman*.

Foucault, in short, suggests that nineteenth-century bourgeois or industrial society "did not confront sex with a fundamental refusal of recognition. On the contrary, it put into operation an entire machinery for producing true discourses concerning it. Not only did it speak of sex and compel everyone to do so; it also set out to formulate the uniform truth of sex"(p. 69). Society produced a "proliferation of discourses, carefully tailored to the requirements of power . . ." (p. 72). In so doing, it also invented a new pleasure: a pleasure in the truth of pleasure; the pleasure of discovering and speaking the truth of sex, of capturing and exposing it.

FOUCAULT AS METAPHOR

It is not possible for me to do justice to the sublety and range of Foucault's ideas in the course of this chapter, but I have presented my conception of some of his ideas that seem valid to me and are relevant to the argument I wish to make. While Foucault's subject is the question of power and control implicit in the "will to knowledge," he does not, with an exception that I will discuss, concern himself with identifying sources or directions or forces of power nor with categories of oppression. Power appears more as passive force in the discourse on sex; it *is* generated, exercised, deployed, and embodied wherever the discourses happen to take place, but by no one in particular, and the specific content of the discourse is irrelevant to the generation of relationships of power. But I believe that Foucault's analysis of the discourses on sex can be used as metaphoric for the discourses on a grand scale between women and men and their generation of patriarchal ideologies and relationships of power, in this case, male hegemony and female subordinance. Foucault would doubtless reject such categorical statements, though he does not reject and in fact invokes, for example, the notion of the hegemonic power of the *bourgeoisie* to foist its ideas about the body, health and sex onto the proletariat. He does state, however,

> . . . there is no power that is exercised without a series of aims and objectives. But this does not mean that it results from the choice or decision of an individual subject; let us not look for the headquarters that presides over its rationality; neither the caste which governs, nor the groups which control the state apparatus, nor those who make the most important economic decisions direct the entire network of power that functions in a society (and makes *it* function). . . . (p. 95)

Nonetheless, granted these complexities and ambiguities and the diffuseness of loci of control, power, and ultimate responsibility (an issue I shall return to), the task to which I am committed here is the attempt to identify and understand the most powerful sources of women's oppression. Consequently, I must concern myself with categories, like patriarchal ideology and power, as well as with the particularities of their expression. Ultimately the most powerful source of women's oppression resides in our own heads, but that derives from and is influenced by certain external realities.

If we return with this perspective to the parts of Foucault's analysis that I have presented, we observe first of all that those in the position to judge, compel, extract, question, punish, forgive, decipher, intepret, treat, and cure have always been men; at the very least half, and in the last century the majority, of those judged, compelled, questioned, punished, forgiven, interpreted, and treated have been women. Certainly all priests and close to 100 percent of physicians and psychiatrists have been men. If, then, the effect of such discourses has been control rather than liberation of the subject, we are looking at a mechanism of construction and control of women's sexuality that spans at least the last seven centuries. Between the power of the confessional (in the form of male authority) and the hegemonic control of the Church over heresy (the sin of which witches were accused for their sexuality, intelligence, independence, or healing skills), women have been the class under surveillance and control for hundreds of years and always under penalty of death.

But while the apparent subject of the discourses may have been sexuality, the issue has always been *woman* herself and her nature. That is, since woman *is* sexuality and untamed nature, the relationships of power embodied in and generated through the confessional and medical discourse, like those embodied in *all* of her discourses within patriarchal societies, constitute an integral part of the system of the social control of woman. And the content and *products* of the discourses have been no less important than the relationships around them. Whatever it was that women have had to confess—their sins of thought and deed, their fears, frustrations, yearnings, aspirations, and dissatisfactions—the "truth" that has been ritually extracted, transformed, interpreted, and revealed to them by those "qualified" to do so (that is fathers, husbands, physicians, and other of society's "experts") has remained insidiously the same: they have been deviant (from the patriarchal mold) and immature (unwilling to nurture without complaint). The degree of their sickness was directly proportional to the degree of their deviance from their natural roles. The "knowledge" that emerged from the psychiatric confessional was "known" to the psychiatrist before the patient arrived, but required the rituals of extraction and interpretation to become known to her; it scientifically validated the results of all her other discourses within her patriarchal world. Thus, the reality and the sources of the degradations, humiliations, self-denials, and self-erosions which women experienced as a result of those daily discourses were medicalized, interpreted, and transformed into her personality disorders, thereby confirming the dependent and immature *nature* of women. The one monolithic portrait, after all, that medicine and psychiatry have drawn is that of *woman*, a very particular disability by all the standards of normality they have constructed. The discourses on sex are but a microcosm of women's discourses with the rest of her world—perpetually validating not her *self*, but her ascribed position within the patriarchal social structure.

Foucault speaks of the science of sexuality's functioning as an erotic art: "pleasure in the truth of pleasure, the pleasure of knowing that truth, of discovering and exposing it, the fascination of seeing it and telling it, of captivating and capturing others by it, of confiding it in secret, of luring it out in the open—the specific pleasure of the true discourse on pleasure" (p. 71). (By his language he seems to attempt to evoke the very pleasure of which he speaks.) The important elements in this erotic art of the science of sexuality have to do with the multiplication and intensification of pleasures connected to the production of the "truth" about sex. But, we may ask, pleasure for whom? From my point of view, this is a constructed male pleasure based largely (at least for many heterosexual men) in the realities or fantasies they enjoy within the context of their representations and constructions of women's sexuality: a fabricated woman and her fabricated sexuality, which has been, contradictorily, represented either as passive and masochistic or untamed fury. Until recently at least, women did not share in those pleasures of revelation (with exceptions, of course), since for many (or most?) heterosexual women sex was either to be neutrally endured or painful or forced and obligatory or fraught with fear of pregnancy. And this multiplication of the male pleasures of seeing, telling, captivating, exposing, and luring in the sexual discourse reaches new heights in the explosion of pornography that depicts sexual violence against women as erotic and natural.

SEX AND THE SOCIAL CONTROL OF WOMEN

Patriarchal institutions and ideology have attempted to make of women objects of contempt—less than fully developed human beings with less than humanly developed intellects and sensitivities. Having attempted to create women to their representations of them by not permitting access to the full range of humanizing experiences, they then construct theories to explain both women's "inferiority" and the practices of men to control, appropriate, possess, degrade, and humiliate women specifically and in general. The fact that women to some extent, either consciously or unconsciously, from anti-feminists to feminists, participate in these systems, believe the constructed image of themselves, and are to one degree or another male-identified and complicit in sexist relationships and representations does not lesson the reality of the generalizations regarding the relationships of women and men relative to power. As for any relationships of subordination or slavery, it is always relevant to raise questions concerning the existence or degree of consciousness, acquiescence, complicity, participation, passivity, acceptance of authority, self-victimization or self-responsibility on the part of the "victim" and the role these play in establishing or enforcing particular power relationships that the victim either desires or accepts. My concern here, however, is to examine ideological sources of the social control of women.

Sex (being symbolic of and identical with love and intimacy, at least for women in our Western cultures) is by its very physical nature the most seductive, private, intrusive, direct, and possessing way to exert power and control. For this reason and because it lends itself so well to the combination of intimacy, psychological seduction, and physical strength, sex is potentially the most effective and abusive way to control women psychologically, physically, or through degradation and humiliation, and to maintain individual women's subjection to a particular man and collective women's social and political subjection. Theories from Sade through Ellis and Freud have explained the "naturalness" ("instinctual" or unconscious) of sexual sadism, without discussing the reality that it had always been male sadism against women (Barry, 1979). While there are many different relationships of power generated by many different discourses on sex, the constant and general relationship of power is the one that enhances the control of women by men. A dominant and pervasive form of that discourse today is aggressive pornography, and the fact that takes the discussion out of the realm of the abstract is that it is not men who are degraded, beaten, and tortured by women or whose lives are snuffed out at the height of orgasms.

Since the sexual degradation of women and physical violence against their bodies is the subject matter of the realities of pornography, prostitution, rape, and battering, and since sexuality is the subject matter of philosophical and scientific discussions, then sexuality is not simply a subject for discourses that generate relationships of power wherever those discourses happen to take place (with the implication of a randomized effect or of potential equality for all). Rather, a particular set of relationships of control is intrinsic to the discourse on sex; sex is the method of the individual and social control of women within patriarchal cultures. The little historical evidence that exists, as I noted in Chapter 6, points to the control of women's sexuality through the legal and physical enforcement of women's monogamy as one of the first steps in the consolidation of male hegemony and state power.

Foucault provides us with an interesting juxtaposition, noting on the one hand the earliest detailed discourses on sex by Sade and the anonymous author of *My Secret Life* and on the other, the medical discourses of Ellis and Freud. The latter directly describe and explain the sexual mastery and superiority of man and the penis over women and the vagina, whether we view the penis as real or symbolic. They make woman's acceptance of that sexual mastery and its extension (penetration) into the rest of her life as synonymous with her normality. We can see here two faces of hypocrisy in the control of women through sexuality: the official, legal, medical face with both its repressive aspects and its discourses that "uncover" sex, establish and enforce relationships of power, and incite sexuality; and the unofficial, sublegal face. The official discourses are important mechanisms for reinforcing patriarchal relations both ideologically—through interpretation of "psychopathology" and prescriptions for treatment and cures that reinforce traditional roles and personalities—and sexually—through reinforcing the primacy of sex and male mastery in sex as the physical and symbolic instruments of male power and control of women. This face is the soft, subtle, *intellectual* control, which through the hysterization and medicalization of women's bodies and psychiatrization of their minds taught women their *need* to be subservient to men, though it speaks the language of love and motherhood. The other face is the unofficial and sublegal one by which sex is used for the *physical* control of women—prostitution, pornography, rape, battering, and sexual slavery—and it teaches that women *want* to be controlled, even violently.

Foucault says that he is "looking for the reasons for which sexuality, far from being repressed in the society of that period [the eighteenth and nineteenth centuries], on the contrary was constantly aroused" (p. 148). Perhaps the clues may be that sex was first discussed in detail, through Sade, as sexual violence against women, and also that sex was the most pervasive and universally available form for the social control of women, yet the most subtle, silent, unspoken, unseen, isolated and therefore protected in the means of its expression.

THE "INSTITUTIONALIZED COMPULSION"[1]: HETEROSEXUALITY AND VIOLENCE

The institutions and ideologies of the state maintain class, race, and patriarchal rule. In particular, the institutions and ideologies of heterosexuality (i.e., heterosexism) are the primary force in the maintenance of patriarchal rule and the social, economic, and political subordinance of women. In the argument I wish to make here, I do not mean to deny the realities of many women's lives: that they have actively chosen, rather than fallen into, a life of heterosexual marriage and children; that they have created a cooperative family life that provides for

---

[1] See Rich (1976; 1980).

each of its members love, support, honesty, friendship, and encouragement; and that, in their heterosexual relationships, they have control over their own sexuality and share equally in the enjoyment of and participation in their sexual relationships. Nor, conversely, do I mean to overlook the realities of some lesbian relationships: that they may lack love, support, honesty, friendship, and encouragment; and that they may reflect and express ideologies and practices of the heterosexist world in which they exist: asymmetries in control and power, oppression, exploitation, manipulation, and even violence. Rather, my attention here is directed at institutionalized heterosexuality as an oppressive force for all women and many men.

The power of heterosexism derives from ideology and violence, the means by which other systems of oppression maintain power. Ideology and consciousness are critical to the success of any system of oppression. A system of ideas, beliefs, and practices must make some sense and offer some rewards or the illusion of reward, to women and men of every class, race, ethnicity, and age in order to perpetuate, without major rebellion, its economic, political, and social subordination. Not only men, but women, must take for granted the benefits to themselves of the gender relationships of their cultures. (Of course, women as individuals or in groups have always rebelled in some way, and a major revolt is presently under way, but the entire class of women has not risen up, and the patriarchy has trembled but not yet collapsed anywhere.) And however great are the particular benefits to the white male ruling class in a capitalist society, patriarchal benefits are seen as shared by men of every class and color.

One of the most powerful socializing forces molding the consciousness and lives of women from early infancy is the ideology of heterosexuality and its practices. So intimate and constant as an influence, a cultural *imperative*, that it is as taken for granted as the air we breathe, and it has remained unexamined until the recent women's movement (and even there has not received the searching analysis it requires just because it *is* so intimate, integral, and seemingly natural a part of every woman's life). While the ideologies, practices, and institutions of heterosexuality specify an enormous number of attributes and behaviors appropriate for women or men, they fall with special force on women, as I previously noted, since the trappings of heterosexuality define the totality of *woman* ("the total woman") in patriarchal societies. From our earliest years, we absorb messages from life in our homes, from school books and school life and from nearly every television commercial and program, advertisement, billboard, and pop song. They unremittingly specify the narrow limits of femininity required for approval, and we early learn that the only important approval is from boys and men. The messages specify how we should walk, dress, talk, think, look, sit, and gesture to be attractive. The potential freedom and creativity of our minds are constrained by the clear message that, if we are to be liked, it will be for being caring and nice, not precocious, argumentative, and challenging (prerequisites for creativity). The primary social task is to make of girls and women soft, compliant, and loving human beings, which requires at the same time discouraging sparks of independence, intellectual risk-taking, and the (male) habits of physical, emotional, and intellectual give and take that sharpen minds and bodies. Our earliest lesson is that we *will be* wives and mothers; and to be that, we must be appealing to men, approved and validated by them. We learn that the only normal way to *be* is to be identified with a man, to have a primary emotional commitment to a man, to take pleasure and pride in utter devotion to a man and in the privilege of emotional, physical, social, and economic dependence on him. It is even taken for granted that *when* we marry, we will simply cease to exist by the name and identity we have had for 20, 40, or 60 years and become instead an appendage to another's name and identity. We are to be pleased and proud to sacrifice our *selves* for love. The degree to which and the ways in which women resist or comply, are conscious or unconscious of, reject or accept this prescription end up constituting, one way or another, the substance, energy, and definition of our lives.

There is a second important source of the power of heterosexism in women's oppression: psychic and physical violence. Every single aspect of male violence against women, as well as the economic and social oppression of women, has existed and can only exist within the context of and because of the ideology of obligatory heterosexuality, which acknowledges, permits, and requires men's unquestioning access to, ownership of, and authority over women's bodies in the service of the bodies and minds of men. Of course, the cultural stereotyping and the cultural violence are closely related; the closer to the patriarchal stereotype of being beautiful but brainless that women become, the more profound the contempt and ridicule with which they are rewarded and the more justified the physical and psychic assaults on their person are made to appear. To demonstrate this claim for the heterosexist basis for all violence against women, I shall have to list the many examples that are already familiar to women, but the length of such a list is itself staggering, as is its underlying base of misogyny. The list includes: anonymous verbal and bodily assault; rape—rape in general, racial rape, marital rape, wartime rape, gang rape, child rape; wife and woman battering; abortion and birth control laws; involuntary sterilizations; unnecessary hysterectomies; clitoridectomies and genital mutilations; foot binding; prostitution and female slavery; sexual harassment in employment; aggressive pornography and snuff films. What is most remarkable about this list of the most common forms of physical violence against women is that they are all sexual assaults. Even when women are the victims of "ordinary" homicide—strangled, shot or stabbed to death—either it is part of rape or it is because a husband or lover has lost, or thinks he has lost, exclusive control of her sexuality. Heterosexual violence and heterosexual consciousness together ensure male dominance and patriarchal control. I shall discuss in some detail only the two most common forms of sexual violence against women; rape and battering.

Rape in General

The story of rape begins with the rage and fear women must live with, are taught by their mothers to live with, along with their first autonomous steps to play out-of-doors. That women are everywhere raped and often also murdered is so integral a part of daily living that the utter horror of this sexually violent act, the contempt and hatred it expresses toward all women, become too debilitating to contemplate more than occasionally. It is the very cutting edge of the social control by men of women as individuals and as a group. The victims are those who are raped and all the rest who are taught both to fear and to love men, who are also seen as their protectors. But while rape profoundly affects *all* women, it has been of no or little concern to *all* men, a curious fact. With rare exception, all men have some intimate relationship with a woman who can be raped at any time, yet it is not a subject that engages the theoretical or active attention of men except for those who rape and some who are engaged in law enforcement and a few others. Men will write to the newspapers endlessly on every aspect of the subject of abortion, but rape seldom appears to be an issue worthy of liberal notice, except perhaps to defend the civil rights of a judge threatened with recall because of his callous treatment of juvenile victims of rape.

A question is, Why the apathy of men in general about a common male crime that keeps all the women around them in a constant state of fear and apprehension? Since the number of men buying pornographic literature and seeing pornographic films is much larger than the number of known rapes and since mass rape in war by troops (representative, after all, of a nation's manhood) is a constant and accepted sociological phenomenon, perhaps the answer is that rape is not far from either run-of-the-mill male sexual fantasies or the realities of the marital and sexual bed. The very existence of rape and its commonness, the ready availability of aggressive pornography, the constant portrayal in books, films, and television of men *taking* women cannot help but create a consciousness that links manhood and virility with mastery, appropriation, and force. That, in fact, may constitute the substance of the struggle for many men who prefer to live more humanely and sensitively than the patriarchal stereotype allows. The ideology of mastery becomes coupled with both feelings and cultural convictions (however conscious or not) about the proper place for women, about women's attempts to be free of male protection, about women "asking for it," and results in an ambivalence that is expressed by apathy or sympathy for rapists. Men who are truly concerned that the feminist movement is not sufficiently "humanist" (i.e., male-oriented) and inclusive have the opportunity to be included by producing insightful analyses of the links between rape, male violence, and sexuality, misogyny, and the appropriation and control of women's sexuality and women through sexuality. Such analyses could provide the bases for changed consciousness and behaviors. At present the male voice that dominates celebrates rape and violence. Only men can change that voice.

In any consideration of rape (and battering), it is necessary to recognize, as MacKinnon (1983a, 1983b) has argued, that our culture eroticizes force and power. Dominance is sexually arousing to many men, as submission is to some women. The work of Malamuth and Donnerstein (1982) and their associates on the effects of aggressive pornographic materials showed high levels of sexual arousal in men exposed to rape scenes and suggested that under varying experimental circumstances, between 33 and 50 percent of nondeviant men classify themselves as likely to rape. Male domination and female submission are implicit in our society's definitions of gender, and that relationship is eroticized. Rape is one violent and sexual expression of that cultural eroticization of gender differences in power. Rape and battery are portrayed as deviant, but they are only expressions of the masculinity that defines men in our society, for which they are otherwise "trained, elevated, venerated, and paid" (MacKinnon, 1983a, p. 643). Since "the state is male" and the "law sees and treats women the way men see and treat women" (p. 644), the laws do not prohibit violence against women. Rather, they have regulated the extent to which the violent sexual control of women by men will be permitted through rape, battering, and pornography and the manner in which abortion, contraception, prostitution, marriage, divorce, and women's employment will be permitted to affect male access to women's sexuality.

Race and Rape

The relationships between sexism and misogyny, racism and heterosexism as necessary elements in patriarchal control lie exposed in the sordid history of sexual violence against black women, institutionalized within the institution of slavery in the American South. The particular ways racism has been expressed and enforced against black women have been sexual. Black women everywhere in this country have always been raped by white men, as well as black, with impunity. Slave women were raped by their white masters, by their white and black overseers and drivers, or by slave men under the direction of their masters for breeding purposes. They were subjected to particularly brutal beatings not merely for minor or nonexistent infractions of rules but for the sexual gratification of their floggers. It was the issue of sex that pitted the white mistress against the black woman; it was the slave who was punished and beaten as a seductress for being raped by her master. As Angela Davis and Bell Hooks maintain, the sexual exploitation of women slaves had little to do with sexual lust and everything to do with "the demoralization and dehumanization of black women" for the purpose of the total submission and allegiance of black and white women (Hooks, 1981, p. 27). Understanding the unrestrained and unpunished sexual violence by white men against black women during and after slavery makes obvious the misogyny that adds special fuel to the mechanisms of racial social control.

From the time of slavery through recent decades, the rape of black women by white men, especially in the South, but elsewhere as well, continues as *the* unspoken and unrecorded crime and was, in fact, an integral part of the judicial system itself of the South. Black women could expect to be raped not only by their white jailers in their cells, but by deputies and sheriffs when they were stopped for traffic violations or for no violations, even when they were accompanied by men. In the conditions of fascism that existed for blacks in the South before the 1970s, there was absolutely no justice within or outside of the judicial system. (I do not imply that there is *now* equal justice before the law; women continue to be raped with impunity.)

There is another particularly excruciating aspect of the combination of racism, heterosexism, misogyny, and the legal system. It was a frequent occurrence in the South before the 1960s that black men were lynched by mobs of white men or by the judicial system (these were often exactly the same—the sheriffs, judges and jurors frequently being members of the Ku Klux Klan) on fraudulent charges of raping a white woman. This was the official punishment for not being sufficiently obsequious—for not stepping off the sidewalk onto the street when approaching white folk, for trying to vote, etc. If they were not lynched and killed first, like 14-year-old Emmett Till (he was accused of winking at a white woman, chained, and thrown into a river to drown), they were found guilty on trial by their white "peers" and killed by hanging, gassing, or electric chair. At the same time, the real rape or murder of black women by black men was seldom or never punished; that is the one freedom that the white judicial system permitted, and still permits, black men. Black and white men can meet as equals in the area of misogyny and violence against black women.

Other Rape

There are many other common forms of rape. Within marriages and other heterosexual relationships, there is a wide spectrum of enforced sexuality, where intercourse occurs because the woman fears violence or other forms of retribution or because of the socially sanctioned power of husbands to exercise their marital rights and of men in general to satisfy their sexual "needs." Only recently have states in the United States begun to legally recognize the entity of marital rape. During wars, the wholesale rape of women is an accepted ritual within the male ritual of war; it is rape that is unpunished and even considered the privilege of both the conquerors and the vanquished. In many societies and cultures, gang rape, along with beating, ostracism, or murder, is accepted punishment for women who get out of line sexually or otherwise disobey or displease men. The rape and sexual abuse of girls by their fathers, stepfathers, uncles, brothers, and family friends were and are common crimes still protected unofficially by silence and officially by policies that, like wife battering and marital rape, place the integrity of the family before the safety and even lives of its children, wives, and mothers.

Wife and Women Battering

As the economic power of the traditional patriarchal family began to decline in turn of the century, industrializing America, the helping services and professions increasingly served to reconstruct and strengthen the private sphere of the traditional patriarchal family (Stark, Flitcraft, and Frazier, 1979). Until the feminist movement broke the silence, social and medical services ignored the "private" brutality that was required to keep women and children in their place. It was estimated in 1979 that between 3 and 4 million women are brutally beaten each year in the United States (Stark *et al.*, 1979). Wife and woman battering is sexual violence. It usually occurs in the kitchen or bedroom, where most murders of women by husbands and lovers also occur, and it is usually precipitated by the woman's perceived failure of some domestic responsibility (MacKinnon, 1983a). It is often followed by rape. To batterers (and perhaps others), beating a woman is sexually arousing; the sex itself reinforces the sexuality of the violence and the violence of sexuality through rape.

Stark *et al.*, through their study of emergency room practices and records in the treatment of battered women, have analyzed the role medical practice plays in strengthening male domination in the home in the face of the struggle of battered women to overcome their problematic status in the family (as indicated by their coming to the emergency room). They believe that along with the disappearance of the family's traditional economic role and the decline of traditional patriarchal authority within the family, male domination has become more extensive throughout life in the United States. They suggest this seeming paradox is reconciled by understanding "the extent to which the social services, broadly construed to include education, religion, and recreation as well as medicine, law, police, and welfare, function today as a reconstituted or extended patriarchy, defending the family form 'by any means necessary,' including violence, against both its internal contradictions and women's struggles" (p. 464).

Stark *et al.* discovered that *after* physical abuse begins, many women turn to self-abuse and other escape efforts: alcohol and drug over-use, suicide attempts, and psychiatric disorders. When a physically abused woman appears in the emergency room, medical practice is faced with an unwelcome challenge to its usual procedures of using all available laboratory techniques to define a physiological disorder, establish a diagnosis, and institute treatment and a cure. There is, however, no physiological sequence to the recurrent condition or "disease" of being beaten nor is there any obvious medical cure. What happens then, upon recurrent visits, is that the woman's problem becomes reorganized by the medical staff as symptoms of her psychopathology: masochism, depression, alcoholism, drug abuse, hysteria, or hypochondriasis. "At this point the woman herself, rather than her assailant, appears as a legitimate object of medical control" (p. 470). Her repeated returns to the emergency room, which are her efforts to escape the abusive situation, become her illness, for which medicine *can* find a diagnosis and treatment. As Stark *et al.* point out and many of us already know, once pseudopsychiatric labels appear in the medical record, such as "patient with multiple symptomatology with psychosomatic overlay," it becomes difficult for patients to receive appropriate treatment. The woman's battering becomes a *consequence* of her "more basic" problem with drugs or alcohol or emotional instability. The majority of battered women seen by the medical profession are given antidepressant drugs, tranquilizers, or sleeping pills and referred to detoxification programs, mental health clinics, mental hospitals, or counselling agencies. The combined effect of these is to help the woman to not recognize or forget her abuse as a political issue and reinforce her dependence on others. She is rehabilitated to resume her traditional roles in the same context within which she is being beaten.

SUMMARY AND CONCLUSIONS

Patriarchal social orders have defined private and public worlds, with women in the world of the family and reproduction and men in the world of politics and production. They define differences in women's and men's "natures" that make the sexual division of labor and power "natural." These definitions then specify the needs and skills of women and men as necessary and complementary to each other (male aggressivity, female nurturance, etc.), and they describe a world that is of necessity heterosexual. Women and men must pair for society (i.e., patriarchal society) to function socially and economically.

To maintain this sexual division of labor and power, it is necessary for the state and individual men to have unquestioned access to women's bodies, their labor power, and the products of their labor. This is done through marriage, divorce, and property laws; through the regulation of abortion, birth control, and sterilization; through systematic job segregation, economic exploitation, sexual harassment in employment, and job training and educational discrimination; and through violence.

Through their discourses on sexuality, science and medicine have played important roles in the social construction and control of women's sexuality and idealized temperament. Through their representations of women as passive, dependent, martyred, and masochistic, science and medicine have reinforced the social stereotype of woman as a subordinate member of the patriarchal household and social order. Through their proscriptions and definitions of normality and maturity, science and medicine have lent tacit support to structures and ideologies that condone direct and indirect violence in the social control of women, and have, in fact, themselves been the instruments of violence against the bodies and minds of women.

Heterosexuality, as institution and ideology, is a cornerstone of patriarchy. Heterosexism provides the forms and consciousness of women's dependence on men—sexual, physical, economic, and emotional. Every productive or economic mode, such as capitalism, fashions its economic, legal, and cultural institutions in ways best suited to strengthen itself specifically and to protect the patriarchal social order of which it is an integral part. Compulsory and institutionalized heterosexuality is also the cornerstone for violence against women. This violence is a logical and inevitable outcome of the assumption that men control, own, or dominate the bodies and minds of women.

Clearly heterosexual relationships in a variety of forms may be important and valid relationships to have and express, just as same-sex relationships may be in the lives of most women and men, however they define their sexuality. Rather, at issue here is the institutionalization of heterosexuality, the cultural imperative that limits freedom of development of mind and body, and that assumes and requires the control of women, even with violence.

REFERENCES

Barker-Benfield, G. Sexual surgery in late-nineteenth-century America. In C. Dreifus (Ed.), *Seizing our bodies*. New York: Vintage, 1978.

Barraclough, C., and Gorski, R. Studies on mating behaviour in the androgen-sterilized female rat in relation to the hypothalamic regulation of sexual behaviour. *Journal of Endocrinology*, 1962, *25*, 175-182.

Barry, K. *Female sexual slavery*. Englewood Cliffs: Prentice-Hall, 1979.

Beach, F. Male and female mating behavior in prepuberally castrated female rats treated with androgen. *Endocrinology*, 1942, *31*, 673-678.

Bullough, V. and Voght, M. Women, menstruation, and nineteenth-century medicine. *Bulletin of the History of Medicine*, 1973, *47*, 66-82.

Dörner, G. Rohde, W., Stahl, F., Krell, L., and Masius, W. G. A neuro-endocrine predisposition for homosexuality in men. *Archives of Sexual Behavior*, 1975, *4*, 1-8.

Ehrenreich, B., and English, D. *Witches, midwives, and nurses. A history of women healers*. Oyster Bay: Glass Mountain, N.D.

Eisenstein, Z. *The radical future of liberal feminism*. New York: Longman, 1981.

Feder, H., and Whalen, R. Feminine behavior in neonatally castrated and estrogen-treated male rats. *Science*, 1965, *147*, 306-307.

Foucault, M. *The history of sexuality*. New York: Vintage, 1980.

Freud, S. *Three essays on the theory of sexuality*. New York: Basic Books, 1962.

Grady, K., Phoenix, C., and Young, W. Role of the developing rat testis in differentiation of the neural tissues mediating mating behavior. *Journal of Comparative and Physiological Psychology*, 1965, *59*, 176-182.

Harris, G., and Levine, S. Sexual differentiation of the brain and its experimental control. *Journal of Physiology*, 1965, *181*, 379-400.

Hooks, B. *Ain't I a woman. Black women and feminism*. Boston: South End Press, 1981.

Hussain, A. Foucault's history of sexuality. *m/f*, 1981, *5-6*, 169-191.

Jeffcoate, T. *Principles of gynecology*. London: Butterworth, 1967.

Jordanova, L. Natural facts: a historical perspective on science and sexuality. In C. MacCormick and M. Strathern (Eds.), *Nature, culture and gender*. Cambridge: Cambridge University Press, 1980.

Koedt, A. *The myth of the vaginal orgasm*. Boston: New England Free Press, 1970.

Kunnes, R. Surgeon remakes vagina. *Seven Days*, 1978, *2*, 25-26.

Leavitt, J. "Science" enters the birthing room: Obstetrics in America since the eighteenth century. *The Journal of American History*, 1983, *70*, 281-304.

Levine, S., and Mullins, R. Estrogen administered neonatally affects adult sexual behavior in male and female rats. *Science*, 1964, *144*, 185-187.

MacKinnon, C. Feminism, Marxism, method, and the state: An agenda for theory. *Signs*, 1982, *7*, 515-544.

MacKinnon, C. Feminism, Marxism, method, and the state: Toward feminist jurisprudence. *Signs*, 1983, *8*, 635-658. (a)

MacKinnon, C. Interview. *Off our Backs*, 1983, *13*, 17-19. (b)

Malamuth, N., and Donnerstein, E. The effects of aggressive-pornographic mass media stimuli. *Advances in Experimental Social Psychology*, 1982, *15*, 103-135.

Merchant, C. *The death of nature*. San Francisco: Harper & Row, 1980.

Meyer-Bahlburg, H. Sex hormones and male homosexuality in comparative perspective. *Archives of Sexual Behavior*, 1977, *6*, 297-325.

O'Brien, M. *The politics of reproduction*. Boston: Routledge & Kegan Paul, 1981.

Ortner, S. Is female to male as nature is to culture? *Feminist Studies*, 1972, *1*, 5-31.

Padgug, R. Sexual matters: On conceptualizing sexuality in history. *Radical History Review*, 1979, *20*, 3-23.

Pollak, E., and Sachs, B. Masculine sexual behavior and morphology: Paradoxical effects of perinatal androgen treatment in male and female rats. *Behavioral Biology*, 1975, *13*, 401-411.

Rich, A. *Of woman born*. New York: W. W. Norton, 1976.

Rich, A. Toward a woman-centured university. In A. Rich. *On lies, secrets, and silence*. New York: W. W. Norton, 1979.

Rich, A. Compulsory heterosexuality and lesbian existence. *Signs*, 1980, *5*, 631–660.

Scully, D., and Bart, P. A funny thing happened on the way to the orifice: Women in gynecology textbooks. *American Journal of Sociology*, 1972, *78*, 1045-1049.

Smith-Rosenberg, C. The female world of love and ritual: Relations between women in nineteenth-century America. *Signs*, 1975 *1*, 1-30.

Smith-Rosenberg, C., and Rosenberg, C. The female animal: Medical and biological views of woman and her role in nineteenth-century America. *The Journal of American History*, 1973, *59*, 332-356.

Sodersten, P. Mounting behavior in the female rat during the estrous cycle, after ovariectomy, and after estrogen or testosterone administration. *Hormones and Behavior*, 1972, *3*, 307-320.

Stark, E., Flitcraft, A., and Frazier, W. Medicine and patriarchal violence: The social construction of a "private" event. *International Journal of Health Services*, 1979, *9*, 461-493.

Willson, J. *Obstetrics and gynecology*. St. Louis: C. V. Mosby, 1971.

Woolf, V. *Three guineas*. New York: Harcourt Brace & World, 1938.

Chapter 8
Patriarchal Science, Feminist Visions

The master's tools will never dismantle the master's house.

Audre Lorde, 1981.

This book has shown that science is *not* the neutral, dispassionate, value-free pursuit of Truth; that scientists are not objective, disinterested, or culturally disengaged from the questions they ask of nature or the methods they use to frame their answers. It is, furthermore, impossible for science or scientists to be otherwise, since science is a social activity and a cultural product created by persons who live in the world of science as well as in the societies that bred them.

Scientific ideas and theories represent efforts to describe and explain the natural world; that is, reality. That reality, in the form of our perceptions and interpretations of it, is like the rest of our culture, a product of human thought. Yet it is perceived as objective reality, which becomes incorporated, in its various forms, into our early and developing consciousness. That consciousness is the medium through which we perceive and interpret the "objective realities" of the external world, learn our individual location within it, and form a world view. That consciousness and its world view, however limited they may be at each stage of our development, provide a framework for ordering and interpreting our experiences, which come to confirm the world view of which they are, in part, the products.

Necessarily incorporated into that world view is the patriarchal ordering of external reality, both natural and social. The language and relationships of dominance and subordinance, control and submission, male and female, become a part of our consciousness that orders and interprets the external world. Thus, while criticisms of scientific investigations and theories have been framed in terms of failures of scientific objectivity, this both understates and misstates the problem because it assumes there is a particular reality to be revealed by another known as objective, value-free research.

In this consideration of the biological sciences, it is necessary to explore concepts of truth and reality, objectivity, and dualisms, since they mystify and impede, rather than clarify, our perceptions of events and relationships in our social and natural worlds.

PATRIARCHAL SCIENCE

The Production of Truth

As discussed in Chapter 7, it is Michel Foucault's theme that what is really at work in discourse is desire and power. Bodies of knowledge represent discourses that reflect, express, and generate relations of power. Discourse unfolds in any society "within the context of external restraints which appear as 'rules of exclusion' " (White, p. 89). The rules determine who speaks, what is or is not discussed, how it is discussed, what questions may be asked, and what is "true" or "false." Thus, while the work of discourse appears to be the *uncovering* of truth, it rests upon and conceals the struggle between those who have the power to discourse and those who do not. Both by their practices of exclusion and their definitions of what *is*, what is to be discussed, and what is false or true, discourses *produce* rather than reveal truth. The conditions and circumstances under which the discourses take place reflect conditions of social power at the time and thus themselves define the theories and practices (such as the scientific methodology) brought to bear in the discourse, consequently determining the outcome. White (1979) summarizes Foucault's view as being that "the modern history of Western man's 'will to knowledge' had been less a progressive development towards 'enlightenment' than a product of an endless interaction between desire and power within the system of exclusions which made different kinds of society possible" (p. 91).

The introduction and use of the IQ test provide a good example of the relevance of Foucault's analysis. Controversies over the IQ test as a measure of "innate" intellectual capacity and over the significance of IQ differences between blacks and whites in this country continue to burst episodically upon the scientific scene and reflect relations of power. The extent to which these issues engage the scientific community at any moment reflects changes in the tension in those power relationships. The IQ test was introduced by Binet in France as a tool for identifying learning disabilities in children and measuring the children's progress after remedial treatment. It was introduced into the United States as an absolute measure of innate intelligence and consequently used to *create* a particular reality for the purposes of racist ideology and practice. (For the history of obfuscation and fabrications of results by celebrated scientists see Billig, 1979; Gould, 1981; Hirsch, 1981.) There is no evidence for the existence of such an entity as "innate" intelligence or for the possibility that the IQ or any other known test could possibly measure the brain's cognitive functioning or intelligence, apart from the effects of learning. The concept of IQ does not reflect or signify or reveal but rather creates a reality. But the question of the relationship between race and IQ would not even arise in a society where race was not an important social problem (Osler, 1980). Scientists would not investigate the question if they had no value judgments about the issue and the outcome, and their conclusions will be critically influenced by their basic philosophical commitment to either the heritability or the learning of intellectual abilities, as well as by their moral commitment to social change.

Similarly, the issue of cognitive differences between the sexes in brain capacities, based presumably on genetic or hormonal factors, is generated by relationships of power, and the immediacy of its discussion fluctuates with changes in the tension in those relationships. To paraphrase Osler, the question of sex differences in intellectual abilities and in our biological *natures* would not arise in a society in which gender were not an important social problem, in which it were not necessary to maintain male hegemony in all aspects of private and public life. A scientific community with the high level of sophistication and understanding ours now has about the structure and functioning of the brain (granted also the tremendous gaps in knowledge) would not tolerate questions about possible measurable genetic or nonlearned components of intelligence were it not for the social context that generates (as it mystifies and obscures) the material and ideological conditions for gender and racial inequalities in achievement and status. These questions emerge and submerge incessantly in different forms and with different language and definitions of what, how, and who is being measured, as the efforts of women or of blacks toward liberation and self-determination wax and wane. Always the "scientific" opinion is polarized, and the questions are basically and ultimately unanswerable scientifically as they are posed. But the questions persist as scientific issues because their significance and purposes are social and political. The very existence of discourse on the subject, the very fact that the question is raised, serves the issue that the discourse presumes to be seeking to understand: the asymmetrical distribution of power between women and men or blacks and whites.

Thus, in Foucauldian terms one could say that truth is not a collection of insights or information floating about, parts of which are sooner or later revealed or discovered, nor does it lie deep within us waiting to be freed. Truth is produced through discourse (based in science upon "proper" scientific methods and investigations), and its production is imbued with relations of power. The role of language in the production of truth may be obvious from some examples I have given. Language in the hands of a scientist, no less than those of a poet, may create a particular reality or view of reality that the writer holds and intends through writing to convey.

Science and Objectivity

Since this discussion started with an examination of the issue of objectivity, we must return to the question of what objectivity is and what is its object. While Foucault, much to our enrichment, has seen and described ever shifting loci for relationships of power displayed by various discourses, I have been concerned here with the manifestations of the relationships of power between women and men in patriarchal cultures. Since women have been historically excluded by men from the philosophical and scientific discourses on *woman's nature*, what was the reality that the fabled male objectivity examined, what does objectivity then mean, and who defined the conditions of the discourses and objectivity? That is, if the reality being examined is defined by some but not others and the conditions of the discourse define who participates, what constitutes objectivity? What, in fact, constitutes reality?

Few would dispute the fact that civilization as we know it, as it has been recorded, has been created by men; that was an enterprise from which women have been, by and large, excluded. It was and is created from the point of view of men, and that creation "*becomes* the truth to be described" (MacKinnon, 1982, p. 537). Objectivity, "the ostensibly non-involved stance," is the male epistemological stance, which "does not comprehend its own perspectivity" (MacKinnon, p. 538). Those who create and specify reality also specify the conditions under which it may be viewed and verified. Truth or its perception becomes contingent on being male. This was assured, since women were excluded from the public world, from the creation of recorded reality, *and* from education for the last 4000 years.

It appears from all of this that truth, reality, and objectivity are all in trouble from our point of view; we see a male-created truth and reality, a male point of view, a male-defined objectivity. We have been led to believe that the discourse on woman and her nature, a discourse, like all others, from which women have been absent and excluded, has been an objective investigation because it was conducted by science. But, in fact, science itself, the tool for the investigation of such natural objects as women, has always been defined as *the* expression of the male mind: dispassionate, objective, impersonal, transcendent. The female mind—untamed, emotional, subjective, personal—is incompatible with science. "The presumption is that science, by its very nature, is inherently masculine, and that women can apprehend it only by an extreme effort of overcoming their own nature which is inherently contradictory to science" (Hein, 1981, p. 370). Thus, science has not only investigated, measured, and constructed gender differences, that is, male-female dichotomies and dualisms, but has constructed *itself* to epitomize and represent that dualism. Science is the male intellect: the active, knowing subject; its relationship to nature—the passive object of knowledge, the untamed—is one of manipulation, control, and domination; it is the relationship of man to woman, of culture to nature. As Haraway (1978) has said, the entire range of the tools of science is "penetrated by the principle of domination" (p. 35). Science then has defined itself as the epitomy of the very gender dichotomies that it sets about to objectively investigate and explain. Its dualisms—subject-object, culture-nature, thought-feeling, active-passive—are all symbolic and descriptive of the central male-female dualism and the oppositional relations of dominance and dominated. Science epitomizes the structure and history of Western civilization. By its objectivity, it is paradoxically able to understand in a unique way both its subjective self—male mind and knowledge—and its object—female nature.

It thus becomes clear that a set of polarized definitions of woman and man has (by defining science) defined the conditions of the discourses on woman and her nature and man and his, as well as the conditions of the scholarly discourses constituting the rest of our civilization's production of knowledge. But equally important, these dualisms have also structured the investigations into and the perceptions of the ways human beings think, behave, and organize themselves. That is, our Western ideologies, philosophies, arts, literature, customs, and institutions consistently express, embody, and enforce female-male differences or dichotomies, and that consistency is taken to reflect the presumed fact that such dualisms exist in nature everywhere and specifically in women's and men's natures. This obscures what I see as the exact converse: the historical separation of our civilization into mutually contradictory spheres—male and female, corresponding to public and private—the maintenance of which required the development of a dualistic mode of thought, the development of concepts and ideologies of oppositions, dominance and subordinance, culture and nature, and subject and object. By examining such dualisms it is possible to come to some conclusions about their validity and their usefulness and then to proceed to an investigation of their origins at the very source of patriarchal thought and consciousness.

Dualisms and Patriarchal Ideologies and Institutions

The basic dualism poses women and men not only as opposites and oppositional categories but as subordinate and dominant relationships, which also underlie and correspond to other dualisms that have been central to Western philosophies, science, ideologies, and institutions: from man over woman follow culture over nature, mind over body, reason over emotion, objectivity over subjectivity, creativity over procreativity, the public and political life over the private life. It is important to examine the possibility that dualistic thinking is a patriarchal mode of thought and analysis that has served the specific historical and political purpose of mystifying and naturalizing as it maintains male hegemony and patriarchal relations by means of a coherent philosophical and scientific mode of discourse and investigation and body of knowledge. Rather than being inherent in nature or the human condition, these dualisms are—like other modes of ordering, describing, analyzing, and categorizing human perceptions and experience— products themselves of human intellect. We tend to mistake our cognitive techniques to comprehend the universe for the universe itself. They are cultural constructions that, like all other such constructions, are intimately related to our experiences and perceptions within the particular social, economic, and political context of our lives. Dualisms that could be posed as hypotheses to be investigated were established as though self-evident truths, inherent to the human phenomena being examined.

Yet, like the genes-environment, biology-learning opposition, these are false dichotomies that serve to order our perceptions of a very complicated universe but not necessarily to advance our understanding of it. As dualisms, they are flawed for different reasons. Some—genes and environment, biology and learning, mind and body, thought and emotion, individual and society, private and public—actually define a spectrum and are inseparable from each other. They are both different yet inextricably related and in constant essential interaction or state of tension with each other. Some dualisms—nature and culture, private and public, in particular, but all dualisms to some degree—are perceived in some cultures but not others. That is, in some cultures, the private and public worlds may be the same world, and the concept of a private-public dichotomy does not exist; in some societies what is defined as natural and as cultural may be quite the opposite of our own definition, and, again, the concept of a difference may not exist; and, finally, the idea of individuality or of personhood in other cultures may be incomprehensible within our conceptual framework and inextricable from the social whole in theirs.

Mary O'Brien (1981) suggests that such dualisms may be products of a genderically differentiated male reproductive consciousness, expressing the need and the struggle to displace women from their material base of power in reproduction and genetic continuity. That is, these dualisms represented the attempt at a philosophical resolution by "male-stream" (p. 34) thought of the basic male-female opposition, in which men, upon the historical discovery of paternity, perceived themselves to be separated from nature and from continuous time because of their alienation from the actual labor process of reproduction and from certain knowledge of their genetic continuity. In O'Brien's view, this basic difference in reproductive experience and knowledge produced a different reproductive consciousness. The male response, in terms of the dualisms I have been discussing, was to separate private from public worlds and exclude women from the public world; to create for themselves their second nature, a cultural nature, as opposed to the presumed single, biological nature of women; to create institutions that would both reinforce the dichotomy between private (female) and public (male) worlds and also provide for men the temporal continuity (through laws, constitutions, monarchies, private property, patrilineality) from which the actuality of reproductive labor had excluded them.

It is a signal contribution to a feminist view of the world, by Mary O'Brien (1981) and also Zillah Eisenstein (1981), to see that the history of Western thought and civilizations has been the history of generic *struggle* that has been presented and viewed (obscured and mystified) as a history of male deeds and thoughts, from which women have been absent as a result of the constraints of reproduction and motherhood. The institutions, philosophies, and ideologies of Western civilizations can be viewed as the products of the historical struggle to resolve that central male/female dualism; to establish, maintain, and continually justify both the man-made division between private and public life and, in the end, male hegemony. Male history, male philosophy, O'Brien states, *is* an ideology of male supremacy.

The organization of knowledge as we know it has been undertaken by men who have translated a male view of the world into universal categories . . . they have internalized their supremacy over women as part of the natural order of things. (Marks, 1979)

As I noted previously in another context, traditional accounts of the course of human *civilizations* in fact trace the chronology of the historical development of *patriarchy*, a coincidence that appears to escape scholarly attention. The reason, I believe, that the identification of Western civilization with patriarchy escapes the notice of scholars is because *that is* their world. To those who describe and theorize, patriarchy *is* the world, it is *reality*, the essence of consciousness. If we were all born into a world where everything and everyone were pale blue, it might never be an issue to understand or explain why things might also be red. Just as the planet Earth forms a certain immutable base of unquestioned material reality, the thoughts, philosophies, cultures, and institutions that constitute our patriarchal civilizations are accepted as the unquestioned circumstance of human life and its social organization. It is assumed that what has developed had to develop. It seems almost self-evident, for example, that once there was a certain level of technology, an inexorable course of human accomplishment followed, leading to the production of surplus goods, accumulation of private property, long-distance trade, wars, expansionism, exploitation, kingdoms, states, and empires. It is a sequence that appears like an unfolding of inherent truth or logic, with an inevitability that does not even need explanation, only ever more detailed description and analysis.

That patriarchal consciousness is our conceptual prison. But if we are born into it and it is *all* we know, how do we comprehend it as a prison, let alone destroy it for a vision of freedom that is not inherently apparent? The fashioning of our own tools, like the finding of women lost to history, has become our feminist task.

FEMINIST VISIONS

Having defined the problem as nothing less than an enveloping patriarchal consciousness and a more than 4000-year-old patriarchal civilization that has ordered social behaviors, forms of social organization, and systems of thought, including science, how can we view the possibilities and directions for change? Over the past decade and a half, feminist activists and scholars have begun a revolutionary movement in thought and behavior so profound and so rooted in a transformed consciousness that it will not stop until all Western consiousness and civilizations are transformed. The main reason for this is that we are seeing a beginning transformation in the consciousness of the half of humanity who, as a whole, has had relatively little *real* (as contrasted with ideologically constituted) investment in or benefit from the dominant patriarchal social order. As subordinate rather than privileged participants in the institutions and ideologies of male supremacy, our changing those ideologies and institutions can be experienced as an act of restoring our individual and collective integrity rather than as the shattering of individual and historical integrity that men may fear.

At this moment in history, we are also aided by the fact that there are others besides feminists who know that patriarchal principles of potency, control, and domination are close to destroying our planet for all future generations. Faced with such obliteration, even patriarchs may consider alternative ways to think, feel, and live.

Feminist criticism of the biological sciences is a relatively young and under-populated field compared with other areas of feminist scholarship, and few have thus far ventured the envisioning of a feminist science. This requires a concerted, collective effort. The following final section is thus a tentative exploration of the conditions and circumstances under which a better science may develop, incorporating some of the recent thinking of other feminist scientists and philosopher-historians of science.

Feminist Science: Change, Complexity, Contextuality, Interaction

A first task in science is to examine the modes of thought that structure science's methodologies and its views of the world. As both Fee (1982) and O'Brien (1981) have also suggested, the historical separation of human experience into mutually contradictory realms, female and male, engendered our culturally inherited dualistic modes of thought, and that male-female dichotomy was built into our ways of perceiving truth. An important task for feminist scientists and, I believe, all feminist scholars is to question and examine *all* dualisms, all dichotomous ways in which nature, human "nature," and human activities are described, analyzed, and categorized. The dualistic mode defines science itself, describes and prescribes participants as well as objects of study and orders and explains the world that science purports to analyze and explain. Not only is the dualistic mode of organizing thought a cultural construction, but the oppositions and universals it poses are themselves culture-bound concepts. Hierarchies, relations of domination, subordination, power, and control are not necessarily inherent in nature but are an integral part of the conceptual framework of persons bred in a civilization constructed on principles of stratification, domination, subordination, power, and control, all made to appear natural. The relationship of culture to nature is not necessarily oppositional; the relationship of the knowing subject to the studied object is not necessarily the dualistic one of activity and passivity or domination and subordinance. These dualisms resonate interchangeably and metaphorically with the female-male dichotomy throughout our literary, artistic, scientific, and other cultural expressions.

Science need not be permitted to specify who does science by defining itself as the expression and epitomy of the male mind, which *it* defines as self-evidently objective, impersonal, and creative. Science need not be permitted to define objectivity and creativity as that which the male mind does and subjectivity and emotionality as that which the female mind is. It need not be permitted to claim that science is or even can be objective, transcendent, neutral, and value-free.

Such dualistic and universalistic concepts and modes of thinking have not only damaged science as well as scholarship in other areas such as anthropology, psychology, and sociology, but they have also structured our social world and women's place in it. They provided the intellectual structure to accommodate the subordinate status of women required by patriarchal ideologies and institutions. Thus, feminist critiques and transformations of science, like feminist scholarship in other fields, will not simply restore missing subjects and points of view, will not simply make science better and capable of a more complete appreciation of the world; they will also transform ideological bases for our Western civilization and for women's place in it.

The problems with a dualistic mode of thought are several. It structures our approach to knowledge of the world, it structures the world itself in an *a priori* fashion and imposes, as premises, dualisms and dichotomies, onto the organization of the natural world that do not exist. Most basically, it obscures a fundamental characteristic of life and matter, perhaps first enunciated by Heraclitus over 2000 years ago: everything is in a constant state of flux, change, interaction. With such a view of reality, we cannot separate genes from environment, culture from nature, subject from object. We cannot view science as an act of domination and objectivity, but rather as one of mutuality and interaction with nature.

Some may view this as an easy mode of thought for women, whose lives are nearly always contextual and interrelational rather than transcendent. As Hein (1981) points out, the requirement to be self-effacing, egoless, objective, and transcendent in order to be a good scientist or scholar is an inappropriate exhortation for women. Since woman's ego or "self has not been abstractly affirmed to begin with, it does not stand in transcendent opposition to its object." (p. 374) So are women's relationships to knowledge, to objects of study and knowing, more usually ones of mutuality rather than invasion or dominance. While women certainly are, as Hein says, educable to male-defined rules, they are more attuned to the fluidity of life, an acceptance of change, fusion, and interaction. Such experiencing of life more easily generates a sense of inclusiveness and contextuality as cognitive frameworks and modes of perceiving and understanding the world, as contrasted with aloofness, exclusiveness, separateness, impersonality. Women's experience, Hein suggests, places them in a perspectival framework different from but no less legitimate than that of men.

That male categories and rules of understanding should appear to have greater legitimacy than those of women can be due only to the political dominance which men have enjoyed. There can be no absolute basis for comparing distinct modes of experiencing, let alone for evaluating them. (p. 376)

This is not the same as claiming for women a particular "inherent" or "innate" way of thinking. We cannot make the important claims, basic feminist insights, that little girls in our Western cultures are socialized from birth to be nurturant, loving, responsive and dependent; that they become, consequently, exquisitely sensitive to the social cues from those on whom they are taught to depend for love and approval; that they learn to define themselves only or primarily in relation to a multitude of others; and, at the same time, believe that such learning has no effect on our modes and frameworks of thinking, and the values and judgments that are an integral part of the process of science and scholarship. If there is a general difference between women and men in their approach to science, it may lie in their different relationships to the concept and practice of control. To be in control of things, people, phenomena, information, and institutions, is an essence of our Western industrial class culture. Since men are the designated actors in patriarchal cultures, they are the ones who must be and are taught to be in control. To know, to be certain, is part of being in control. It is important to know *causes* for events and phenomena, for without that "knowledge" one cannot know how to intervene effectively in order to remain or be in control. To be concerned with understanding process, change, and interaction, rather than causes and effects, is to relinquish the need for control or to acknowledge the implicit irrelevance of the issue of control. For women in general, control has been a non-issue. Just as men were not taught or expected to think about parenting as a relevant issue for their lives or their self-definition before the contemporary women's movement, the question of being in control (of anything or anyone, including their own selves) was never part of women's frame of reference for conceptualizing or realizing their own relationships to others or to nature. Since interaction and concern with process characterize the generally accepted (if not required) mode of women's social responses and interchanges, they are seemingly our natural modes of thought and conceptualizations.

Other philosophies and methods—Hegelian dialectics, Marxist dialectical materialism, phenomenology, hermeneutics—also appreciate the realities of change, interconnectedness, and contextuality, but they are not modes of thought that are part of mainstream biological and social science. Hein believes both that women's experiences of life generally engender such modes of thought and that their experiencing of life, of nature, of the world is yet to find expression, since

female frameworks have been so profoundly devalued that neither women nor men have found it worthwhile to try to transmit them, and so there is not even a language in which they might be expressed. Since women have been dispersed throughout the dominant culture, they have not formulated a distinctive and common tool of communication. (p. 376)

If nondualistic, contextual, interrelational cognitive modes were to prevail, if women were to find expression for *their* experiencing of life, a process that has begun, sciences could become whole.

Whether one is attempting to explain the development of tuberculosis in humans (the majority of whom in the United States are exposed during their lifetime to the tubercle bacillus but do not acquire active tuberculosis), the gradual development of sedentarism and villages, or the development of patriarchal ideologies and cultures, it is important to recognize that there can be no single "correct" explanation, no simple, dramatic "cause." Rather, there will be an array of factors, some more important than others, each factor having its own historical course of development and its own situational specificities, interacting with other such factors over time and eventually leading to the phenomenon under scrutiny. We can use the example of lung cancer. There are people who get lung cancer who have never smoked and others who smoke two packs a day and don't get lung cancer. In the smoker who gets lung cancer, smoking has interacted with a particular combination of biological and environmental factors that may very well be a unique combination for each person. Biological factors would include immunological, anatomical, hormonal, and genetic characteristics; environmental factors could include air and occupational toxins and pollutants, viral and bacterial infections of the lungs and bronchial tree, nutrition, drugs, and stress. Environmental factors all have an effect on one or another of the biological characteristics. Some particular coincidence of several such factors constitutes the complex "causation" of cancer in any particular person.

It follows from this that no single individual scientist, scholar, or theorizer can produce the "whole truth" about a given phenomenon. Each of us brings to the inquiry, to the investigation of a particular phenomenon, our own life history of experiences, knowledge, and attitudes as well as our particular skills and training, and, consequently, each illuminates one or another facet of the complex phenomenon we are trying to explain. Together we illuminate many different facets, all varied aspects of the "truth." It is through this plurality of shared views and voices that we come to some understanding of nature, society, and ourselves.

After this critical examination of the dualistic/universalistic mode of thought and the limitations on its usefulness, as compared with concepts of change and interaction, it is important to examine particular dualisms that mold our approaches to science and knowledge and our perceptions of natural phenomena. Two that leap to mind in association with doing science are the dualisms of objectivity-subjectivity and dominance-subordinance. As one approach to knowledge of nature and society, science relies on methods of rationality, logic, empirical testing, and objectivity. Throughout this book, I, like others elsewhere, have criticized particular scientists and sciences for their false claims to objectivity and neutrality and for their role in providing unwarranted "scientific" authority as legitimization for social and political beliefs. However, both Fee (1982) and

Keller (1982) warn against a nihilistic retreat into cultural relativism and a wholesale rejection of science and the possibility of comprehending the world in rational terms; and Fee outlines the characteristics of an ideal and useful scientific approach:

> The concept of creating knowledge through a constant process of practical interactions with nature, the willingness to consider all assumptions and methods as open to question, the expectation that ideas will be tested and refined in practice, and that results and conclusions of research will be subjected to the most unfettered critical evaluation—all these are aspects of scientific objectivity which should be preserved and defended. The hope of learning more about the world and ourselves by such collective process is not one to be abandoned. (1982, p. 7)

While in most scientific efforts we cannot exclude the self (i.e., subjectivity), we can at least insist that our thoughts become "conscious of self," that "critical self-reflection" be part of our scholarly inquiry (Keller, 1982, p. 594). A part of this process is recognizing the degree to which investment of ego and pride in one's previously stated beliefs and theories may corrupt the scientific approach outlined above by Fee. Objectivity and subjectivity are inseparable parts of the thought processes and inquiries of women and men, scientists and nonscientists alike. To believe otherwise is to believe in myths. Individuals differ primarily in the levels of their consciousness and acknowledgement of self (with its history, experiences, values, beliefs, hopes, and desires) in their private and public judgments and acts and their scholarly productions. The experiences, values, and ideas embodied in the self can, as an integral part of any scholarly inquiry, help to illuminate some facet of truth or reality or, on the other hand, act to distort and torture reality in the service of personal, social, or political needs. In the former case, the "critical self-reflection" can be and usually is a freely acknowledged (and clearly unavoidable) part of scholarly inquiry and has been an important feature of feminist scholarship. In the latter case, the experiences, values, and beliefs of the self are not acknowledged as such but rather are universalized as objective truths about society, nature, and human nature and have been an important feature of Sociobiological and other biological determinist theorizing.

The other important dualism that has molded scientific thought and methodology is that of dominance and subordinance (Haraway, 1979). In other chapters I have provided examples of the extent to which dominance and dominance hierarchies have served as organizing principles and causal explanations in the fields of anthropology, primatology, and Sociobiology. Evelyn Fox Keller (1982) also discusses the importance of the ideas of power, control, and domination, both over nature and other humans, in the goals, theory, and practice of modern Western science. She documents the early expression in our modern scientific tradition of the combined patriarchal view of gender relations and science with a quotation from the philosopher of science, Francis Bacon (1561-1626), who spoke of science as "leading to you Nature with all her children to bind her to your service and make her your slave" (p. 598). The themes of domination permeate the sciences both as explicit principles of social organization assumed to exist among primates and other species of animals, as though inherent in nature, and also as metaphoric assumption, such as in the "Master Molecule" concept of the action of genes. Through this concept, Keller nicely illustrates two different ways of conceptualizing and approaching the investigation of natural phenomena. In the face of a dominant paradigm in the field of molecular biology that posits a linear hierarchy in which genetic DNA encodes and transmits all instructions for cellular development, the research of biologist Barbara McClintock, who spoke to Keller of her scientific approach of "letting the material speak to you" and having "a feeling for the organism" (p. 599), led her to a different view. In this view, DNA is "in delicate interaction with the cellular environment"; master control is not found in a single component of the cell; rather, "control resides in the complex interactions of the entire system" (p. 601). The focus of importance is on the organism and its environment, not on a Master Molecule.

Over the past several years, the fields of biological development and ecology have undergone dramatic change in their concepts and approach from mechanistic and deterministic explanations to a fuller understanding of the importance of change, context, and interaction. It is recognized that genes do not *determine* events, but that genetic mechanisms are "turned on" by environmental events and constantly influenced by them.[1] Historians or scientists in these disciplines may be interested in discovering the degree to which these trends have been influenced by the work of scientists like McClintock and Rachel Carsons and other women active in these scientific fields, which may have a larger than ordinary proportion of women.

Both Fee (1982) and Haraway (1979) suggest that it may not be possible for us, immersed and marginalized in a patriarchal capitalist system and ideology of dominance, to conceptualize a feminist science. It would be, Fee says, "like asking a medieval peasant to imagine the theory of genetics or the production of a space capsule" (p. 31). On the other hand, certain themes emerge from the work of Fee and Haraway and other feminist philosophers and historians I have discussed, as well as from the rest of this book, which reflects my own perspective as a feminist scientist. These are themes that point toward a better science, one that includes and encompasses women, but these themes do not by themselves constitute a feminist science with a uniquely, radically feminist philosophy and approach. It does not seem unreasonable to expect that the development of feminist scientific theory and philosophy will proceed hand-in-hand with the feminist struggle to change the conditions of our lives and work and with the development of feminist theory in general: a theory that articulates the new

---

[1] I am indebted to Cindy Cowden for this information.

self-conscious destiny of women, points to the abolition of barriers "between public and private, between production and reproduction, between women and men" (O'Brien, p. 193), and makes impossible both the appropriation of women and children and all systems of dominance by any group over others.

Doing science well requires what women, in general, have: the ability to listen and hear, to be aware and perceptive, to understand and appreciate process and interaction. It is "letting the material speak to you" and having "a feeling for the organism," whether that material or organism is another human being, a chimpanzee, genes, or the unexpected signals from a radiotelescope. It has to do with not imposing the ego in the form of preconceived, unalterable, unacknowledged, and constraining belief systems on the subject matter, but rather creating the circumstances that permit the matter to reveal some of its characteristics to you. This means the courageous and difficult task of examining and questioning all of our assumptions and the very structure of our thought processes, all clearly born and bred within a profoundly stratified, hierarchical, patriarchal culture. These include assumptions about dominance and subordinance, women and men, objectivity and subjectivity; about causation, truth and reality; about what is "normal" and "natural"; about control and power; about reproduction and motherhood. Doing good science involves an appreciation of the complexity of all phenomena and the constancy of only the process of change.

While similar critiques of science have been made by scientists of the political left who would not necessarily call themselves feminists, what is potentially and ultimately revolutionary in the feminist critique is that the patriarchal structure of science, its theory and practice, will not be left intact. What is developing as a unique emphasis in feminist scholarship is the value of and the necessity for the plurality of our views. If indeed the phenomena we examine are multifaceted in their complex reality and their causal forces, if indeed we are validly different from one other, each bringing our unique coincidence of history, experience, belief, and skills to our joint efforts, then we know we must turn our enormous learned capacities to listen and nurture to an attentive appreciation of each other and our different views and approaches, which, together, will illuminate important realities. The answer to Haraway's question, "How can feminism, a political position about love and power, have anything to do with science as I have described it?" involves the idea of our collective approach to knowledge of nature and ourselves and the survival of both. It involves the breaking down of hierarchies, the changing of boundaries and definitions, since, as Fausto-Sterling (1981) suggests, women entering a non-hierarchical science in large numbers will have their own ideas about the subject matter of science and the language it will use. "The ideal of individual creativity subjected to the constraints of community validation through a set of recognized procedures" (Fee, 1982, p. 7) can guide us toward a better and more humane science; and the contours of a feminist science will emerge as more feminist scientists, scholars, and practitioners turn their attention to the problem.

REFERENCES

Billig, M. *Psychology, racism and fascism*. Birmingham: A. F. & R. Publications, 1979.

Eisenstein, Z. *The radical future of liberal feminism*. New York: Longman, 1981.

Fausto-Sterling, A. Women and Science. *Women's Studies International Quarterly*, 1981, *4*, 41-50.

Fee, E. A feminist critique of scientific objectivity. *Science for the People*, 1982, *14*, 5-8, 30-33.

Gould, S. *The mismeasure of man*. New York: Norton, 1981.

Haraway, D. Animal sociology and a natural economy of the body politic, Part I: A political physiology of dominance. *Signs*, 1978, *4*, 21-36.

Haraway, D. The biological enterprise: Sex, mind, and profit from human engineering to sociobiology. *Radical History Review*, 1979, *20*, 206-237.

Hein, H. Women and science: Fitting men to think about nature. *International Journal of Women's Studies*, 1981, *4*, 369-377.

Hirsch, J. To "unfrock the charlatans." *SAGE Race Relations Abstracts*, 1981, *6*, 1-65.

Keller, E. Feminism and science. *Signs*, 1982, *7*, 589-602.

Lorde, A. The master's tools will never dismantle the master's house. In C. Moraga and G. Anzaldua (Eds.), *This bridge called my back*. Watertown: Persephone, 1981.

MacKinnon, C. Feminism, Marxism, method, and the state: An agenda for theory. *Signs*, 1982, *7*, 515-544.

Marks, E. The courage to see. *Statement to the University of Wisconsin Board of Regents' Task Force on the Status of Women*, 1979.

O'Brien, M. *The politics of reproduction*. Boston: Routledge & Kegan Paul, 1981.

Osler, M. Apocryphal knowledge: The misuse of science. In M. Hanen, M. Osler, and R. Weyant (Eds.), *Science, pseudo-science and society*. Calgary: Wilfrid Laurier University Press, 1980.

White, H. Michel Foucault. In J. Sturrock (Ed.) *Structuralism and since*. Oxford: Oxford University Press, 1979.

Author Index

Subject Index

Adrenogenital syndrome (AGS), 98–103
Aggressivity, 95–101
Androgens
  and aggressivity, 95–101
  and IQ, 102–103
  organizing effects on developing brain and adult behaviors, 85–86
  prenatal effects on "tomboyism," 97–101
  problems in theories about organizing effects of, 86–90
  See also Hormones, sex
Anterior pituitary. *See* Pituitary gland
Anthropology
  biases, 121
  ethnocentric biases in, 138–142
  evidence bearing on hunting, 129–130
  feminist scholarship in, 138–160 *passim*
Anthropomorphizing, 27–28
  in primatology, 28–31
  in the language of Sociobiology, 31–34
Antislavery movement, 5, 49
Archeology
  evidence bearing on hunting, 123–126
Aristotle, ix, 3
Australopithecus, 53–57 *passim*

Baby slings, 131
Bacon, F., 204–205
Barthes, R., 12
Battering of women, 181, 182, 188–189
Behavior, human, effects of biology or learning on, 51–53
Biases in science, 1–5
Binet, A., 51, 194
Biological determinism, 5, 15–46 *passim*, 49
  in feminist thought, 11–13
Blacks, biological determinist theories about, 2, 5, 49–51
Body politic, viewed as physiological organism, 117–119

Brain, effect of environment and learning on structural and functional development, 6–7, 62–67, 74–75
  evolution of, 54–62, 74–75
  evolution of in relation to hunting, 124
  fetal development of, 62–63, 74–75
  gene-environment interactions in development, 43–45, 52, 63–67
  lateralization, 92–93
  postnatal development of, 64–67, 74–75
  relationship to "innate" nature, 49–76 *passim*
  sex differences in, 49–51, 91–93
  structural and functional plasticity, 63–68, 74–75
  structure and function, 49–76 *passim*
Brain size, and intelligence, 58–59
Burial sites
  in Catal Hüyük, 153
  Chinese Neolithic, 153
Burt, J., 173

Carpenter, C., 118
Carrying devices, 131, 133, 134
Carsons, R., 205
Casserly, P., 104
Cerebral cortex, 59–62
  and culture, 62
  and flexibility, 61–62
Chiefdoms, 151, 152, 153, 158, 159
Chromosomes, 41
Civilizations, Western
  as generic struggle, 198–199
  traditional histories of, 150–152
  viewed as synonymous with patriarchy, 199
Clark, L., 104
Class stratification, evolution of, 151–154
Clitoridectomy, 169
Clitoris, 170–173
Cobb, J., 104

About the Author

Ruth Bleier is a professor in the Neurophysiology Department and the Women's Studies Program at the University of Wisconsin-Madison, and is currently the chair of the Women's Studies Program. She received an M.D. at the Women's Medical College of Pennsylvania (now the Medical College of Pennsylvania), practiced medicine for eight years, and, after postdoctoral study at the Johns Hopkins University School of Medicine, held a research position as an experimental neuroanatomist at Hopkins before moving to Madison. Her area of specialization has been the mammalian hypothalamus, on which she has published three monographs and a number of articles. Long a political activist, Ruth Bleier was one of the founders and leaders in the women's movement on the Madison campus that was responsible for changes in the early 1970s in the position of women and in their conditions of employment and study and that led to the establishment of the Women's Studies Program in 1975. In recent years, she has been engaged in the critical examination of the biological sciences and their Western androcentric and ethnocentric assumptions concerning issues relevant to human behavior and presumed sex differences, and has written and lectured on this subject.